typo p108

PANORAMA
of the Nineteenth Century

PANORAMA
of the
Nineteenth Century
by Dolf Sternberger

INTRODUCTION BY ERICH HELLER

Translated by Joachim Neugroschel

MOLE EDITIONS
URIZEN BOOKS · NEW YORK

Originally published in Germany as
Panorama oder Ansichten vom 19. Jahrhundert by Claassen Verlag
© 1955 Claassen Verlag GmbH, Hamburg

© This translation Urizen Books, Inc. 1977
© Introduction Erich Heller 1977
All rights reserved

First American edition published by:
Urizen Books
66 West Broadway
New York, New York 10007

Printed in U.S.A.

Library of Congress Cataloging in Publication Data
Sternberger, Dolf, 1907-
    Panorama of the 19th century.

    Translation of Panorama.
    1. Nineteenth century.   I. Title.
CB415.S713   909.81   76-30922
ISBN 0–916354–24–5

CONTENTS

PANORAMA
of the Nineteenth Century

INTRODUCTION

How many American or English readers have come across any of the writings of Dolf Sternberger, one of the most remarkable, most accomplished and most productive essayists of Germany? Probably some scholars who have sampled his many articles on the theory and practice of politics—a small number of them have appeared in American journals —and some readers who are able to read German literature in German: all in all, only a few. It was high time that at least one of the books of this important author should become available in English. Even so, younger readers may not know the "technical" meaning of "panorama" in the title, a word that seems to have freed itself of its "artificial" associations and, taking an unusual route, turned "natural" (if a view from a lookout tower or a panoramic road is a gift of nature). Yet in 1883 it meant, for Germans, above all a vast painting in the round, complete with three-dimensional trees, armies and military machines arranged against the circular backdrop, showing the Battle of Sedan of 1870 in which the French were catastrophically defeated by the Germans. And for Americans, also in 1883, it meant the same kind of pictorial exhibition of the Battle of Gettysburg to be seen in the Pennsylvania town itself while Sedan, with elaborate "mimesis" was built up in Berlin and unveiled by the victorious nation's emperor.

In either case the definition of the encyclopedias applies: "Panorama, the name given orginally to a pictorial representation of a whole view visable from one point by an observer who in turning around looks successively to all points of the horizon." The German subtitle of this book that takes its cue from the Panorama of Sedan is "Aspects of the Nineteenth Century" and its author-observer, even if he does not look to *all* points of the horizon, opens up more vistas than would any merely academic—and assuredly less entertaining—treatise on that epoch's cultural history.

Will Dolf Sternberger mind my calling him an essayist? He is much more than an essayist. He is also the author of books knowledgeably *and* essayistically sustaining one theme over many pages: *Panorama* (1938), for instance, or his most recent (1972) work, *Heinrich Heine und die Abschaffung der Sünde* [*Heinrich Heine and the Abolition of Sin*]. But even to say this is to pander to a prejudice tenaciously held not only in Germany: that the essay is a literary form necessarily inferior to fiction or protracted volumes, more often than not inflicting scholarly boredom upon an unwilling public. Surely, Montaigne and Pascal, the great essayists, are less tedious and intellectually more nourishing than many an academic tome. So be it: Dolf Sternberger is a master essayist, even when his essays, as in the present book, are clustered around an important historical theme and dispense surprising riches of information and scholarship—surprising because their provider is not immediately identified as a scholar, writing as he does with felicitous urbanity. In his *Kriterien* (1965), what he confesses in concluding a delightful *and* thoroughly informed feuilleton on Goethe's last words tells us a great deal about the writer: He had "researched" his subject, he says, not as much with the intentions of earnest scholarship as with the *pleasure* he derives from "*Akribie,*" that is, from assembling and tracing to its real or illusory sources all that can be known about it. He could have said this of many of his works. Often they look like serious parodies of didactic pedantry, the metamorphosis of pernicketiness into literary freedom. (Flaubert in *Bouvard et Pécuchet* tried to accomplish such a transformation on a scale too vast for him to succeed.)

Much more than an essayist: Two weeks before Paul Tillich's death in October 1965, Dolf Sternberger, then holding the Chair of Political Science at the University of Heidelberg, received the last letter of his older theologian-philosopher friend. In this letter from Chicago, the indefatigable Tillich, 79 years old, spoke of a new series of lectures he was preparing: "The religious dimension of political ideas." Unsure whether he would be able to do justice to the demanding theme, he added: "I should give these lectures together with you and Hannah Arendt." It was in such a triumvirate that, as the celebrated teacher of Divinity believed, Dolf Sternberger would have had his place, together with Hannah Arendt, one of his closest friends from their student days and to whom he dedicated his *Kriterien*. While Hannah Arendt wrote her doctoral dissertation on St. Augustine, Sternberger's subject was a critique of Heidegger's "existential ontology." His thesis appeared as a book in 1934 under the title of *Der verstandene Tod* [*Death understood*]. No wonder that Tillich thought of him as a possible collaborator in his theological and politicological pursuit.

Yet, four years after the book on Heidegger, he published *Panorama*, a work philosophically as removed from existential ontology as, historically, the Battle of Gettysburg is from the peaceful occupation in 1977 of the White House by Georgia. The change shows the author's ever greater width and variety of vision. It stretches not only from death, ontologically understood, to the vagaries of political theory and practice, or the *Panorama* scenes of the *Gründerzeit*, a time boasting of capitalist affluence, power and confidence, abounding with bad taste, scientific-technological ingenuity, expansive foreign politics, but also giving rise to artistic adventures as pervasive as *Jugendstil*, the German branch of *Art Nouveau*. This epoch has provoked some of Sternberger's most penetrating observations and elegant prose. Indeed, he has made his home in the capital of German *Jugendstil*: Darmstadt. Accommodating in his writings, seemingly without the slightest effort, such weighty figures as Lessing, Goethe, Schiller, or such a coruscating, independent and unreliable genius as Heine, Dolf Sternberger likes to relax (if writing brilliant feuilletons can be called relaxing) in the contemplation of great entertainer-artists such as Charlie Chaplin or Marlene Dietrich or Gustaf Gründgens, the incomparable Mephistopheles and tragic Wallenstein of the German stage and a director from whose demise it has not yet recovered.

This unyielding and yet unstrained energy of the intelligence and the imagination, assimilating or, as the case may be, rejecting the offerings of the epoch and its tradition, has characterized Dolf Sternberger throughout his career as a student of philosophy, literature and politics,

as a member of the editorial staff of the intellectually most distinguished
newspaper of Weimar Germany, the *Frankfurter Zeitung* (Walter
Benjamin was one of its literary contributors), or finally as an acade-
mician of Heidelberg, influential in the affairs of the University, the
German Academy of Language and Literature, and the German *P.E.N.*

Panorama was re-published soon after Hitler's fall: in 1946, and
then again in 1955. There were not many German books written under
the rule of National Socialism that would have cared to be seen in 1946
without having first undergone radical cosmetic surgery, and certainly
very, very few that cited at the outset an event as dangerously over-
charged with nationalistic sentiment and patriotic passion as the Battle
of Sedan (by then a plural: for it was again Sedan where in 1940 the
German invasion of France began.) Indeed, it is all but incredible that
the book could have been printed in the Germany of 1938, one year before the beginning of Hitler's wars. Much more understandable is the
fact that its author was eventually not allowed to publish. He and his
Jewish wife had to withdraw into anonymity, the precariousness and
the humiliations of underground existence. The wonder of their survival
will be a telling chapter in Dolf Sternberger's biography; in addition to
telling once again of the abominable state of Germany during those
years, it will tell also of his courage and endurance, as indeed do many
of his subtly "underground" contributions to the *Frankfurter Zeitung*
during the initial years of the Hitler regime, articles which made their
way into print apparently by following Karl Kraus' maxim that satirical
writing proves its literary worth by the censor's not understanding it.
They are contained in *Figuren der Fabel*, a book that came out in 1950.
Later, in 1957, there appeared one of Sternberger's best-known books:
Aus dem Wörterbuch des Unmenschen. His co-authors were W. E.
Süskind, the writer and translator, and Gerhard Storz who became
Minister of Cultural and Educational Affairs in the *Bundesstaat* of
Baden-Württemburg and afterwards Professor of German Literature
at the University of Tübingen. Revised and enlarged editions of the
book appeared in 1962 and 1968.

Wörterbuch des Unmenschen—even its title is untranslatable:
"From the Dictionary of the Inhuman"? No, "*Unmensch*" is exclusively
German. It is an annotated list of collector's items that were first pub-

lished in consecutive issues of *Die Wandlung,* a journal that Dolf Sternberger founded immediately after the war. More generally, the book is a glossary on the language of *homo administrator* and *administrationis;* but above all, it comes from the very center of Sternberger's intellectual fascination and intent: to diagnose the character of an age by examining its language; and if we agree to extend the meaning of "language" to include other forms of expression, painting, for instance, or fashion, or science, or technology, we also understand the diagnostic method of *Panorama*: to interpret the handwriting of an age, to contribute to the graphology of an epoch.

Whether Dolf Sternberger examines the ever deeper cleavage between the domains of the "natural" and the "artificial", the "organic" and the "technological", or scrutinizes the ever more ostentatious displays of souls clamoring for "higher values" while greedily pursuing lower but materially more rewarding goals, his *Panorama* encompasses a wide vista of scenes, internally coherent in all their external variety. What comes into view, each time focused with precision, is the *one* meaning of such seemingly diverse fascinations as that which the garish colors of the exotic held for the inhabitants of the new industrial cities in their gray monotony; or the touching sentimentalities of *Uncle Tom's Cabin* for the ever more prosperous exploiters of labor; or Darwin's "Natural Selection" for entrepreneurs anxious to justify their struggles for ever more power over life by appealing to the ruthless practices of Nature; or the literary cult of purity and innocence, poverty and blindness, for those who made their gains in the daylight of ever subtler blatant acquisitiveness. In allowing the *idiom* of the epoch to reveal this, Sternberger differs profoundly from the Marxist interpreters as well as the "linguists" of the age through his conviction that language—meaning, once again, not only words but the manifold means of expression—reflects the spiritual nature of the person, or the group, or the society, that speaks it. Dignity, nobility, goodness show in the "dialect of the tribe," and so does the corruption of its soul and mind. Heaven forbid that "scientifically" concerned linguists alone should control the concerns of language! We need to be reminded not only of the aesthetics but also of the *ethics* of speech and writing. Dolf Sternberger does it—as a student of history, a professor of politics, and a writer of words.

A PANORAMA

Anton von Werner, of whose vast oeuvre only the *Imperial Proclamation at Versailles* is still generally known today, rendered an account of panorama painting in his memoirs,* an account inestimable in its theoretical and practical, i.e. historical, value. It was he who designed, led the execution of, and partially painted the most famous and important panorama during the era of the new German Kaiserdom: *The Battle of Sedan,* ceremoniously unveiled in Berlin, on September 1, 1883, in the presence of the Kaiser. "The cyclorama" (according to a contemporary description selling at the entrance for a few pfennigs) "shows that moment in the Battle of Sedan during the afternoon of September 1, 1870, between 1:30 and 2:00, when the French Army, namely the VIIth French Corps . . . enveloped by the left flank of the German army and pushed back to the Plateau of Floing-Illy, is making its last desperate attempt to smash through the Prussian lines and gain an avenue of retreat." This straightforward statement sharply focuses the expectant viewer's attention on a highly specific historic situation precisely delimited to, if not the minute, then at least the half-hour. The compulsion for utter illusion becomes all the more obvious in the next few sentences: "Upon stepping out on the platform, the spectator gazes far over the delightful Valley of the Maas; in the depth below him lies the hamlet of Floing, which has been totally occupied by the Germans since 12:30 P.M. In front of the church, the 2nd Comp. of the 82nd Inf. is emerging from

* *Erlebnisse und Eindrücke* 1870-90. Berlin, 1913.

the depths. Ibidem: Captain Bödicker (3), Commander of the 5th Rifle Battallion, whose 4th company is stationed on reserve in the village."

Thus carried away (if not beyond space and time, well then from everyday life to a time thirteen years earlier and a place several hundred kilometers away), the visitor is almost casually changed from a passerby to an eyewitness of highly significant events; he finds himself surrounded by none other than the "delightful Valley of the Maas" and the military operations unfolding therein. The Kaiser had a special treat on opening day, a small heightening of the platform, which, on request, would slowly revolve, "affording the spectator with no effort required on his part, a round-robin view of the panorama"— a circumstance apt to more greatly ensure his being carried away, or rather detached, from himself. This same goal dictates the technique of this painting. "Nothing can be done here . . . with the subordination, sketching, or suggestiveness permitted in easel pictures," says Anton von Werner. And what a strange blend of real, measurable, spatial distances and their depiction in the pictorial surface; of the imperfections in the human eye and an objective structure in the things it perceives! What a strange blend in the panoramist's expectation of an observer who, as though standing on the generals' promontory, scours the scene with a telescope. Werner reports that Eugen Bracht, his chief collaborator, felt obliged to paint a huge nut tree in the foreground leaf by leaf and to take utmost pains with the slate roofs of Floing. Werner himself, at maneuvers, which he often had permission to attend and where he, the artist, was so amiably assisted by the general-staff officers, studied quite specific phenomena such as the amount and extent of the powder smoke from the guns. In order to arrange the countless figures in the exact perspective size, he used a strategic map, accurately measuring the distance between the various fighting areas and his own standpoint, which would after all be that of the panorama viewer.

While such topographic and chronometric reconstruction claimed full attention from the painters involved, Werner's account does contain a single, almost miniscule point feebly recalling higher illusionary arts and rapture goals. Not satisfied with the traditional rendering of light and shadow by the black-and-white palette, Werner hit upon the idea of sculpturally modeling the lights—especially the weapons and musical instruments flashing in the sun—and then adding silver or gold. Such scattered brilliance in a space otherwise filled with uniform studio light is faintly reminiscent of the admittedly more powerful light effects at which the older panoramas and dioramas had excelled. The panorama, dating back to the late eighteenth century,[1] was actually refined with a certain illumination technique by Daguerre, the inventor of photography. Daguerre had first gained renown with his *Diorama* in Paris, an opus his comptemporaries so meaningfully dubbed the *Salle de Miracle*, a genuine home of the wondrous. The pictures on exhibit—Edinburgh in the ghastly glow of a conflagration, or Napoleon's tomb transfigured by the natural aureola of a blood-red sunset—flickered with the more brilliantly Bengal, supernatural lighting that had once accompanied an Assumption, a Crucifixion, or the dawn of Judgment Day. Such a waning but still blood-curdling sign language of light, which, after the decline of the spiritual theater of Baroque church decorations, found a more fleeting refuge in those Miracle Rooms, is now wrested from heaven, here in Werner's demiraculized illusionism, and attached to the trumpets and drawn sabers of the glorious Prussian batallions. But still, a vestige of transfiguration, which the military band partook of for a long time. The same motif reoccurs in the band's most famous glorification, Liliencron's poem "Clingaling Boom Boom,"[2] although here it may be construed quite differently, as impressionistic joy in the play of light, or as the poet's shimmering merriment. "Bengal" crops up again here quite literally: "Is the Persian shah triumphant?" And in a playful simile, a memory comes drifting by, almost casually in this unexpected place, recalling the violent omens of supernatural, eschatological events:

> *And round the corner, bursting, boom!*
> *Like tubas on the Day of Doom.*

In the painted panorama, however, Nature was preponderant. An enclosing artificial Nature, whose relentless illusionistic unity forbade even the faintest hint of a frame and required negating the pictorial character in any way whatsoever as well as reducing or bridging the viewing distance, which was usually taken for granted. So it seems quite consistent for the painted surface to have things added to it, sculptural components in the foreground or actual pieces of nature transported there, stones, bushes, even tools. Daguerre had already enhanced the impression of Swiss scenery, to the total enchantment of visitors, by constructing the façade of an Alpine house in front of the backdrop and distributing rustic implements nearby—a chopping block, an ax, and some hewn wood. You could almost hear the bleating of a goat in the stable and the melodious jingling of the cowbells in the distance. "It was," wrote a German traveler after viewing the diorama, "as if our unannounced arrival had frightened away the timid dwellers."* Anton von Werner, too, made use of this tradition, at least in the three huge scenic pictures, which he installed in other rooms of the building where the painting-in-the-round was being shown. Those pictures portrayed "the three great historic moments following one another at five-hour intervals, like the final three acts of a drama, after the decisive end of the battle at 2:00 P.M.; at 7:00 in the evening, the handing of Napoleon's letter to Kaiser Wilhelm; at 12:00 midnight, the surrender negotiations between Moltke and Wimpffen; at five in the morning, the meeting between Bismarck and Napoleon." The dioramas were erected in such a way as to be brightly illuminated from above, while the viewer stood in an absolutely darkened room, at the exact horizon level of the paintings. This arrangement achieved a startling light effect, even though immediate nimbuses or annihilating fires were no longer aimed at, and it seemed worth concentrating artistic ambition on a highly natural portrayal of evening light in the open country, a misty midnight room lit by kerosene, and a bleak dawn. The nocturnal picture in particular, according to Werner's report (below), produced an illusion no less effective than Daguerre's magic room of fifty years earlier and was described in a way amazingly reminiscent of those masterpieces of deception and entrancement.

> The lamp on the table actually shone, and its reflections on the weapons and uniform buttons of the officers flashed towards the spectator with deceptive authenticity. When an international jury gathered here in 1891 for the International Art Exhibition, its members, including Alma Tadema, E. La Chaise, Juliaan de Vriendt, and others visited the Sedan panorama, and it was only

*   August Lewald: *Gesammelte Schriften*, Part VIII, p. 388. Leipzig, 1845.

by climbing into the pictorial space and touching the canvas that they convinced themselves the lamp was simply painted and its effect not due to artificial devices, transparency light, or anything of that sort.

One point, however, quite crucially distinguishes this account from that of the German traveler who had visited the Salle de Miracle. Daguerre's sorcery carried the viewer away to Switzerland, the land of yearning, and the effort was so perfect that a sentimental Englishwoman believed she had reached the valley of Chamonix, the destination of her consolatory escape from the metropolis—or at least she owned to being truly enchanted. In Berlin, on the other hand, a few practiced experts and acknowledged authorities on the craft (which is described more like a black art or superior legerdemain than a fine art) climbed into the roped-off area, backstage as it were, to fathom the machinery and ferret out the secret. It was the simplicity of the devices used—the lamp being merely painted and no "artificial" additions heightening the effect—that elicited their admiration, and they were far from even covertly wishing to really succumb to the illusion itself. In a word, illusionistic virtuosity became an end in itself. In all passages of his memoirs dealing with the panorama, Anton von Werner never quotes the voice of naïveté, never once cites any evidence that visitors were really deceived and felt transported to the place of battle, or even alleged having been deceived—and this circumstance characterizes the painter's "objective" aim and the expectation of contemporaries. Instead, Werner compiled a mass of testimonials by domestic and foreign colleagues, all of them very impressively confirming that this art of deception was done for its own sake and not—to deceive.

The rejection of "artificial" aids for the lighting did not go so far as to make Werner's ideal a total confinement to paints and brushes and thus a return to "pure" painting albeit in the service of illusion. "The natural, sculptural foreground of grass, earth, rocks, weapons and the like, imperceptibly blending into the painted foreground, achieved a pretense of reality in a fashion unattainable for paintings in exhibits and other environments."

The elucidator of another panorama goes even further (if the reader permits this insertion): the *Crucifixion of Altötting*, which is still shown today at that Bavarian shrine. At a certain point in the tour, the guide urged his audience to note a stone stairway where the artist did a wonderful job of imperceptibly blending art and reality. "The first three steps," he would say, more or less, "are reality, the others are art." Here concepts and meanings are confused. What the Altöttinger guide casually termed "reality" was what Anton von Werner more subtly or professionally distinguished as "natural, sculptural elements," thereby of course linking nature and art in one breath. In the diorama, however, stones, grass, and weapons do not form a smooth transition to the surrounding reality—such a surrounding reality is abolished to the ultimate possible degree, shrouded in darkness, annihilated, virtually withdrawn or cut away. The spectator's eyes have no purchase on anything familiar. They are drawn solely to the illuminated scene in front of them. The situation thus resembles a theater or a peep show more than pictures in a studio or a museum.

Integrating pieces of nature in art works has a long and involved history—recall certain Baroque buildings such as Munich's *Johanneskirche*, Church of St. John, by the Asam brothers, with its façade that starts below with hills of natural rocks; or those paintings in Weltenburg's monastic church, where, not so very differently from the panoramas, the painted crag continues into the space of the church with "real" sculptural rocks. This history alone should prevent our understanding such "naturalism" all too literally, neglecting the programs and intentions of the panorama artists because of the strange sight of their works, or taking at face value the "reality" they attempted to produce or imitate. No indeed: Werner's peep shows were so far from being a "mock-up of nature" that they actually exerted a magic of their own, inherent in neither nature nor art. Such magic persists today in the peculiar chill that sometimes overcomes us at the sight of these arrangements. The esthetic question whether this is really art yields no approach to such painting, for the esthetician, after answering No with good reason, has to get down to more serious business, and the panorama is null and void for him.[3] Werner, to justify his life's work against later esthetic detractors, merely cites his industry, output, technical skill and care, all of which makes him more of a virtuoso performer than an artist. Indeed, the products of his care and industry are quite outside modern art history, although now and then haunting it, alien and irksome. What Werner practiced was nothing but a black art or alchemy, an art of mixing and combining natural and artificial elements—and its goal is not art or even beauty and enjoyment of beauty, but a new and different, a manmade nature. A mirage of nature, admittedly, for everyone—the industrious creator and the admiring observer alike—is from the very outset aware of, and agreeable to, being deceived, Again, such deception is not meant to deceive (Werner says that painting a panorama requires utmost veracity and honesty) but to exist for its own sake, and it is content to amaze the viewer. For this black art has become modest.

Seduced by the mirage, those international authorities groped along the canvas to track down the light of the diorama lamp. In vain! No other ray illuminated the scene but the painted one, the natural/artificial ray caught in the scene.

Meanwhile, we have learned the ways of this alchemy. We know the elements assembled in this kitchen—topographical surveys and the system of perspective proportions; eye-witness accounts; "true-to-life" portraits of the individual participants, made from models or photographs and then integrated; studies of uniforms and sketches of landscapes; and finally rocks, grass and earth. All these things were melted and mixed. Truly, a wealth of sedulous preparations, whose purpose was as self-evident to the people involved as its essence was obscure to them. Aside from his closest collaborator Professor Eugen Bracht, who together with the painter Schirm did the landscapes for two of the dioramas, there were, according to Werner, no fewer than nine young academics helping with "the details of weapons and the like" for the great battle panorama itself, while Werner himself only supervised the overall execution. Thanks to this division of labor, which subjectively illustrates the character of the alchemical compound, the grand panorama could be completed in the brief period between late January and August 18, 1883. And the shiny new element emerging from these crucibles was: the captured historic moment.

This mirage of the moment was not useless, for the moment was renowned. Of course, the renown and the name, *The Battle of Sedan*, were lost in the carefully enumerated detail of a particular strategic situation, whose drama could be evoked only by explaining the before and after, since the moment per se, with its semblance made visible, cannot have anything dramatic in it. Still, this industrious wizardry did enjoy the very good graces of rulers and commanders because it immortalized not so much their deeds as precisely those tiny, the tiniest of, circumstances, "the way it really had been," and also because it promoted Fatherland feelings. Werner tells about a second visit by the Kaiser to the panorama, and this elucidates the characteristic contrast between the attitude of the sublime patron, who now appeared in twofold guise, and the attitude of the audience itself, who at times seemed dissatisfied with the spareness of the mere moment:

> Even though the public had been denied admission for half an hour, the platform was fairly crowded with visitors, who were rather delighted at this unexpected opportunity of viewing not just the painted but also the actual glory-crowned hero of the historic drama, and being so charmingly greeted by His Majesty. The Kaiser once again had a detailed conversation with me about his experiences and impressions on that memorable day. I remarked to His Majesty that, among other things, the public had not been finding enough battle turmoil and butchery in the picture, to which the Kaiser replied that it was well nigh more than enough and true. Most of all he surveyed and followed, as at the opening of the panorama, the ride he had taken with his retinue during the afternoon of September 2, for five hours, from Donchery across the battlefield. Again he was particularly amused by the flashing of the weapons, musical instruments, cuirasses, etc., and he asked in what manner these effects had been achieved.

Incidentally, Bismarck also visited the panorama and had a comprehensive talk with Werner about the third diorama in particular, which depicted his meeting with Napoleon III. He felt, for instance, that his mount, "good old Rosa," was finely captured: "She was a big-boned creature, only she was a mare—her head is somewhat masculine here—she just died last year," the imperial chancellor added softly by way of correction. There were other instances of his memory not quite tallying with the picture in single minute points, each of which must have been of major importance to the artist. Napoleon's barouche, according to the chancellor, had stood on the highway, facing Sedan, so that Bismarck had ridden up from the back, whereas in the painting, the vehicle was turned the other way. Werner, to justify this change, follows the report of the conversation with a rather detailed discussion of possible reasons for this "conspicuous circumstance": the early morning hour no doubt induced the coachman to move his horse back and forth, and Emperor Napoleon, no doubt because of his bladder trouble, left the wagon, freezing—a swarm of disparate facts quite graphically demonstrating the drudgery of reconstructing a moment.

The might of princes also protected these new alchemists, who certainly did not have to wait as long for the success of their efforts as the old adepts.

The actual exhibitors of such mirages were not the princes appearing in them nor the painters enjoying an admittedly short-lived glory, but rather the entrepreneurs of the panorama—in the case of the Sedan battle as doubtless in most others, a stock corporation. The board of directors, in plain mufti, attended the opening-day celebration, receiving some best wishes from the smiling Kaiser for the "material reward." This entrepreneurial manner went with the style of the presentation, which, modeled after the great industrial fairs included a restaurant on the ground floor and all kinds of roaring and radiating accessories, described in the official printed cicerone: the mezzanine sported an orchestrion, and the evenings featured "electric incandescent illumination" and "an electro-fountain with an arc lamp." The magic of both electricity and mechanical music thus helped to considerably intensify the enchantment of the visitor and the mirage quality of the panorama.

Poignantly, Anton von Werner laments the destruction of the panorama paintings, a good number of which he counted as the most important creations of their artists: "All these works, spatially and artistically powerful, vanished after the sight-seers had seen their fill—and the stockholders had no further prospects of high dividends. I wonder if some future book on art history will mention any of them as a characteristic phenomenon of the last third of the nineteenth century?" I cannot say whether any rolled-up remains of those unbridled paintings-in-the-round will ever be unearthed in a cellar somewhere. The panoramas still shown in Europe today can be counted on the fingers of one hand. We may forgive the artist's melancholy at this destruction, for he did not realize what handiwork he was serving. Nevertheless, the transience of this vanishing is quite different from the kind we usually bewail when viewing the ruins of past glory and grandeur. The mirage has the peculiar trait of vanishing the way it came.

I

NATURAL
ARTIFICIAL

In January 1875, at the founding festival of the Prussian Verein für Gewerbfleiss (Union for Business Diligence), the most important industrialists in Berlin listened to a speech by Dr. Ernst Engel, director of the Prussian Statistics Office, who in his time was regarded as the most outstanding German statistician* and who along with Franz Reuleaux, the director of the Berlin Business Academy, had an important say in everything concerning Prussian industry. At the centennial banquet commemorating James Watt's invention of the steam engine, he offered a toast that was in many respects extremely peculiar.†

> Gentleman! I have requested the floor for the purpose of inserting a toast between the official ones, and my request has been granted. Let us raise glasses to a couple celebrating the hundredth anniversary of its union this year, a jubilee couple whom you all know, to whom you owe a great deal, and for whose children and children's children our organization has performed no small amount of nursing. Since the celebrating couple are not present, please allow me to introduce them to you. The husband is a true child of Nature, of ancient stock. His forebears claim to have witnessed the first and grandest of all foundings, the Creation of the world. All the offspring of this dynasty have one thing in common: they

---

* That is how he is described, say, in *Meyers Konversations-Lexikon*, third edition, Vol. VI, p. 107. Leipzig, 1875.

† In: *Das Zeitalter des Dampfes in technisch-statistischer Beleuchtung*. Berlin, 1880. Verlag des Königlichen Statistischen Bureaus.

are very hot-headed. Now, to be sure, our man was forced to be somewhat well-behaved upon entering matrimony, and he still is, on the whole. However, at times, when neglected, and especially when short of drink, he gives vent to his native temperament, smashing everything around him to smithereens and sparing nothing that stands in his way. . . . The wife is altogether different. Her family is much younger than her husband's, although her ancestors could easily go back as far as the Freytags. Still, ages and ages ago, they were very simple and roughhewn people.

After the humorous speaker finishes summing up the background of Watt's invention and his application for a patent, disguised as "banns" and "nuptials," he continues:

One hundred years have elapsed since then. The marriage performed in 1775 is, despite the vast difference between the spouses, one of the happiest on the face of the earth and is still in its heyday. And it is also the most fruitful. Its offspring number in the hundreds of thousands. With very few exceptions, they are the best bred, hardest working, and most docile of creatures. They never rest by day or night and are veritable models of obedience and temperance. . . . Wherever we build huts for them and treat them properly, their entrance is followed by success and abundance close at their heels.

Allegory of the Steam Engine

Like Dr. Engel's audience, the reader has readily puzzled out this teasing conundrum. In a thoroughly reified world, in which natural forces are usually seen as nothing but quantities of work energy, and which is determined by physical and technical units of measure and, ultimately, by manufacturing costs, such personifications of steam and the engine have to be reserved for hours of cheery leisure. Once these hours are past, we have to get down to business, and business, in this case, means boiler statistics; though Dr. Engel reports that his little joke did help to "bring some life into the bleak world of boiler and steam-engine statistics." This may relegate allegory to the realm of non-committal humor and thus, even more important, debase it to a mere "disguise" of "naked" facts; this may make the costumed facts sound like a rather silly painting of bourgeois marriage, akin to dressing up bears or elephants in dainty petticoats and Tyrolean pants. Yet, remarkable for its rarity, this attempt at a direct allegorical apostrophe of technology and nature conceals a very serious meaning. The humor masks the sinister and enigmatic face of technology—or nature—which serves for a long time and then, unexpectedly and unforseeably, flies into a destructive passion. Tracking down the laws of this change from peaceful usefulness to sudden, erruptive annihilation, hunting out the reasons for the damage by observing and counting, and thereby finding ways to improve the equipment—those, after all, are the tasks of the boiler statistics for whose animation the toast was offered. Far from belittling the engima of that double face, Dr. Engel's allegory, by its very tone of innocuously smirking banter (especially when telling about the "old gentleman's furious outbursts" or the occasional "stumbling of the offspring"), reveals the underlaying demonic nature all the more frighteningly.

Of course this double face belongs to Nature rather than to modern technology, insofar as Nature presents itself to humanity in the changing light of hope and fear. Even if there ever existed a man with no tools and no drive or need to cultivate nature, a man picking his fruits wherever they happen to fall his way in the wilderness, such a paradisal picture cannot lack lightning and hail, which "unexpectedly and unforseeably" rob him of the wild garden and its nourishment. The novelty of Dr. Engel's allegory (let us inspect it against this foil) is the distribution of the two faces: the friendly and useful face belongs to the "wife," the engine; the dangerous or, as he puts it, "hot-headed and ill-mannered" face belongs to the "husband," steam. In this way, the steam engine appears as a "copulation" or union of a natural and an artificial element, whereby the disturbing factor of relative unpredictability, which the statistician must constantly try to restrain, is attributed to Nature. This twofold creature, humorously costumed, yet emerging with all the force of an allegorical figure, once again evinces that character of a natural/artificial fusion which the reader recalls from Anton von Werner's panorama.

That character recurs here in an object whose realm is quite remote from the earlier one and which above all belongs to an obviously so much more stable and more thorough "reality"—and the recurrence is by no means owing to that random and curious toast by the statistician Dr. Engel. It is not just due to the sprightly allegory that this orator devised about the steam engine or, more generally, about the relationship between technology and nature; it is not just due to some imaginative opinion or witty notion that the machine appears in this fusion and that this hallmark of the panorama crops up again: The real Technology and the real Nature of the nineteenth century are characterized by that view and figure.

For never before was nature a single and equal figure or power confronting the human race as the field of its work, the means of its existence, and the image of its perception; nature had always and incessantly entered new constellations. And these metamorphoses do not fluctuate beautifully past the motionless eye as in the magic lantern; in them, man, always busy changing nature, is himself remade and remolded.

For the man dealing with steam engines and railroads in this time always felt a keen urge to have these machines come forth as allegories and to give them a seeming life and dual being. Max Maria von Weber, Carl Maria's first son, named after the hero of the *Freischütz*, played a major international role as a railway expert from the mid-century to his death in 1881. The boy's astonishing and fully independent resolve to take up the technological sciences is described by a contemporary biographer as "typical of a phenomenon decisive in our culture: the transition from the sphere of fancy and thought to that of applied activity, realistic creativity." Now this man, for over two decades the director of, first, Saxon engineering and then Saxon railroads, an official in the ministry of finances, later called to Vienna, to Turkey, to Berlin, also emerged as a writer, in a rather odd way. "Max Maria von Weber discovered the poetry of rails!" wrote a Viennese critic, and the publisher of some of his works credits him with having produced the "technological novella." It is actually an allegorical poetry that he "discovered," in the specific sense that elements of technology, joined to those of living nature, achieve a new autonomous existence and a "double-faced shape" in the metaphors. "Equipped with a well-nigh ghostly life, searing breath, and boundless strength" (thus he writes, in 1880, in an essay* on James Watt's epoch-making invention), "[the steam engine] is our faithful and obedient servant, whose might and reliability often allow us to triumph in the struggle against the forces of Nature—always, however, interceding with a gigantic ghostly hand, it relieves man of the hardest, most soulless, most ignoble drudgery." Such a sentence (containing, of course, other, at this point irrelevant motifs) evokes the steam engine—now powerfully growing into an alien if helpful spirit, now sinking back into a plain, harmless servant—as a virtually semicorporeal being, detached from the calculating and constructing activity of the human mind, to which it does owe its existence after all. The paradox of the mighty servant and the double game of giant stature and faithful obedience may in part derive from the memory of Aladdin's powerful and yet ministering genie; but the echo of magic is merely one more sign that this freshly discovered "poetry" is not so harmless as to pass for simply a decorative touch. If the engine has a "well-nigh" (though not altogether) ghostly life of its own, it may be a menial, but one with searing breath and boundless strength; yet for all its protestations of loyalty, it does not seem to enjoy full trust, and this undertone of eeriness is what lends the quoted sentence its weight and color. In moral terms, the responsibility and liability of man the builder for possible although unnamed accidents (boiler explosions, railroad catastrophes) are generally and providently laid to that powerful, then all-too-powerful, but otherwise ministering genie. Taken as a mere construction, the machine could not assume this vicarious role. It should actually be described as it really was described in the poem that J.A. Stumpff, the royal British harp-maker, indited on the steam engine:

> *Der blanke Stahl steigt auf und nieder,*
> *Belebt zum Streben alle Glieder*
> *Nach einem Ziel. Der grosse Bau*
> *Folgt stets des Meisters Sinn genau.*
>
> *The shiny steel moves up and down,*

---

*   Printed in the collection *Vom rollen Flügelrade*. Berlin, 1882.

It animates all parts behind
A single goal. The huge construction
Always obeys the master's mind.

These harmonic and idyllic verses, composed as early as 1827, struck Goethe's fancy and were reprinted in Ottilie's journal in *The Elective Affinities*. But enough—for moral observations ill behoove us here.

THE STYMPHALIAN

The allegorical figure of the steam engine thus presented itself in two ways and with enough clarity. But as to its diacious nature, dubbed "copulation" in Dr. Engel's toast, we still have to pinpoint what that was all about. After Max Maria von Weber's death, a collection of small pieces on various themes came out, and the title enunciates the crucial motto and designates virtually the concise figure of speech for the railroad as a whole insofar as it belongs to the nineteenth century. The name of this book is *Of the Rolling Winged Wheel*. Every German knows the winged wheel as a symbol on timetables, prospectuses, and official uniforms in the German railroad system; and yet here, where the otherwise mute sign has found utterance and appears as a literary metaphor, it seems to divulge its own nature. Seen soberly, as an image, the winged wheel is a curious and even somewhat awkward object. Both the wheel and the wings stand for a motion, and yet it is not so easy to imagine the copulated whole as really able to move. If one tries, one finds oneself in something of a predicament: Do the wings actually follow, and turn along with, the rolling wheel, or is the wheel carried off by the wings? Probably the best way to understand this is that the wings, connected by a solid axle and beating with the help of unseen muscles, are a kind of organic engine, making the wheel roll over the level ground. Which is why that book title speaks of the rolling winged wheel and not, say, of a flying wheel, much less rolling wings.

In contrast to the Stymphalides, those mythical birds with brazen pinions and plumes which Heracles brought down, this creature here has living wings, but artful iron in lieu of a head and body.

The fact that the wings actually represent the motor energy is confirmed by a not infrequent simile, which also recurs in the introduction to Weber's posthumous book. The publisher, Major Max Jähns, writes: "Mightier beyond compare than steed and chariot, than oar and sail, is the new and powerful motor of our day: steam, which, with aquiline speed, guides ocean castles and rolling towns." Steam is like an eagle, which supplies the heraldic rudiment of the wings—and not Mercury's feet as one might think. It is part of the same eagle whose roaring flight one so often encounters in the poetry and painting of the developing, and then certainly of the completed German Kaiserdom, especially in glorifications of imperial unity. Always and everywhere, regardless of its position, whether soaring skywards or, with sparkling eyes, flying ahead of army hosts and heroes, the eagle never freezes in the heraldic rigidity whence it derives, it moves vividly like a real bird. This eagle, moving and metaphorically held fast in its movement, cropped up in all areas of contemporary life, in politics, art, and also technology. It was the totem of male song ("Like a haughty eagle see this song soar high") just as it aided Crown Prince Friedrich in the fight against the foreign dragon (on one of Anton von Werner's street paintings to welcome the warriors returning from the Franco-Prussian War. And, like the symbolic oak tree, the eagle brings to the established and unified Reich something of that primordial landscape of dense jungles, hurricanes, and wild beasts, a landscape in which the early pioneers of national freedom and unity felt at home, at least metaphorically.

Something of the creature itself and not just the blazon was preserved in the railway logo (despite the loss of the freedom of soaring), since the wings remain earthbound with the wheel. After all, Max Maria von Weber is concerned not so much with the wings as with the animal character of this natural half of the railroad allegory—he often speaks of the "iron pet," and the earnestness of the metaphor comes forth when it is used to support a highly concrete argument about traffic management.

The iron pet must conform its entire being so precisely to circumstances of place and time that its construction must, so to speak, be as carefully acclimated as the nature of the live pet, and that, like the pet, if it is to develop the full measure of efficiency and performance, it achieves physiognomical features by the way it is used, the kind of nourishment, the time and place of its utilization —features characterizing it as a variety of the same species. The juxtaposition of these things in the various branches of the railroad forms the geography of the railroad system, just as the geography of flora and fauna is shaped by similar influences and phenomena in the organic world.

Obviously, this is the diction of an "individualizing" railroad policy, which, economically and technologically, perfers a network of manifold structures to a centralistic and monopolistic system, from the great main lines down to the local and subsidiary routes.

The metaphorical urge is, however, not limited to the steam engine and the railroad. The term "steam-horse," still used today, though not grandiosely but with a pinch of humor, is, needless to say, of the same sphere. This urge also takes over the entire elaborate system of rails with their accompanying telegraph lines. One cannot help but admire the sovereign daring of an image that fuses this phenomenon of developed technology with the element of a natural living creature, an image yet again coined by the man who discovered the "poetry of rails": "But just as the muscle of the human body would be a lifeless mass of flesh without the nerve drawing through it, so too the flying muscle, which Watt's and Stephenson's inventions have brought to mankind, would be only half as powerful if the guiding thought, on the nerves of telegraph wires, did not pulsate through them and control them." Here, the entire technological landscape stirs like one powerful body with muscles and nerves, and even though the "thought" guiding it comes from man, nay, even if man himself is represented in the image by that "guiding thought," this technological body is still the body of, and an undetachable part of, "Mankind."

Hence the artificial and technological element, which in all those metaphorical figures at first appeared to be the underlying, poetically disguised, hard, namely iron-clad reality, soon boomeranged, and, in reverse, became equally serviceable for addressing the live human being and the organism per se and not always just metaphorically. It is as yet a very harmless and truly "poetic" example of this process when Weber applies the epithet "iron-headed" to such important constructors as the builder of the Thames tunnel, Sir Marc Isambart Brunel. It may be due to that fresh enthusiasm for mechanical engineering and to the faith in the unsurpassable permanence of its materials that the attribute "brazen" or "iron," in regard to the natural as well as the human and historical, pops up wherever irrefutable validity, utmost energy, and necessity have to be made evident. "Iron" describes the laws of nature as much as, subsequently, the "March of the Workers' Batallions"; "iron" describes political deeds, particularly the yearned-for unification of the Empire (". . . and when our Germany is rejuvenated by iron action* . . ."); and "iron" describes Chancellor Bismarck, who performed this action.

But the blend of the technological and the organic goes much further, especially into the science of man, into physiology and psychology; and just as the technological apparatus was metaphorically combined with the organic body into a single figure, the human body, in contrast, is permeated here with apparatuslike elements. It is the language of telegraphy, coming into stronger or weaker play whenever the nervous system is described. A single quotation may suffice. It is culled from the renowned magnum opus of a writer who set out to refute philosophical and anthropological "materialism," to justify, nay, prove the spiritual will and source in all living things. This work was Eduard von Hartmann's *Philosophy of the Unconscious*, and it promptly forestalls the perhaps likely assumption that the technological permeation of the organic is a trait of explicit "materialism." The lines in question are:

> I wish to raise my little finger, and its rising takes place. Does my will move the finger directly? No, for when the brachial nerve is cut through, the will cannot move the finger. Experience teaches us that for every movement there is only one single place, namely the central ending of the nerve fiber, capable of receiving and executing the voluntary impulse for the specific movement of the specific part of the body. If that one place is damaged, then the will is as powerless over that part of the body as when the nervous circuit to the specific muscles is interrupted.

* From a letter of Victor von Scheffel to the Schleswig patriot Esmarch in 1850.

What he has in mind becomes absolutely clear a bit later. "Thus it is the excitation of the center from which the current generates." With a minor and insignificant shift from the rigorous telegraphic imagery, the immediate activity of the will in relation to the central nerve endings is depicted in the following suggestively obvious and solid way: "We can think of the central ending places of the motor nerve-fibers as, so to speak, a keyboard in the brain; the touch, aside from its strength, is always the same, only the touched keys are different."*

What dangerous glittering, flashing, sparkling in body and brain! Transmitting, receiving, current, circuit, damaging or interrupting the circuit pressing the Morse key—all these things effortlessly combine into the picture of a psychophysical telegraphy. For our present work, it is not important to examine the role that Hartmann's construction assigns to the mind and the unconscious over, in, and with that apparatus.[4] The author, of course, in formulating that last-quoted sentence, applies a certain caution ("We can think of the [matter] . . . as, so to speak, a keyboard"), since, after all, no such keys can be found in the brain. But this simile is more than a simile or a mere *façon de parler*, as we see from its not being interchangeable and being scarcely variable and persistently recurring not merely in this author alone. Once muttered and applied, it cannot be excluded without crucially changing the character of this analysis of the body-soul connection, without radically modifying this theory and figure of humanity. Any attempt to exclude the "telegraph allegory" while retaining the thing itself makes obvious how fast it adheres and how indispensable it is to these observations. Were we to cut or remove all these words, the scattered, ubiquitously inserted and imprinted bits of technical language, then the subject of Hartmann's investigation, the human nervous system, would be totally obscure and unintelligible. In point of fact: metaphor, and this metaphor in particular, makes up the notion here rather than serving as its illustration. Certain consequences of that theory of voluntary human movements come of their own accord when the same image is carried further. Thus Hartmann offers an explanation of what is now called a *Fehlleistung*: a "mis-

* Eduard von Hartmann: *Philosophie des Unbewussten. Versuch einer Weltanschauung*. Quoted from the fourth edition of 1872, p. 63. Berlin, 1869.

action", a slip, a blunder, a lapse of the pen, a lapsus linguae. His analysis, inconceivably remote from the one forwarded by the modern psychology of the unconscious, nevertheless seems fully cogent and surprisingly plausible under the given metaphorical circumstances: Such inadvertent "misactions" supposedly occur when the wrong keys are struck on that keyboard.

Later on, the peculiar mythology of nerves, the nervous cult of the *fin de siècle*, with its utter awareness of refinement and pure soulfulness, preserved this image of telegraphic variations. Strindberg's second wife Frida, in her recently published memoirs,* says the dramatist's nerves were so sensitive to atmospheric electricity that a storm communicated itself to them as though they were wires.

Which came first, the semicorporeal allegory of technology or the semitechnological figure of the body, cannot be resolved. It suffices that in both cases, both elements, the natural and the artificial, adhere as tightly to one another as the Magdeburg hemispheres and are so inextricably enmeshed that the seams could no more be detected than the border between the sculptural and the painted steps of that stone staircase in the Altötting panorama could be perceived by the naked eye. This combination or intervolvement of the simultaneously distinct areas, this natural/artificial and artificial/natural, this copulation, this Stymphalic is, as an element of the panorama, a hallmark or feature of the epoch being investigated here.

One could still assume that this feature is intrinsic to the reflection of the historical man, a poetic and scientific reflection to be sure, but still merely a reflection. Yet so much and such specifically tinged naming, designating, considering of things cannot leave them unshorn. Man, acting, shaping, learning, delving, boring and building, separating and joining, alters the visible nature that is given to him and that carries him: the landscape.

Transformation of Work

The violently and thoroughly altered landscape of the nineteenth century has remained visible until today, or at least traces of it have. It

* Frida Strindberg: *Lieb, Leid und Zeit*, p. 34. Hamburg, 1936.

was shaped by the railroad. Not only was the railroad "epoch-making," as Sombart said; it was also, if the expression be permitted, "nature-making." Wherever a mountain and a tunnel, a gully and a viaduct, a torrent and a cable-car, a river and an iron bridge enter a peculiar and intimate union, we find the focal points of this historical countryside, its sublime vistas, which, in their darkness à la Ruysdael, drew all contemporary attention and were viewed, copied, and flaunted in myriad peep shows.[5] In all bizarreness, they testify that the victory of technological civilization did not plunge nature into namelessness and amorphousness, that it is not the pure construction of a bridge or a tunnel that elicits curiosity, admiration, and pride and remains above all a feature of the landscape, but rather that the construction was instantly joined by a river or a mountain, which came not as the vanquished to their conqueror, but as a friendly power asserting its prestige in this new proximity. The names of the Saint Gotthard Tunnel, the Ravenna Viaduct in the Black Forest, or the Rhine bridges of Kehl-Strasbourg and Mannheim-Ludwigshafen immediately recall these prospectlike vistas, where the heroics of the high mountains and the macabre blackness of the road blasted into the rock, the peril of the abyss and the massivity of the brick pilaster arches, the broad, raging speed of the river and the dusky latticework of the bridge and the smoke ribboning from the lurching train are bound in an inextricable union of dark, equivocal, ominous energy. The iron train, passing through the walled-in gates of the mountains to vanish for intervals in their sunless interior, running this same route into darkness, between Offenburg and Singen in the Black Forest, thirty-eight times in a row, seems to be returning, just as often and ever anew, to its home, where the material it was made from lies in the ground.

And the power moving it, the "unruly" steam, "King Steam," that the revolutionary song[6] of the English Chartists cursed by denying its natural origin and raising it to an unfeeling tyrant over "white slaves"— this power, visible in its lavish violence as it belches from the smokestacks of locomotives, seeks and, by driving the train across the bridge, finds communion with the germane element of the water rushing in the depths or hurtling and foaming from the crag. Thus civilization did not, as claimed by its most recent and aestheticizing enemies, expel and extinguish the "images" of nature; rather, the works of civilization, at their early appearance and procession across the earth, intensely entrusted themselves to the bosom of nature, and the landscape of the nineteenth century shows the traces of such allegorical "copulation" in its specific vistas.

For all the triumphant awareness of the age of technology or science, its foremost machines and achievements show no sign of trying to levitate; in dark materiality and with their so tangible dynamics, they adhere to that other mass, the earth, reveal the earth and especially its innards anew, look for and glorify, rather than break the spell of, "energy," and thereby merge into an artificial/natural hybrid, increasing their might, since the elemental seems to elude the intellect with both robustness and agility. The song of the Chartists or the fury of the Silesian weavers who smashed the machines (plus, of course, the house of Zwanziger the manufacturer) was aimed precisely at the autonomous creature, which actually ruled more by the grace of nature than of man.

All this is hardly poetic allegory and nothing less than late metaphysical transfiguration. Science itself, which gave the era its bombast, drew an abstract outline of the landscape we have tried to depict, and, through knowledge, it developed the fundamental concepts that, as key words, named the combined natural/artificial reality and also founded that reality in the more general and more profound being of an itself combined nature: the just as snugly copulated notions of "energy" and "matter."

Helmholtz, though not the first to discover the law of the preservation of energy[7] (whose explanation can no longer be delayed here), did more than anyone else in Germany to propagate the comprehension of that law—its scientific, not its philosophical or ideological comprehension. In 1847, at the Physics Society of Berlin, he delivered his famous first treatise on the law, equivalent to an original and independent discovery because at that point he must have known nothing or next to nothing about the previous work done by Robert Mayer, Colding, a Dane, and Joule, an Englishman. Eventually Helmholtz, aside from conclusions and further developments within experimental and theoretical physics itself, came out with a whole series of explanatory and elaborative lectures and writings, some of which were explicitly labeled "popular" and thus meant to disseminate the idea. Only this "popular" presentation, which fairly omitted the mathematical formula of the law and its consequences, and only this notion of energy, which was soon commonly known, will now be discussed, since the average and ordinary and for that very reason often hidden or neglected features of the epoch are our topic, rather than its far-reaching deeds and discoveries. One of Helmholtz's explanations, a lecture given in Koenigsberg in 1854, is of great relevance for our characterization of historical nature because of a very odd view it develops on the historical origin of the discovery of that truly "epoch-making" law of nature. The lecture is entitled "On the Interaction of Natural Forces and the Latest Pertinent Findings of Physics."* The term "interaction" may be, if not misleading, then too concrete to offer any of the specific abstraction that those latest findings of physics had produced as an actual result: the equivalence relationship between the various known "natural forces;" thermal, magnetic, electric, electromagnetic, and mechanical energy, and as the expression of that relationship, the concept of "energy," which unites all these so disparate "forces" by transforming itself and specifying itself in every single one of them as its measurable generality. The transformation—and preservation—of energy, this subsequently so cultivated, nay, adulated creature, was, as we know and can see, first recognized and investigated in machines, albeit then subsequently in the processes of nature itself, nay, the processes of the universe.

And thus Helmholtz begins his presentation by analyzing and clarifying a specific simple machine, a forge hammer: "If the example I base this on, a water mill with a forge hammer, still looks tolerably romantic, I must, alas, neglect the dark woodland valley, the foaming brook, the spark-spurting hearth, and the black Cyclopean shapes, and request a moment of your attention for the less poetic sides of the machinery." The scientific lecturer's jest was ascribable to his "popular" intention and apparently aimed at the ladies in the audience. By excluding the "poetic" or "Romantic" from this small, sketchy picture of industry, he all the more clearly brings to the fore the casually and matter-of-factly listed props of its graphic natural half, in the negative. But still, he does

---

* In: H. Helmholtz: *Populäre wissenschaftliche Vorträge*, no. 1. Brunswick, 1865.

leave out that side of the matter and, while presuming a universal interest in it, he nevertheless makes that interest seem ever so slightly ridiculous—which, after all, quite befits the scientist pursuing rigorous concepts. But what remains of the picture after that initial reduction? We can skip the details and observe the results. "While the work of our forge hammer consists in raising the heavy hammerheads aloft, its driving force is created by falling masses of water." Here, both things are visibly together—the working hammer and the plunging water, mediated by understanding the falling water as the "driving force." But then: "If we multiply the weight of the falling mass of water by the height of the fall and regard it as the measure of its work, such as we have done with the hammer, then the work performed by the machine as it lifts the hammer, expressed in footpounds, can at best be as great as the number of footpounds produced by the water falling during the same time." The equivalence is first set up here, namely in that the water itself performs "work" by falling, nay, that this plunging of the water masses can be broken down or translated into a measure of work. The third phase of the process is still missing, the falling of the hammer, and its work quantity turns out, in Helmholtz's presentation, to be determined by the speed of its dropping motion. "The motion of a mass, insofar as it represents work energy, is the living energy of the mass." Everything, nature like the art of machines, seemed to be evaporating into numerical relations, but at the very same instant, the term and concept of "energy" are introduced, tucking the world of formulae up again: "Thus, in our forge hammer, we had work energy first in the form of a falling mass of water, then in the form of a rising hammer, finally in the form of the living energy of the fallen hammer."

This wording, today, may sound anything but odd, anything but unusual; yet, if we step back, it shows in all precision that the breakdown of the so-called wealth of nature into quantitative relations is only one side of the issue. It is a mistake of our newest cultural critics and irrationalists to see only this one side in the natural science of the age of technology. The other side is represented here by the conception of universal work energy and its "forms"; though not openly cropping up in the mathematical formulas that express loss and balance and equivalence of energy, this other side does form their background. For this physics as a whole—it is the modern mythology—speaks as much in words as it does in numbers.

In Helmholtz's above-quoted sentence, universal "work energy" is the operating principle, so to speak the inside of the entire process that he analyzes; yet the principle itself never shows up, it is realized in "forms" alone, and these can be either natural or artificial, a plunging brook or a hurtling hammer—no matter. These forms, however, albeit "mere" forms, do matter for theory and maintain a certain independence, which is shown in that their mutual relationship is taken as one of conversion. "We would be able to convert only the third form back into the second, if, for instance, we let the hammer drop upon a highly elastic steel girder strong enough to withstand it. The hammer would bounce back, at best to the height from which it fell, and never higher." Hence, it is, mythically speaking, the spirit of work energy which can assume different shapes in these forms, mechanical forms with the example at hand, and otherwise the forms of heat, magnetism, or electricity as well. Compared with the metamorphoses of a real mythical spirit, these forms differ only, but of course quite essentially, in that man can guide them by setting up the proper conditions, here, say, by bringing in an elastic girder. In another passage, Helmholtz is right on target when he speaks of "the Protean way in which the effects of a cause in nature can change under altered outer conditions." "Energy" tarries in this twilight between autononomy and maneuverability, and that is precisely the most outstanding feature of both nature, as understood and appearing in the light of the new law of physics, and the machine, as reinterpreted by the same law. The point of that law is stated in the following lines from Helmholtz's lecture:

> We human beings cannot create work energy for human purposes, we can only take possession of it from nature's general storehouse. The woodland brook and the wind that drive our mills, the forest and the mineral-coal deposit that fuel our steam engines and heat our homes, are all merely bearers of a part of nature's huge energy reserve, which we exploit for our purposes and whose effects we try to maneuver according to our will.

Thus there is no work energy that is not transformed natural energy;

but then of course the converse holds equally, namely that natural energy, indeed nature itself, insofar as its being is "energy," enters both knowledge and practice only as work energy.

The interchange between man, technology, and nature can also be heard quite readily in peculiarities of language. For the generally prevailing use of the terms "work" and "energy," Helmholtz offers the following explanation, which sees its own essence in translation from one area to the other:

> The concept of work was transfered to machines obviously by likening their performances to those of the men and beasts they were supposed to replace. Even today, we reckon the work of steam engines in horsepower. Now the value of human labor is determined in part by its expenditure of energy (a stronger worker is more highly esteemed), but in part also by the required skill. Skillful workers are not available in sufficient numbers at any given moment; they must have talent and instruction, their training requires time and effort. A machine, on the other hand, that does well at some sort of work can be manufactured at any time in any number; that is why its skill does not have the preponderant worth that human skill has in such fields in which it cannot be superceded by machines. We have therefore, in regard to machines, restricted the concept of work quantity to observing the expenditure of energy, which was all the more important since most machines were actually intended to surpass men and beasts with the power of their effects. That is the reason why, in a mechanical sense, the concept of work has become equal to the concept of the expenditure of energy.

Through this figurative use of the name, both the mechanical and the inorganic-natural—the forge hammer and the forest brook—have something semihuman or, better, semiorganic about them. And of course, the reverse is true: man and beast, as other, specifically defined "forms" of energy transformation are virtually drawn by the established equivalence into the artificial/natural figure of the natural-force machine. For "what can we say about the motions and the work of organic beings?" asks Helmholtz towards the close of his lecture in popular science.

Having learned about the origin of work energy by observing the steam engine, we must ask: Is it any different with human beings? In point of fact, survival is tied to the continual intake of nourishment, combustible substances that, when totally digested, enter the blood, then undergo a slow burning in the lungs, and form wellnigh the same combinations with the oxygen in the air as would arise from burning in an open fire. Since the amount of heat generated by combustion is independent of the length of burning and its intermediary stages, we can calculate on the basis of the material consumed how much heat or its equivalent in work can thereby be produced in the body of an animal. Unfortunately, the difficulties of such experiments are still very great; yet within the limits of precision hitherto attained, research shows that heat generated in an animal body matches that supplied by chemical processes. The body of an animal thus does not differ from a steam engine in the fashion in which it gains heat and energy; it does differ, however, in the purpose and the manner for which and in which it then uses the energy gained. Moreover, in its choice of fuel, it is more restricted than the steam engine.

The gist here would certainly be poorly grasped or caught were we merely to leap to the general, always correct, and indefinite conclusion that man is simply a natural creature and hence subject to natural laws; yet it would be just as inaccurate to read those lines as merely demoting the living creature to a machine. If that were so, moral indignation or an opposing ideology could do little, since we are not dealing with arbitrary opinions here; but aside from that, such an exegesis would simply talk past the peculiarity of these sentences. They actually transpose the character of the energy machine to the organism, and in a thoroughly conclusive, experimentally attestable fashion at that.

For the singularity of this both natural and mechanical "energy," it is revealing that, at the very start of his reflections, Helmholtz himself pointed out the contradiction to a then prevailing medical theory of an independent "life energy."[8] "Most physiologists had resorted to claiming it was the physical and chemical energy of the organs and matter that operated in a living body, but that the life soul or life energy dwelling within is able to bind and break up the effectiveness of this energy.

Something about this explanation strikes me as contrary to nature"* This wording, as sharp as can be, indicates that the entrance of the engine, the "energy machine," into the organism spelled both the end of its special position and a return to the one and universal Nature.

Nonetheless, by interpreting the animal body as a steam engine, Helmholtz is not claiming thereby to understand the essence of the living organism as a whole. His explanation merely pertains to the feature of "survival," and not, say, to death. The element of the machine is embedded, as it were, in that "animal body," but without becoming fully one with it.

Above all, it seems necessary to be more familiar with the new interpretation provided by physical science for the essence of the machine itself, since this knowledge will prevent all too hasty judgment.

THE END OF PERPETUAL MOTION

Helmholtz's intelligent historical observations in his lecture are of great value for characterizing this new position of the machine in regard to, and within, nature. The law whose explanation is the theme of his talk is at one point formulated thus: Research discloses "that the whole of nature possesses a supply of operative energy that can in no wise be increased or diminished so that the quantity of operative energy in inorganic nature is as everlasting and immutable as the quantity of matter. With these words, I have stated the universal law of the principle of the conversation of energy." The same lawful framework (the peculiar term "the whole of nature" is discussed more thoroughly below) is stated negatively by Helmholtz in this original form: "Throughout the processes of nature there is no circular way of gaining mechanical energy without a corresponding consumption. The perpetuum mobile is impossible." The experience of myriad abortive experiments, to wit, that one cannot construct perpetual motion, the finally disabused hope, is, for Helmholtz, the historical point at which the discovery of the new law commenced.

Leaving the factual issue aside, we can see that the new figure of

*   cf. Ellen von Siemens: *Anna von Helmholtz, Ein Lebensbild in Briefen*, Vol. 1, p. 86. Berlin, 1929.

the power machine looms clearly before the background of perpetual motion, the ideal of a purely "mechanical" engine, which enchanted men for centuries. There were so many astronomical timepieces rich in forms, there were such artfully constructed automata, of which Helmholtz cites a few examples widely renowned in the eighteenth century: for instance Vaucanson's duck, which ate and digested, or his flute player, who moved all his fingers correctly. If we take all these clocks and robots as approaches to the ideal of a perpetuum mobile, they seem to express the hope of producing spontaneous motion and life with mathematics and mechanics and of ultimately imitating the Creator's work, itself a huge machinery which men thought they had penetrated. Every astronomical timepiece, every artificial wonder, is thus nothing less than a self-revolving miniature effigy of the self-revolving universe—an effigy, to be sure, which lacked only one thing for perfection: the ability to get along without being wound or set off. Nevertheless, this was somehow justified in the idea that once God's finger must have nudged his grand wonderwork to get it going. In this way, briefly, the machine was a copy of the universe, and the universe itself a machine. A propos, it would not be quite accurate to label the construction of perpetual motion in the described sense as a mere dream, whose futility was finally and inevitably proven: for the Baroque understanding of nature, it was first and foremost the highest expression of a principle tangibly verified in every smoothly functioning clock.

With the burial of that hope, the machine itself quite generally entered a new order. The clock, this most precious tradition of the mechanical age, behaves quite differently now that its imperfection vis-à-vis the universe has been discovered and the impelling finger of man has lost its glorious arrogance. Helmholtz interprets the timepiece as follows: "Our wall clocks are driven by sinking weights, our watches by tensioned springs. A weight lying on the ground, a relaxed elastic spring, can produce no effects; to achieve these effects, we must first lift the weight, tense the spring. This happens when the timepiece is wound. The person winding it imparts a certain amount of work energy to the weight or the spring, and the exact amount imparted is gradually expended by the timepiece during the next twenty-four hours when it slowly utilizes the energy to overcome the friction of the gears, the air resistance of the pendulum. The clockwork thus does not operate any work energy not imparted to it, it simply doles it out equally over a longer period of time." No different from the steam engine or even the "animal body," the clock has become a vessel of work energy, its construction reveals itself as the mere production of conditions useful for transforming and guiding the energy in the desired manner. What was previously its imperfection in regard to perpetual motion, its sore point, now becomes its glory, as it were, or at least the clearest expression of its share in the entire process of nature. By being wound up, it shows, if we may say so, its navel cord. The muscular energy needed to wind the clock is, for its part, the product of transformation, of chemical combustion in the body; the nourishment taken in by the body is ultimately sunlight converted inside the plants, and so on ever further back.

Every station of the energy metamorphosis concretely illustrates yet again nature and the machine as being comparable, nay, interchangeable. The truly powerful dominion of the steam engine, for instance, emerges in a way that might sound dreadful to modern ears, but that had nothing offensive for Helmholtz's listeners: "Indeed, the sun, here, on earth, drives a kind of steam engine whose performance is by far superior to those of artificially constructed machines. You see, the water circulation in the atmosphere brings . . . the water evaporating from the warm tropical seas to the heights of the mountains; this circulation virtually constitutes a grandiose hydraulic engine to whose performance no man-made machine could even remotely hold a candle."* It has already been explained that the steam engine could not have offered a valid metaphor for such a natural process if it had not itself been legitimized

Pursuing energy through all its transformations leads the physicist upwards to the cosmic and cosmogeonic spheres, and even the dimensions of the planetary system turn out to be "imperfect" in the same sense as, previously, the clock; for the enormous amount of heat generated at the birth of the system from the cosmic mists must have "lost" a great deal as radiation to make possible the union of the masses. But not even this loss of heat can, for Helmholtz, "gainsay the principle of the conservation of energy": "The heat was lost for our solar system,

* *Populäre wissenschaftliche Vorträge*, no. III, p. 124. Brunswick, 1876.

but not for the universe. It radiated out and is still moving out into unending spaces, and we do not know whether the medium carrying the vibrations of light and heat has any frontier where the rays must turn back or whether they will continue their journey to infinity forever." This "universe," endless in time and space, thus remains the only perpetuum mobile, as well as the only place in which natural energy or work energy is truly "conserved" without losses, the place containing the "energy reserve" which both living creatures and machines draw upon. The law under discussion has really full validity only for that utterly remote realm of a nevertheless closed infinity; when the law is applied to that realm it becomes a law in the most literal sense of the word. The moment the horizon of this "whole nature" is even slightly restricted, whether to the notion of our planetary system or even to the conditions on earth, then the otherwise "timeless" formula of the principle brings forth conceptions and strictly necessary reckonings of the beginning and the end of the world, a death by heat, exhaustion of energy, in short, calculations of natural history.

"Whole nature" (whose immensity does not so greatly strain the imagination as to keep from playing a cardinal role under the name of "universe" in all the enthusiasms of the century) is something in which the engine participates. This factor constitutes the essential notion and the historical peculiarity of the engine. And thus, a hybrid of natural force and the conditions of its transformation, the engine has a double face, just like the cosmos, in whose unendingness alone perfect economy prevails and the search for lost work energy comes to a rest.

II

O'ER
LAND AND SEA

Engines, especially trains and steamers; rails and the other daring constructions that smoothed their paths—tunnels, bridges, viaducts—did not just alter the face of the landscape. In a new and novel fashion, they opened up the world, the lands and the seas. The history of these triumphs is well known. The first railway boom in Great Britain occurred during the 1840s, whereas the expansion of the continental network followed in the decades after midcentury, reaching its highpoint in the seventies, the era known in Germany as the *Gründerzeit*, the period of promoterism. From 1890 into the new century, the non-European countries (America kept up a fair pace with Europe) were opened and occupied by and for the railroad.[9]

The railroad elaborated the new world of experience, the countries and oceans, into a panorama. It not only connected previously remote places with one another by freeing the vanquished route of all resistance, disparity, and adventure; but, more important, since traveling became so comfortable and universal, it turned the eyes of travelers outward, offering them a rich diet of changing tableaux, the only possible experience during a trip.

Everything already within, or gradually drawing into, the realm of such traffic was soon an effortless part of the sphere and procession of tableaux; but as a result, the world, known in this way and yet unfamiliar, lost its colors, the charms of foreign places grew interchangeable, and the lands of dreams and yearnings, the actual homelands, moved further away, to the impassable Alpine peaks, the Orient, or the Nile. The railroad made hope a fugitive.

Ever driven on in quest of the incessantly approaching distance, more and more painters and writers (plus explorers and industrial colonizers, of course) headed for a south that was no longer the home of models and rules like classical Italy, but rather an inexhaustible and steadily increasing storehouse of colors and passions. The "South," hitherto represented only by Italy, the land of art, now widened unforeseeably and fused in every way with the Orient, whose exploitation (we can speak of both artistic and industrial exploitation) retroactively sent the taste for Italy in a new direction. Europe became gray, and exoticism radiant.

FREEDOM IN THE DESERT

Delacroix had gone on ahead, guided and promoted by the colonial expansion of France. In 1830, Algiers had become French. Just two years later, the painter went to Morocco with a French delegation, and, amid limitless, fiery yellow desert sand that swirled around the Arab horseman in their fluttering white burnooses, he captured freedom itself, a hectic, gaudy freedom, in his paintings or converted it into paintings, helping willy-nilly, as the illustrator of expansion, to curtail this freedom in the political reality. Freedom here was nothing but liberty of passion, ardor, savagery, heroism, as well as fanaticism and cruelty, jealousy and sensuality. For Delacroix and his more subdued descendants, tigers and Arab stallions were equally valid subjects, bearers, vessels of such freedom as the Moroccan horseman themselves with their long, thin, silver-studded flintlocks. And in the wealth of glistening African color, the Frenchman, strangely, found the simple outline of antiquity, the Homeric era, the same ancient world that was kept in rigorous custody in the halls and cabinets of the Academy of Paris. The same? A friend of the port director of Algiers, who had gotten Delacroix a long-desired admission to the arcana of a harem, reports that this man of passion, upon viewing the voluptuous inmates in their gold-brocaded silks, exclaimed over and over: *"C'est beau! C'est comme au temps d'Homère!*

*La femme dans le gynécée s'occupant de ses enfants, filant la laine ou brodant de merveilleux tissus. C'est la femme comme je la comprends!"**
(It's lovely! It's like the days of Homer! The woman in the gynaeceum taking care of her children, spinning wool or embroidering marvelous cloths. That is woman as I understand her!) What he gazed at here was not an antiquity of white, frozen ideality, but an antiquity of relaxed living—an Oriental antiquity, the same one manifest in the tensed strength of his tiger bodies and the hot savagery of fighting Arab horses. He spoke about them to his biographer Silvestre: *"ils se prennant à belles dents comme des tigres and rien ne peut les séparer; les souffles rauques et enflammés qui sortent de leurs naseaux écarlates, leurs crins épars ou empâtés de sang, leur jalousies féroces, leurs rancunes mortelles; tout en eux, attitude et caractère, sent l'héroïsme de la nature primitive."†*
(They get embroiled in one another like tigers, and nothing can pull them apart, their raucous and burning breath that tears out their scarlet nostrils, their thin, blood-matted hair, their wild jealousies, their mortal grudges; everything about them, their bearing and characters, reeks of the heroism of primitive nature.) Heroism of primitive nature, intensity of instinct, *férocité* and *verve*: those are the categories of this Orient. On the streets, writes Delacroix in a letter from Tangiers, you can see the sublime running about alive, and it strikes you dead with all its reality—*"et vous assassine de la réalité."*

Here, African Romanticism and political usurpation hard on its heels far outraced the railroad, the first Algerian line not being put in service until 1862. Delacroix remained an early forerunner; the great procession of painters, especially Germans, to Africa and the Near East, only started after the midcentury. It was as if the railroad, the visible seal of industrial conquest, had driven along these seekers and quick capturers of the exotic subjects that rather peculiarly became the epitome of a rich life violently striven for; it was as if the railroad both caused and helped and outstripped their flight.

In 1856, the very first African railroad was opened, the Alexandria-

---

*   Raymond Escholier: *Eugène Delacroix*, Vol. II, p. 87. Paris, 1926-27.

†   Ibid., p. 35.

Cairo line. That same year, the rich, beautiful, and eccentric young Dutchwoman Alexandrine Tinne took her first trip to the Near Eastern Orient and Egypt, with the scientific rather than esthetic goal of finding the sources of the Nile. Nevertheless, while undertaking the most perilous and yet scientifically profitable expeditions to Upper Egypt, this woman, with unparalled persistance and determination, took the Orient seriously as the home of passion. She lived in Cairo surrounded by Arab servants and black slaves in a dilapidated Egyptian house, wearing Oriental garb and fully resolved never to return to Europe. During her third expedition, she was killed on the edge of the Sahara by the Tuaregs accompanying her, and this death ratified her metamorphosis.

In the sixties and seventies, Cairo, and Egypt in general, became the pre-eminent goal of painters voyaging from faraway Germany. One of the first was Wilhelm Gentz, a Berliner, who likewise sought out Nubia, Asia Minor, and Turkey, eventually using his experiences to supply illustrations for Egyptological novels by Georg Ebers. Later, around 1870, came Leopold Müller, painting camels and camel markets; after 1870, when the rail network had grown considerably, Adolf Seel from Wiesbaden, who explored the harems from the inside, providing them with decorations; and finally, in the winter of 1875-76, Lenbach and Makart together with Müller. Makart was not interested in the country itself; he actually appropriated the authentic prospect in front of which Cleopatra, awaiting Marc Anthony, was to be arranged with her retinue. The painting, displayed in Munich after his return in 1876, shows the "ancient cruise down the Nile" combined with a crocodile fight that occupies the foreground. What was hitherto a locale of liberty is now a backdrop hurriedly brought home. The courage and headiness of the first thrust had already been caught up with—by the railroad.

The colonizers entrenched themselves, and the freedom of passion shrank down or dried up into an ascertainable if continually and willingly noted ethnographic peculiarity; and at the same rate, the bewildering and overwhelming colors previously discovered in the African scenery, the colors at home in such an Africa, fully belonging to, expressive of, and inherent in, that passion—these colors passed into the craft and technical skill of each painter representing the profession of Orient painting. Splendid color and glowing light became stereotypical features of this professional art rather than of the world in which this painting eagerly and assiduously bestirred itself, ever intent on precise observation and newsy information about manners and mores.

In 1871, the exhibit at the Academy of Berlin included a picture by the Orient painter Wilhelm Gentz, showing a storyteller at the gates of Cairo. The reviewer from the *Zeitschrift für bildende Kunst** wrote: "A simply wonderful, one may say thrilling painting was his *Storyteller Near Cairo*. The motley listeners at the city gates, the phantastic and vividly reciting rhapsode, the color blaze of the costumes and of the ardent evening light: everything joined together to even further transfigure the poetry of the East, despite the quite tangible manifestation. Gentz has most likely never produced anything so perfect." Color and desert light adhere densely enough to the scene, which, however, is frozen, a snapshot from a train compartment, though meticulously accoutered by a man who, for this very purpose, got out of the train and settled down here to study, and who arranged those many figures, all "interesting" at least for their costumes, in a horizontal plane, while the gaze yearning for primitive savagery and Homeric existence cannot infer any depth, and no freedom of even full color springs from the depth. Here everything seems attached and fettered to the spot, "at the city gates of Cairo." This Orient releases neither light nor color, but both are squeezed into it, and there they shall remain.

It is merely a confirmation of that fact when color blaze and ardent evening light in the critic's sentences seem for an instant almost like maneuvers of the knowledgeable painter, useful "to even further transfigure the poetry of the East." This scarcely emerges with any verve from the locale itself, so that the painter has to coat a ready-made glaze of tranfiguration over the "quite tangible manifestations." The "ardor" in both senses, of color and of light, thus becomes and remains long through the nineteenth century the abstract seal of an Orient that was brought back and made available; wherever there's ardor, there's Orient.

Nine years after that write-up, the same reviewer praised another picture by the same painter, and now he was fully outspoken about what

*   Vol. VI, p. 172. The magazine was edited by Prof. Dr. Carl von Lützow in Vienna and published by E.A. Seemann in Leipzig.

had earlier been hinted at: the picture struck him as a "thrust into the hustle and bustle of the life of Algerian people." Only those who have been totally subjugated can be made into an object of study, nay, inventory as now described:

> With the keen characterization peculiar only to him among the Orient painters, Gentz has lent each of the countless figures an individual life, an interesting physiognomy. What a wealth of observations and studies . . . must have preceded this! What a spiritual energy that can penetrate the soul of the people with such understanding! Far from offering us a shiny photograph of nature, the artist, by having the sunlight pour its vast floods over the motley scenery, has introduced that phantastic and poetic element which wraps the perfectly realistic depiction of folk types in, as it were, an ideal aura.*

The subjugation of the free Orient could apparently not be driven any further than here, where its most intrinsic element, light, has been volatilized into an "ideal aura," which the artist has in stock, so to speak, for glazing his actually "realistic," i.e. obviously gray or certainly lightless, at best just motley scene. The Oriental or African mood has now become an attribute, fully passing into the capturing, coating, transfiguring, illuminating power and glory of the artist. In the following years, "a wealth of types" and "a lush brilliance of colors bursting with energy" were the critical judgments passed on the Orient paintings that Gentz exhibited, and finally it was settled that Gentz's pictures once and for all "radiated a replete brilliance of colors." No longer as in the past (during his youth in Paris, Gentz copied Delacroix's Algerian women) does the painting hunger and thirst for freedom; no longer as in the past is it full of lust; truly "replete," it now radiates a preserved heat, a coloring lent by the painter and even applied with energy.

THE BOREDOM OF SAVAGERY

The hot and yellow "South," thus expanded, was not the only climate where savage life was sought and ultimately subdued. Theodor

---

*   *Zeitschrift für bildende Kunst*, Vol. XV, p. 47. 1880.

Horschelt, for instance, a Munich artist, who together with two colleagues had followed in Delacroix's footsteps by "choosing" (as a contemporary account accurately put it) Spain and Algiers "for his locales,"
later preferred the Caucasus, greedy for adventures, of which there was
no shortage then during the Crimean War. Horschelt remained there
for five years, 1855 to 1860, and his pen-and-ink drawings, *Memory
Leaves from the Caucasus*, were awarded the gold medal at the Paris
World's Fair of 1867. "Whosoever wishes to make the acquaintance of
the Russians or their savage, fanatic foes," wrote Pecht (the historian of
Munich painting in that century) about the Crimean War paintings,
"must study these pictures, which will tell him more than any books."*
A few lines later, however, the author goes on to say (and I quote him
because of this judgment, printed in 1888): "Unfortunately, they [the
Caucasian sketches], any more than the works of others cannot disguise
the monotony required for depicting such savage peoples, who possess
no spiritual life or only one that inspires our repugnance. None of the
Orient painters has ever managed to get past this stumbling block of
rapid boredom."

An astonishingly blunt word, and all the more astonishing after the
foregoing praise: the interest in foreign savagery has paled, or is at
least overriden and overlaid by the national *Kultur* pride of a man who
feels attached to, and subservient to, the might of the German Empire.
He puts Adolf Menzel above any other painter, and not for his artistic
qualities, but for his ardent patriotism; for this and no other reason,
Menzel means more to him than "all those artists whose painterly concern is more important to them than anything else, and who depict Circassians today, Bedouins tomorrow, and their foes the day after, with
the same peace of mind with which they might paint flocks of sheep."
What is here labeled "painterly concern" was that urge previously
spurred by colonial expansion and paradoxically encouraged by the
railroad, that urge for another, still unoccupied, untamed world. But
now that Circassians and Bedouins are no longer the bearers of a color-
blazing freedom, no longer the nomadic dwellers of a dream homeland

* Friedrich Pecht: *Geschichte der Münchener Kunst im neunzehnten Jahrhundert*, p. 230. Munich, 1886.

without settledness or security, all 'savage peoples" are lumped together. In this aspect, the painters do not differ in the slightest from industrial entrepreneurs: Siemens, in his memoirs, calls it a "bizarre coincidence" that in the same Crimean War—whose painterly results induced Pecht's remark—"the two hostile camps in Sevastopol and Balaclava employed [telegraphic] apparatuses from Berlin with successive serial numbers."*

In short, the views from Europeans windows had lost their depth, becoming part and parcel of the same panorama world surrounding them and constituting a painted surface everywhere. That was why Friedrich Pecht, who threw the whole bunch of Orient painters in one pot and reproached them as boring, needed another value, patriotism, to take a new and superior position. Nonetheless, it is as if the ardor, hunted for such a long time and found in the Sahara and elsewhere, has passed into this patriotism, so that he can term it "ardent."

Although no doubt, in metaphoric linguistic and emotional usage, the "ardor" is given a more lasting location, a more solid niche here than anywhere else, that passage into patriotism is not just figurative. It takes place literally and palpably wherever Orient painting, that is to say, both the painting and the Orient, enter the service of the Fatherland: in depicting scenes from German colonizing. The politics of colonization had a whole pavilion for itself, the so-called Kaiser diorama, at the Jubilee Exhibition of the Berlin Academy of the Arts, in 1886, around the very time that Pecht wrote those scornful lines about the whole Orient "profession." The diorama building, aping an Egyptian temple in form and decoration, solidly erected in plastered brick, iron, and sheet metal, concealed in its interior (two naves with a long row of columns straight down the center) a different shrine from the one in the original temple. One aisle contained five big diorama pictures, separated by carpets hanging crosswise to ensure an effect of closure for each picture; visitors wandered through the other aisle. The first picture, *Stanley's Arrival at the Congo Cataracts,* had been painstakingly prepared with detail studies by a painter whose journey to Central Africa had been generously financed by the corporation; Gentz and his son (baptized

* Werner von Siemens: *Lebenserinnerungen,* p. 124. Quoted from the fifth edition, Berlin 1897. The manuscript itself dates from 1889-92, Bad Harzburg.

with the desert name of Ishmael) had done the figures, "Stanley and his muscular, brown companions"; and a third painter had done the landscape. Nachtigal's corpse on the gunboat *Möwe*; an elephant hunt on the Congo River by François's expedition; the blood brotherhood of Dr. Peters and the sultan of Nguru, amid utterly picturesque rock formations and a luxuriant tropical vegetation. And last but not least, the naval demonstration at Zanzibar, a focus of universal applause, according to the reviewer from the *Zeitschrift für bildende Kunst*. "The surface of the sea," he says, "which the German man-of-wars are plowing, is alive with tropical solar ardor flashing in a thousand lights; and the watery vapor, the picturesque city in the background, and the imposing display of might by our Fatherland's fleet are all depicted with a virtuosity that knows no hindrances, no difficulties."* The entire tropical landscape is the setting; and likewise, the ardent light, covering this scene with its "ideal aura," is merely the transfiguring attribute of patriotic power display. The poetic lights of the subjugated Orient play around the armored turrets of the war vessels.[10]

TRAVEL BUREAUS

In the sphere of the newly won world, it was not only the painters who had started out early to travel and look afresh at the changing images. In November 1864, five years after the first ground was broken for the Suez Canal, Louis Stangen, together with seventeen other people, conducted the first of his popular tours to the Orient, traveling through Corfu to Alexandria and Cairo, from where they went on the often described outing to the Pyramids of Gizeh. The Sphinx had been discovered long before, but not fully excavated until 1886.[11] And in 1876, when Stangen, an inventive beneficiary of the railway, published his *Life Sketch*, his brother Carl led the twenty-eighth tour to the Orient. The usual Egyptian route ("there stood the cradle of spiritually developing Mankind," he wrote) had meanwhile been expanded "with a journey through Palestine, from Jerusalem to Damascus." That same year made obvious the financial bankruptcy of the Khedive of Egypt and thus the end of the independent realm of the Orient. Stangen no longer sent his

---

*   *Zeitschrift für bildende Kunst*, Vol. XXI, p. 210. 1886.

parties to an oasis of liberty, but to a country at the mercy of the European powers; even though this crucial change did not yet dim the view of caravans, camel markets, and pyramids, of yellow sand and blood-red sunsets.

Louis by now was specializing in Italy, i.e. the old South, which, presented as new and more comfortable, stood its ground next to the more lavish Orient.[12] A good notion of the arranging skill deployed by this panorama entrepreneur is offered in the following self-assured passage from his memoirs:*

> The Venetians still have not forgotten the great Stangen cruises down the Canale Grande in 1864, a trip that took place in gondolas and barques adorned with gaudy lanterns in a moonlit night, and that left the Hotel Bauer to the accompaniment of music and singing, and lured myriad Venetians, men and women, to the narrow banks of the canal and the Ponte di Rialto to watch those eager travelers, the *Prussiani*, amusing themselves in the Queen of the Lagoons and enjoying the far-sounding barcaroles of the Italian choral group.

In this way, Stangen showed not just his Germans, but also the Venetians themselves, the real Venice.

One section in that life sketch of the former railroad official is entitled "In Civil Life and In Travel," implying that he himself did not reckon "travel" as part of civil life. Actually, travel in one form or another was not always such a generous and expensive affair as for Stangen's clients, but usually leading out and into a prepared foreign world, it was simply not to be forgone as a pendant to, and accessory of, bourgeois life during this epoch. In Germany, Louis Stangen was the missionary of this perfectly circular road to salvation, this trodden path of untroddenness.

The perfection of the rail network over the earth robbed travel, at least in its methods, of the sting of adventure. Werner von Siemens, who had played an outstanding part in linking countries and forming the world panorama, who not only drew his wires over the mainland but

---

*   Louis Stangen: *Auf gebahnten und ungebahnten Wegen*, p. 17. 1876.

also laid cables through seas, the Mediterranean and the Red Sea, thus tying continents to one another—this man, looking backward at the age of seventy-four, bade farewell (what an odd paradox) to travel, which he had so greatly promoted. During the sixties, he had twice visited the Caucasus, where he owned a copper mine in Kedabeg, and his memoirs explain: "With these two Caucasian journeys, I regard my actual travel days as terminated, for today's European travels in comfortable train compartments or stagecoaches can only be called pleasure rides. And the third journey to Kedabeg, for which I gird myself in order to take leave of the Caucasus for the rest of my life, will scarcely be anything else." That was written in the year 1890. Transportation had put an end to traveling.

The brief outline of travel, with a few dates serving as markers, is meant to analyze how the world of lands and seas opened and closed at the same time. This very phenomenon is identified by the name "panorama." The case of the Orient, the "greater south," was not just a random example, but of huge historic importance, since the Orient, both outside and inside (of homes and people), held a major rank in the nineteenth century.

The Tableau of Passion

That passion, as whose place and new embodiment the Orient was first opened, also began (while the locale turned into a panorama surface) to withdraw from this image, or at least vascillate peculiarly between the image and its viewers. Within their souls, the contemplation of the ardent-hued painting was bound up with their own desires; and as Oriental "luxuriance" was brought into European rooms and studios, as the objective color and the desert light were left to the painter's transfiguring technique as a coloring and an ideal aura, the intrinsic savage wealth of life vanished from the African or Egyptian-Nubian setting, and there remained scenes or figures that were really alluring objects of desire rather than powerful utterances of a free and savage realm of nature. Far from amassing passion in themselves as its original home and then radiating that passion out again, the scenes of the Oriental panorama become the goal and food of a roaming lust that hoped to find indemnity for what was denied by a bleak Europe with its system of inhibitions.

All those myriad women—Egyptian slaves, Turkish songstresses, dark and frivolous Venetians, dreamy and passive Spaniards, defiant Gypsies —painted and exhibited in Munich, Düsseldorf, Berlin, and everywhere else, whether as props for a southern countryside and architecture or as fateful coquettes or seductive sufferers in genre dramas—these females were just so many dream objects of a "free" love that procured itself both a field of action and an alibi in the so willingly and so frequently emphasized ideality of art. Erotic and exotic became quasi-synonyms.

Gypsydom, too, the "Bohême,"[13] is in part a special case of such an Orient—a case we moderns remember personally. With a certain characteristic infatuation, people peered over at that unsettled, roving, and generally unsafe life, every last detail of which seemed opposed to a bourgeoisie that, in property and security, was locked up against all chance: the Gypsy world was a nomadic paradise, in which one could sense paradisal feelings, intact, untainted by any commercial corruption. At the already mentioned Berlin Jubilee Exhibition of 1886, a painting of *Captured Gypsies* (a small procession of noble, defiant men, ardent-eyed women, and weeping children, spitefully eyed by burghers) was commented on by Ludwig Pietsch in the great catalogue: "Things that are an abomination to the authorities watching over public order and security in our modern well-policed European states tend to offer the artist subjects of keenest interest and a treasure-trove of the best motifs. If artists had their way, the wandering Gypsy bands would have to come much more frequently and in much greater numbers into our bleak, sober, formless, colorless, unpicturesque modern existence, and they would have to be cordially invited, rather than intimidated, persecuted, tormented, hindered in their living habits and even jailed and penalized."* This is doubtless a quite average and popular (incidentally rather late) utterance, characteristic of the most non-commital variety of cultural criticism, which the bourgeois capitalist society can only file under "bleakness and sobriety," and whose alluring counterpicture is hardly a picture any more, but merely the general picture-hungry and

---

* *Deutsche Malerei der Gegenwart auf der Jubiläumsausstellung der Königlichen Akademie der Künste zu Berlin 1886.* Heliogravure edition, p. 131. Munich, Hanfstängl.

motif-craving notion of the "picturesque" as an itself totally reified lump sum of color sensations.

That, of course, is how this very casual and not very earnest critical remark on behalf of artists scarcely differs from later comments made with more pomp and circumstance. Playing a mythical, spiritual picture-world against a modern existence that is ruled by murderous abstraction and at the mercy of mechanical technology has never managed until today to really invoke mythical motifs again—just as that hunt for the "picturesque" could never wangle any more from its motifs than a basically powerless decoration of the bleak Europe on which it was meant to bear. Any sharpness of opposition, moreover, is blunted in those lines by Ludwig Pietsch, the interpreter of artists. He gazes amicably at his protégés, gladly allowing them the harmless freedom of feuding with police opinion.

Here, as I have already said, only a very summary concept of the picturesque catches the joy in a vagabond Orient, a pleasure long since pertaining as well to the existence of the motif addicts themselves, the painters of the picturesque, the world of artists and studios, the earlier relationship having been essentially more intense, and more dangerous too. Sensuality, sucking hard on the picture of the Gypsy girl (and Oriental woman in general), emerges perhaps most solidly in Spielhagen's *Problematical Natures*. Here, the "tawny countess" roams through the Brandenberg forests and domains with her boy Cziko, who, as an illusionistic child of nature, knows how to imitate the voices of birds, and who is actually a girl in disguise, the natural issue of the Gypsy and Count Oldenburg, an eccentric landowner who scorns society. The hero of the novel, a private tutor, has dozed off in the forest meadow, his street clothes dusty, his hat hanging from a branch, the entire scene forming a somewhat frugal tourist idyll. When he awakes after a brief nap, he finds himself in a completely transformed scenery, an Orient of nature: With red cloths and garments, the tawny Countess has set up her camp on the outskirts of the woods, and from afar we can make out the bird-calls of Cziko, the unseen boy-girl. Here, the picturesque is in full flower, and the colors conceal the mysteries of sensuality. The Oriental girl has stepped out of a painting, and the viewer of the panorama, in this case Count Oldenburg, has sired a child with her, under the patronage of all the ardor of the Orient painters. That was how the novel managed to get merely painted figures into motion, to make the otherwise esthettic voluptuousness *pro*creative.

IIII

GENRE

The instant in which the Oriental woman presented herself here was quite literally fruitful. At bottom, however, all the women smiling from countless paintings with gestures frozen in the act, all such "instants," seem to be awaiting some kind of fulfillment. The target of this expectancy is not in the picture—it is the viewer. The painting and fiction of the later nineteenth century, whether claiming to be "realistic" or "idealistic" or "purely poetic," whether operating with models or out of the imagination, had no more universal or more typical peculiarity than this need for an arranged, expectant scene—in short, genre. Everything is filled with it—not just exhibits, periodicals, novels, and verse, but also the most ordinary workaday bourgeois life. The impact of genre on the thoughts and feelings of this age can scarcely be overestimated: That is to say, genre not in the sense of a special branch of art or learning, but as a form of viewing, a form of human conditions, of life itself.

The arrested moment was, after all, the subject and object of the Sedan panorama—here it was a historic instant, the afternoon of September 1, 1870, between 1:30 and 2:00. Everyone coming to view the panorama could—and had to—be expected to visualize the situation and supplement or complement it backwards or forwards in time. Actually, of course, there was nothing to see but a field and a village, fighting soldiers, powder smoke, and glittering musical instruments. The view of the frozen moment was composed of all those things, but as a whole it was itself merely a slice of time and of the historic process; the artistry had consisted in picking out the piecework in such a way that the viewer would be able to eke it out in any direction. For the panorama could not otherwise get along.

Apart from such a reconstructed historic moment, the instants in need of completion, the genre pictures, are mostly quite different. They are instantaneous pictures of beauty, childlike innocence, scenes of vice, lushness, and lust, cold cruelty, poignant compassion, and pure goodness. Hence, "living pictures," *tableaux vivants,* not allegories, but human models playing allegories. Or else allegories admitted into, locked up inside, human figures and scenes. Earlier personifications of Beauty, Vice, and Virtue, as in the Baroque, had an inherent permanence that cut straight across all time, remaining independent of human change and occurrence, and it was only such permanence that made the figures allegorical. This permanence is lost in the "living pictures"; it could not be retrieved by these wandering, seemingly live phantoms. They strove all the harder towards the instant, the ephemeral, transitory instant, to replace their lost rigorous validity with the most poignant appeal to the spectator. Halted in mid-motion, these figures and scenes absolutely beg the viewer to add to them.

Nor is any delight without interest here. Quite the opposite: in the genre, the interest of the viewer, of the reader, of the thinking, touched, indignant, lustful third party, is everywhere at work. Just as the frozen scene, the living picture, requires supplementing, so too this interested spectator is eager to supplement and keen on activating his feeling in order to fill the gaps with the challenged lusts or tears and close the breaches in the patchwork of the picture.

All that is human has disintegrated into such scenes. The world of human relations in the late bourgeois nineteenth century is like a hubbub of genre scenes. Goodness and nastiness, beauty and inner suffering, innocence and cruelty can be found galore just about anywhere, wept for, sighed over, and cursed at. No one was capable of thinking, say, "mother love," without envisioning the mother about to shield her baby from some brutal attack or being torn away by harsh fists from her child's cradle and sending back a last doleful glimpse. Ideas and experience knuckle under to such a mania, slip into the element of genre. It is also the form in which "human values" are negotiated, in which good and evil lead their confused imitation of life. The outstretched little arms of that infant and the doleful gaze of the mother do not reach out to one another so much as to the ever-present onlooker—his interest and commiseration, which needs the imagined cruelty in order to start functioning, are what must heal these wounds. Also and above all, the wound of time, gaping here as a frozen instant.

THE VENUS DE MILO

So great is the familiar lust to supplement and assemble the ruins of human order with and in feeling, to round out the depicted instant backwards and forwards into a complete scenic event, that such desire busily takes control of what would have permanence by itself and consistency in itself. The damaged idol of the Venus de Milo, unearthed in the second decade of the century and surrounded with ever-increasing, ever more general, ever more urgent interest, is no exception to that rule.[14] Had anyone been willing and able to prove that this statue was nothing but an immobile and inactive, nonexpecting and nonfearing, totally sculptural being, just a statue and no more—then interest, as if struck by a cold ray of disenchantment, would perforce have subsided. Instead, the ruined quality of the figure lastingly aroused the desire to complete it. One could do so in various ways, a different notion of the scene or situation of the figure implied a different possibility for joining the missing arms: and that was what made up the much-discussed "enigma of the Venus de Milo." It so enflamed the passions that one could detect it, almost with dismay, even in systematically and purposefully founded expositions by archeologists and anatomists involved ex officio.

The century brought many such scenic readings of the Venus de Milo, each rejected after much bitter controversy and supplanted by new ones. Was Venus gazing at her own reflection in the shield of Ares; or about to get into her bath, or, vice versa, "just now" leaving her bath? Was the figure merely the remnant of a group, "held fast" by the artist in the moment of warding off an attack by Mars on her chastity? And what about that peculiar cloth or garment around her hips; was it falling or was it fastened, and if so, for how long? These were some of the questions challenging minds.[15]

Typical in all of them is that "just now"—an expression that could really serve as the motto of scenic genre. Common to all of them, likewise, is the desire for completion, which could not restore to the ruined shape the permanence that the living statue, even as a torso, once possessed. This desire placed the goddess into the strangest, the most embarrassing "situations," as a beauty taking a bath, looking at her own mirror image, protecting her chastity, but in any case "a beauty." For that precisely is the name of such a *tableau vivant*: once again an allegory, disguised as a single person existing as a piece among pieces. An allegory representing neither Beauty nor a beautiful woman; the former would be truly allegorical in the precise old sense, the latter merely human and thus a subordinate object in an art composed of higher values. But "a beauty"—that is an allegory demoted to a shadowy existence, having bartered its permanence and rigorous validity for a mess of pottage—its life. Yet this allegory needs to be completed and staged, and it requires the curious interest of the viewers, who alone can render such assistance. For the interpreters, it was an advantage that the excavated goddess had no arms; who knows whether she would otherwise have become so interesting and so popular?[16]

Now art as a whole in that later nineteenth century was nothing but an arsenal to store all the occurring human costumes for allegorical figures. In this era, art, as has often been written and said, experienced the return of beauty—this time, however, not as its demanding law but as a piece in its store of figures. Since beauty does occur, it is a sort of living creature (a model), at the same time, however, also an isolated, impuissantly gesticulating fragment, uselessly casting about, forlorn, with no one approaching it except for the lustful, who take clear interest in such beauty. Seldom before has there been such directly erotic painting as in this epoch (it suffices to cite Makart). But all those beautiful bodies in Makart's bacchanales and in other scenes of voluptuousness, bodies offered and drawing the "completing" gazes and feelings, were and are scraps, pieces, set pieces in the artistic world that was crammed to the hilt with them and their sort.

UNCLE TOM'S CABIN

However, the borders of this artistic world, as I have already said, were in no way identical with those of exhibits or literature; they lay much further out, undetectable, in the thicket of the most normal weekday life. Not only did the burgher hope to find the voluptuousness of the painted beauties in the studio and in artistry, but virtues and vices, for the most part allied clearly enough with the beauties and atrocities, went about in the same way everywhere. How many slave markets in Cairo and other places, painted, written about, or merely conceived, appealed (genre scenes that they were) for lustful pity with the fearful ardent eyes of dusky slave girls, for the ready-for-action disgust with the brutal and cynical miens of traders and buyers? Because here, sweet suffering and cold cruelty, sensual pity and humane indignation are inseparable.

Slavery, that inexhaustible quintessence of suffering and cruelty, was a "problem" insofar as it was the object of a practice aimed at abolishing such torment—a practice of evolution (evolution—"the magic word of the century," cried the "materialists") or ennoblement. A man was ennobled by changing from a vessel or seat of cruelty to one of compassion, and this shows that even humanity, once the sharp blueprint of human nature, sparking hope and action, blurs here in the scene and in genre.

The sublime death scene of Uncle Tom, who has been mortally beaten (in Harriet Beecher Stowe's famous novel,[17] a basic book in that era for Germany no less than for the United States and other nations)—this scene, called a scene and sublime one by the author herself, and meant to crown the entire work in the way of loftiest ennoblement, culminates in an emphatic utterance from the moribund's mouth: "O Mas'r George! What a thing 't is to be a Christian!"* And these are the words dominating young Master George's mind after Uncle Tom's death—a clear sign of their importance even if they are not printed in italics. They are treacherous words.

To measure how treacherous, how instructive they are, we must first determine what this "being a Christian" means and what function it has in the genre of slavery and also for the problem of slavery. Tom's long-practiced Methodist piety and psalmodizing expectation of the heavenly Jerusalem remain constant under the scourge of the devilish

* Quoted from the text of the first edition of *Uncle Tom's Cabin*, published in 1852 by John P. Jewett & Company of Boston and Cleveland. The German translation appeared the same year as the American first edition.

slave owner Simon Legree. He manfully refuses to obey Legree's order and wield the whip on his comrades since he considers violence sinful; he also holds his tongue when harshly importuned to reveal the escape of two beautiful slave girls. The Satan Legree, infuriated, ignores any possible economic qualms to spare this valuable and expensive piece of manpower and, with the help of his two Herculean Negro foremen, has Uncle Tom flogged to death. Waiting for, even yearning for the end in an old shed, Tom has made these two "savage men" weep, shed tears of repentance and compassion, at the tale of Jesus' death and his power to save—the kind of tears whose richly flowing gush is the start and sign of "ennoblement," the binding agent of genre or the warm solvent for hardened human conditions, washing away the settled allegorical cruelty and bringing an angelic, compassionate goodness.

This goodness, however, is so overpowering in Uncle Tom that he need not strain himself to forgive his tormentor and murderer, notwithstanding the latter's total indifference to that. The forgiveness does not manifest itself as a deed or process, it is nothing but a self-evident function and a necessary appurtance of Tom's utterly ennobled nature. It does nothing and is meant to do nothing but demonstrate to the readers, to whites throughout the world: There are such people among slaves!

> "The old satan!" said George, in his indignation. "It's a comfort to think the devil will pay *him* for this, some of these days!"
> "O, don't!—oh, ye mustn't!" said Tom, grasping his hand; "he's a poor mis'able critter! it's awful to think on 't! O, if he only could repent, the Lord would forgive him now; but I'm feared he never will!" (Chapter XLI)

This excess of forbearing love, of unwavering compassion even for cruelty, its own counterpart, does not prevent Tom's best listener, that young Mas'r George (who eventually frees all his slaves), from having the following scene with the murderer scant minutes after the pious demise of the ebony saint:

> "After all, what a fuss, for a dead nigger!" said Legree.
> The word was as a spark to a powder magazine. Prudence was never a cardinal virtue of the Kentucky boy. George turned, and

with one indignant blow, knocked Legree flat upon his face; and, as he stood over him, blazing with wrath and defiance, he would have formed no bad personification of his great namesake triumphing over the dragon.

This behavior is hard to tally with the earlier example of nonviolence, and yet, as proven by the rapid transfiguration of the resplendent man into a new icon, George's action enjoys full approval from the author and doubtless, from the readers. No indeed, there is no real Christian experience here, no submission of passion to humility, no actual repentance or true breaking of human willfulness. This is the perfect genre scene. Here it is, with all its elements gathered together. Cruelty incarnate right next to miserable and commiserating goodness incarnate, each of the two figures driven to its utmost expression by the thickening of the plot to catastrophe. And right in their midst, the necessary observer in person, the representative of an entire civilized world of the observers of slavery. Young Master George; full of mellow commiseration at the side of the dying man, full of blazing indignation at the sight of the cruel man.

"O Mas'r George! What a thing 't is to be a Christian!" Thus speaks the sufferer in genre, who after all, cannot cease suffering. However, this suffering does not, in a Christian sense, constitute the thoroughly experienced essence of all salvation-needy creatures; it only fills out half of a to-be-completed picture. That is why being a Christian is merely (in the German translation) a *wonderful* thing; otherwise it would be a dangerous and difficult thing. And that is why this *wonderful* thing is merely called "being a Christian," since otherwise, at best, it would have to be known as "certitude of forgiveness." This would be an objective hope, leading clearly and sharply from the dungeon of pain and from the gush of tears. The wonderful thing of being a Christian, however, remains a subjective quality, a kind of sense of self in the suffering part of genre, the universally and sentimentally observed allegorical soul of the black man.

Still, action is possible for the observer, young Master George, who goes and k.o.'s cruel Legree. No forbearance here, now indignation speaks, and it is a good thing about the novel that the observer is personally present in the scene and can give instant vent to his feelings. Indeed, pity and indignation were challenged throughout the world by Harriet Beecher Stowe's novel, pity and indignation were expected to solve the "problem" of slavery. This could be called a Christian or even humane demand—it was at any rate a genre-Christianity and a genre-humanity.[18]

THE PRECIOUS MEMENTO

In *Uncle Tom's Cabin,* only the planter Legree remained on the side of personified cruelty. Of the male and female slaves, however, there was not one whose evil side did not melt away under tears, whether at the sight of the Christian Tom (like the two brutalized blacks, Sambo and Quimbo) or the no less supernatural love of the beautiful soul of the child Evangeline, which love could touch even uneducatable Topsy, to be sure a comical, but also a thieving, mulish, lying, and as it were, intentionally heathen darky.

In this case, too, a death scene was necessary to lure forth tears and, at the same time, to let Little Eva forever remain a tender, beautiful child, an angel on earth (she could be an angel *only* on earth—in the world of genre!) her transfiguring agony leaving an unforgettable stamp on all witnesses of her demise, those in the novel and those who read the novel. "Has there ever been a child like Eva?" we are asked, and then told:

> Yes there have been; but their names are always on gravestones, and their sweet smiles, their heavenly eyes, their singular words and ways, are among the buried treasures of yearning hearts. In how many families do you hear the legend that all the goodness and graces of the living are nothing to the peculiar charms of one who *is not*. It is as if heaven had an especial band of angels, whose office it was to sojourn for a season here, and endear to them the wayward human heart, that they might bear it upward with them in their homeward flight." (Chapter XXII)

Despite this idea of otherworldly origin, the emotion is quite worldly, namely the misery that even such an angel must die, the misery in the face of her nevertheless easy death, the hearts rent at hearing her suffering and compassionate farewell and her—almost precocious—knowledge of imminent death, which is what really makes the effect. It is not Little Eva's death that constitutes the sacrifice for purging the slave souls (though such was probably the pious author's goal); but rather, her own long, protractive and attractive expection of death is the object of a general, self-gravitating, addictively painful emotion felt by all observers of the talky and teary scene; hence also the slaves. Eva herself exploits the situations of her poignant death in order to speak many last words; she presents her tender and fading existence, her own dying scene, as the object of a lifelong mellow memory for those present; and this remembrance, hazily including the vague promise to be a Christian, is meant to form a virtual oasis inside every single heart-wrenched spectator, an oasis of softness and goodness, of emotion, which is held to be good in itself and vouchsafes that the person feeling it will occupy the gentle, compassion-arousing place in genre for the rest of his life.

> "I sent for you all, my dear friends" [the dying child says to the gathered household], "because I love you. I love you all; and I have something to say to you, which I want you always to remember. . . . I am going to leave you. In a few more weeks, you will see me no more."

But the soulful value of such remembrance is not merely spiritual. It is captured in a thing—and this thing, the "precious memento," will from now on be worn on each rent heart as the token and object of its introspectiveness.

> "There isn't one of you that hasn't always been very kind to me; and I want to give you something that, when you look at, you shall always remember me. I'm going to give all of you a curl of my hair; and, when you look at it, think that I loved you and am gone to heaven, and that I want to see you all there." (Chapter XXVI)

That is the close of Eva's address, and the author continues, by yearningly and relishingly taking up her role as observer, as an involved audience of the second instance (the first instance being, of course, the darkies themselves):

It is impossible to describe the scene, as with tears and sobs, they gathered round the little creature, and took from her hands what seemed to them a last mark of her love. They fell on their knees; they sobbed, and prayed, and kissed the hem of her garment; and the elder ones poured forth words of endearment, mingled in prayers and blessings, after the manner of their susceptible race.

The bosom in which the tiny blond curl is kept, memory, is the only place where the heart-rending scene can gain any kind of permanence. For that reason alone, the "precious memento" (which plays such a crucial part not only in novels, but also in daily circumstances, in the real human relations of the era) *is* so precious, because it painfully re-lives the sweet sensations and once again sheds the long-dried tears, in short, because it evokes the totally bygone "scenes" and lends genre an admittedly specious permanence—for many, the only lasting good in their lives. And the "precious memento" was indeed of great signifi-cance—for who could possibly enumerate all the curls, yellowed letters, preserved childhood garments, dried clovers, withered roses that formed an ever-accumulating, nostalgically redolent mass of memory stimuli?

Eva's farewell to the slaves is sheer genre and the classical quintes-sence of the precious memento. For here, the scene and the pathos alone do not suffice; here the desire for giving permanence to the scene and the pathos in the locked-up interior, for making sighs and tears repeat-able till the end of life, giving introspection a tangible possession—that device, the memento, has once again become a scene. The demise of the angelic child was not mute, it was taken into, and dissolved in, the fluid medium of the dying speech and the emotions of countless participating spectators, but that wasn't enough: To fully ensure the effect, above all to tie the many participants in the scene to genre, the object of so much cathartic compassion, Little Eva herself, makes the doling out of me-mentos to the spectators the substance of the scene.

That is a great deal of precaution—so much so that all harshness of the action retreats. And yet not all that precaution, not even owning the dear pledge of the transitory scene, can give the permanence of the perished allegories back to the instant, which is completed by twofold feeling. The instant remains a mirage.

Vivisection

The knowledge about automatic natural laws advanced into the realm of living creatures, producing a picture of the organism as a system of reactive mechanisms, each one able to be determined and measured by experiment. All subjectivity was virtually snuffed out of these living creatures and removed from the sole area worthy of knowledge, the domain of casual connections, because it was regarded as a singular, perhaps sublime, but usually distracting frill. And so the body became a dismountable patchwork, even though each element—nerves, muscles, bones—urgently needed the others. The actual dismemberment of live animal bodies for investigating or demonstrating individual reactions is, so to speak, only the necessary, obvious outer side, the experimental correlative of the theory of the organism, life, and disease. Theory, long before experiment, had always performed vivisection by making living creatures mere objects of natural science or grasping the mere object in life.

However, the sight of veritable dismemberment in the dissecting room reactivated compassion and indignation— under the name of humanity. The physiological laboratory, under the glare of such observers, turned into a "torture chamber," in which the professor as personified cruelty did his horrifying work and the natural object as a suffering, otherwise so friendly animal gazed beseechingly and cried for help and revolt. It was Ernst von Weber's famous *The Torture Chamber of Science** that first aroused German indignation against vivisectors; and the primitive woodcuts he included always show the experimentor in rolled-up shirt sleeves, lifting the knife, and, with a brutal expression, ignoring the looks and gestures of the dog on the dissecting table.

Yet these animals themselves always seem about to offer a paw or lick the spectator's hand—and that scene was what so strongly and repeatedly moved not just Ernst von Weber but the widest lay audience as well as writers like the great Darwin. "Everyone has heard" (writes Darwin in *The Descent of Man*, p. 70) "of the dog suffering under vi-

---

* *Die Folterkammern der Wissenschaft. Eine Sammlung von Thatsachen für das Laien-Publikum von Ernst von Weber, Verfasser von "Vier Jahre in Africa."* Berlin and Leipzig, 1879.

visection, who licked the hand of his operator." Himself touched and
ready to be indignant, although cautious about a possible scientific rationale, he goes on: "This man, unless the operation was fully justified
by an increase of our knowledge, or unless he had a heart of stone, must
have felt remorse to the last hour of his life." This was written by the
man who made the cruel relentlessness of the struggle to survive the pre-
eminent object of his anything but bitter, pessimistic, or even cynical
research, which was actually attuned to "civilization" and "ennoblement." And if Darwin reacted like that, then how much greater must
have been the agitation of normal citizens!

Even today it is not possible to avoid the painful impression aimed
at by endless lists of vivisections in the reports of physiological journals
and other sources. Truly a horrific battlefield! Ernst von Weber, aided
especially by the great official English examination reports of 1876,[19]
combed every part of that battlefield, singling out the methods and
equipment in experiments and the observations of the response and further life span of the animals used, and making that great misery and accumulated cruelty the basis of his public denunciation. One example
can stand for hundreds:

> The renowned Professor Magendie indulged in such horrors
> against the unhappy animal victims that I for my part must reckon
> him in all seriousness among the most reprobate of sinners. Thus,
> for instance, he took a fine, nervous spaniel, a puppy he had pur-
> chased at an auction, and nailed its four paws and long silken ears
> to a table, without anesthetizing it, mind you, in order to demon-
> strate to his students, comfortably and without interference, how
> to sever the ocular nerves, saw open the skull, cut apart the spine,
> and expose the various nerve fascicles. And then he put the wretch-
> ed, still living creature aside for the next day's experiments! *

Over and over again it was dogs, evidently favored in experiments, who
aroused sympathy and excitement, since the signs of their pain are familiar to people, and people feel, as it were, personally affected by ca-
nine woes. That dreadful account about Professor Magandie cites an

---

*   *Die Folterkammern der Wissenschaft*, p. 15.

especially aggravating as well as infuriating circumstance, the fact that the victim was such a tender, lovely, and sensitive little spaniel, an animal that brings joy to the everyday world with those very traits, has feelings of the human owners in its image, and hence is far more heart-rending than any marten or raven or even fish. It is the loyalty of the dog, so flattering to human beings, and constantly reiterated in myriad anecdotes and pictures, that seems tormented and disdained here, and such loyalty therefore becomes the gist of the ever-present positive pictures retorting to the scenes of vivisectional cruelty. The Saint Bernard that has saved half a hundred lives, the intelligent fox terriers or poodles that one could sometimes watch doing such astonishing tricks at county fairs, as well as the "darling puppy of elderly women leading bleak and lonely lives"—all such poignant memories are not merely evoked as propaganda against that "disgrace to civilization," they are actually the images to which the sliced and twitching limbs on the dissecting table are completed in the souls of the observers.

"The method that has achieved a fine success particularly in England," said Herr Von Weber to his audience at Dresden's Humane Society,

> is putting up large pictures of the horrors of vivisection at street corners, on kiosks, in railway stations, hotels, and restaurants. I have some of these pictures here, to be sure in reduced dimensions, and I take the liberty of asking you to view them. What warmth radiates from the little picture of the dog with a tobacco pipe in his mouth and the stein of beer before him, and how suitable seems the appeal: "Shall such animals be cut up alive?" Likewise the picture of the faithful hound digging about on his master's grave and not letting anyone stop him, or the big Newfoundland who has saved dozens of people from drowning. Only a totally heartless and unfeeling barbarian can calmly and indifferently see such pets, endowed with such deep emotions, exposed to the frightful tortures of vivisection, only a man in whose soul every moral feeling has been completely throttled.*

In a note to this store of cherished ideas that are meant to advance as a

---

*   Ibid.

procession of images and drive out cruelty as the other half of the genre world, the author quite openly reveals the interest essential in all genre: "And if the vivisectors refuse to show consideration for dogs, they at least owe consideration to those of us who are interested in, and arouse interest for, these dogs.

What Herr Von Weber's agitating lectures and writings lacked to complete the picture of the struggle of compassion against cruelty, to fully stir up the feelings of hearers and readers, to make the observers's mind burrow even deeper into those dreadful scenes, plunge more thoroughly into the action and counteraction of suffering, horrified indignation, and addictive goodness—what Herr von Weber's work lacked was made up for by something else: Marie-Espérance von Schwartz's novella *Gemma or Virtue and Vice*, which, published a bit earlier in Munich, under the *nom de plume* of Elpis Melena, was intended, so the foreword indicates, as a counterpart to *Uncle Tom's Cabin.*

> No less saddened than dismayed by atrocities committed daily against innocent creatures by human aberration and heartlessness, we appeal to our readers, of whom, for the sake of the cause, we desire a very large circle on all levels of society and in all age groups—and, ridden with fear, we call to them that it is our bounden duty to liberate our century from a scourge which, in its criminal truculence, is no worse than the slave trade—a scourge which, wielded by brutality, nips in the bud all compassion, that lovely wellspring of virtue, which everyone tries to bring into the heart of his child—a scourge which, were the wounds struck by it rendered visible to all the world, would long ago have been forbidden by law and condemned by the voice of the people, the highest tribunal of justice.*

The novella, curiously linking two locales, England and Italy (the latter chiefly as the homeland of daring Garibaldi), completes the ensemble of satanic cruelty and, like the more epic and more inventive Harriet Beecher Stowe, it does not fail to introduce the indignant observer physically into the scene. Corresponding to Little Eva in *Uncle*

* Elpis Melna: *Gemma oder Tugend und Laster*, p. viii. Munich, 1887.

Tom, we have Gemma, a lovely, innocent, compassionate maiden; the bestial slaveholder Legree is matched by the vivisector, who unfortunately in Gemma's father, a man personally acquainted with all the vices on this earth—adultery, gambling, drinking, and all manner of churlishness and odiousness, lust and cynicism, all of which is marked on his face as a "sardonic smirk" and a warped grimace—and the young Master George of this tale, the just man who, sympathetic and indignant, steps between the innocent girl and the inhuman father, is Osvaldo Santacroce, an ex-Garibaldian, also wrapped in the shimmer of a onetime free life as a brigand, the fiery lover of animal-loving Gemma, who eventually, thus heightening her innocence, turns out to be her very own brother.

Harriet Beecher Stowe of course made her task of depicting slaveowners and their helpers more difficult by presenting an entire host of harsh and mild, skeptical and humane, patriarchal and reformist planters, in order to drive home her message, total abolition, despite even the finest and kindest masters, and to subvert arguments from advocates of a humane slavery by proving the ultimate consequences of the whole system. Elpis Melena, however, knows only the "bestial" vivisector, and this name is always synonymous for her with lecher and downright devil:

> "What can you expect of a man" [says she] who tramples on the most sacred laws of Nature, a man whose every last grand and noble feeling has died in him, who cannot even appreciate the wonderful spiritual qualities of a daughter worthy of worship, a man who seeks his pleasures in the lowest debaucheries and gory orgies, whose conscience and hands are forever smeared with blood . . . in short, what can you expect of a vivisector?"*

"Debaucheries of all kinds" and "gory orgies" now dubbed "scientific studies" are equivalents here.

That is why the book bears that explicit and unvarnished title *Gemma, or Virtue and Vice*, whereby, more specifically than ever, the allegorical origin of these genre figures is evoked or revealed afresh.

---

* Ibid., p. 117.

Here too, the story does not fail to have personified Virtue, the beautiful daughter, put to death by personified Vice, the satanic father in intoxication; and Gemma, too, faithful to her position in genre, forgives her tormentor on her deathbed. Still, there is no conclusion of any moment for the participating observer Osvaldo, or for the authoress and her readers; all forgiveness notwithstanding, the final chapter is called "Nemesis," and shows Vice punished, namely the conscience-panged vivisector bestially dying in madness.

> "Look at them, look at them" [he raves], "they are coming at me in mobs, in legions of all kinds, all breeds, those accursed beasts! Oh save me, save me, they are surrounding me, seizing me, they want to tear me apart; free me from their claws! Did I not nail you down, torture you, and mangle you with my own hands, and yet you still have the strength to pursue me! That is your vengeance for the scorn with which I ridiculed your suffering and exulted in your convulsive struggles, that is why you grant me no rest, no peace!" . . . And thus ranting, he collapsed and uttered a howl that would have frightened and terrified even the wild brutes in the desert.*

This bloodcurling picture is confronted with that charming other picture: the maiden Gemma on her beloved pony, accompanied by the devoted dog, which she, as a little girl, ransomed from drowning, and which later saved her (as well as the loathsome father) from the raging torrent. United with these two animals, Gemma can also be seen on the frontispiece of the book. It is the—often varied—genre of Virtue.

THE WOMAN'S PRIVILEGE

"Vivisection is a crime, solely the work of man; woman, who ought to excel in loftier compassion and tenderer feeling, is dutybound to distinguish herself as an apostle of humanity by exorcising this evil.—Is it not befitting that a woman should unfurl the standard of feeling and preserve it in its immaculate purity?"† Thus goes Gemma's "Memorial"

---

*   Ibid., p. 258.
†   Ibid., p. 148.

to the queen, to induce her to pass a bill against vivisection. This petition, unmailed because of the father's intrigues and therefore never reaching its destination, occupies the center of the story; coming to naught in the plot, it is meant instead and all the more urgently to reach the ears and hearts of the ladies and gentlemen reading it.

The peculiar humanitarianism of the nineteenth century, exiled to the oasis of feelings, reveals its forlornness in nothing more explicitly than the very fact that women had to set themselves up as its apostles. That humanity per se, rather than being an issue for all human beings, became the special mission and function of the sex known as the tender or weaker one. And it was that "standard of feeling" under which the woman as such emerged from the darkness of the private sphere in which she had been lingering for so long, stepped forth with the hope of melting the hard reality that she considered the work of men and of the mind.[20] It was her gaze from within the family cell that projected all the sharp focusing of social conditions, all the objective mercilessness of power struggles, all the reifying of science (hence also vivisection), into the "hardened male heart" as the source of so much mischief. Feeling is the new privilege, held up against that of the economically managing and ruling intellect and of the possession of usable education, and put up with the claim of loftier moral value: the woman's privilege.

Compassion, the "wellspring of all virtue" and the "fairest flower of civilization," is nothing less than the expanded ultimate consequence of rediscovered Christian commandments; it is the powerless solvent of hardened social conditions, a means of compromise and defense against criticism, the reservoir—willingly and well-meaningly viewed—of the humanity fleeing the market and stock exchange, an ineffectual physic and a feeble arcanum. Insofar as the woman is called upon to preserve that, every marriage virtually formed a latent genre, consisting of both halves of the scene: the hard man with the cold eye and ruthless reason —the gentle woman, a priori suffering and compassionate.

The prototype of the "interesting female martyr," the suffering beauty, was repeatedly depicted as an ideal object of interest by several painters, with Gabriel Max in the lead. Not infrequently, the expression of mute sighs, of beseeching meekness, of voluptuous sorrow suffices to give the virgin tarrying in the picture an aura of holiness. Yet scarcely ever is the cause of such suffering to be seen, true affliction of pain or maiming bodily wounds, blood or convulsion. Even the female "martyr on the cross" offers herself in unscathed beauty to the lustful and compassionate gazes of the spectators. Her pain is purely inward and merely contributes to making her all the more desirable. Likewise, at the demise of the angelic girls Eva and Gemma, those pure sacrificial victims, little was visable of the consumption that felled them: one more sign (if still required) of their concealed allegorical nature. With these women displayed as pictures, some vestige seems to be at work of the cruelty that was once a counterpart to suffering virtue, but now, turning into compassion, reaches out from the gazes of the sepctators.

But enough. We still have to cite a document in which the battle against vivisection was substantiated and supported by an explicit theory of compassion, or in which this category of the genre became the kernel and content of a special religion.

THE RELIGION OF TEARS

We have been so informatively enlightened about the dreadful bungling of the "science" recommended for uncommon esteem and inviolable guardianship to the "greater public," and especially to our ministers and princely councilors, our enlightenment coming from several general practitioners already outstanding for their noble German style, and thus we can regard ourselves as justified in hopefully assuming that the specter of the "utility" of vivisection will no longer frighten us in our further efforts; instead, all we shall care about from now on is to allow the religion of compassion, notwithstanding the advocates of the utility dogma, to gain powerful ground for our new cultivation thereof.

This sentence and this enthronement of compassion are by Richard Wagner, who in 1879 published an "Open Letter"* in reply to Ernst von Weber, who was writing to countless prominent personalities for energetic support of his efforts. The religion of compassion, propagated here and having its mystery in *Parsifal*, is not really the Christian reli-

---

* Richard Wagner: *Gesammelte Schriften und Dichtungen*, vol. X, p. 253 ff. Leipzig, 1883.

gion, in that neighborly love and compassion are as sharply differentiated as revelation and feeling. It actually showed certain concepts of Indian self-dissolution as transmitted by Schopenhauer and likewise made evident—peculiarly enough and without ever being specifically named—in the figure of Darwin as the "wise man of Down" to his disciples and admirers.

Darwin, according to Bölsche's biography* of him, was haunted until old age by nightmares about the screaming slaves whose agonies he had grown familiar with during his world voyage—and he was similarly tortured by the sight of brutal draymen maltreating their horses. And indeed, his work contains no small amount of clear evidence for such sensitivity. This author, who, just like his "materialistic" successors, never tired of depicting the relentlessness of that objective law of Natural Selection, which operates blindly and coldly with death as its favorite instrument—this author, inwardly and in some of his scientific pictures, exhibits an exceedingly vulnerable moral sense, even towards animals, whereby, to be sure, he always strives to justify these protégés of his with a comparison to human vices. Here is a typical passus (*The Descent of Man*):

> It is often difficult to judge whether animals have any feeling for the sufferings of others of their kind. Who can say what cows feel, when they surround and stare intently on a dying or dead companion. . . . That animals sometimes are far from feeling any sympathy is too certain: for they will expel a wounded animal from the herd, or gore or worry it to death. This is almost the blackest fact in natural history, unless, indeed, the explanation which has been suggested is true, that their instinct or reason leads them to expel an injured companion, lest beasts of prey, including man, should be tempted to follow the troop. In this case their conduct is not much worse than that of the North American Indians, who leave their feeble comrades to perish on the plains; or the Fijians, who, when their parents get old, or fall ill, bury them alive.

That is the blackest fact in natural history, whereas at the same time, ac-

* Wilhelm Bölsche: *Charles Darwin. Ein Lebensbild.* Leipzig, 1898.

cording to that same Darwin, that same natural history is made up of an
endless chain of black facts: nothing but ruthless expulsion and extinction of relatively unfit or feeble organisms. But this nervous compassion
with the individual scenic case is here too, merely the subjective compromise for the necessary recognition of that objective large-scale
cruelty of nature. Just as the gushy compassion with slaves could make
up for acknowledging, as a matter of course, the ruthless mechanism of
the labor market on a large scale; and the no less lively feeling for the
tortured animals on the dissection table could balance the quite useful
medical analysis of the organism. Such compassion virtually made caves
for itself within the social edifice, on whose walls, as though projected
by a *laterna magica,* the scenes of a genre world passed and whose interior is flooded with the tears of that compassion. The observation of animals evoked the Brahman echo that also occurs in Richard Wagner's;
and just as Darwin's biographer considers him a kind of gentle saint, or
at least a sage, so too Wagner explicitly cites not just "the wisdom of the
Brahmans," but also an imaginary sage (it could almost be Darwin himself), who first sympathized with the animals and also knew the happiness of suffering.

> This sage had to own that the rational creature attains its loftiest
> bliss through voluntary suffering, which he therefore sought with
> lofty zeal and ardently grasped, whereas the animal faces absolute
> and (for it) useless suffering only with dreadful terror and hor-
> rible resistance. And that sage found man to be even more lament-
> able for deliberately torturing an animal and remaining indifferent
> towards its sufferings, for the sage knew man to be endlessly more
> remote from salvation than even the animal, which, by comparison,
> seemed as innocent to him as a saint.*

Misery, however, that evokes commiseration, and compassion that is itself a passion—compassion and suffering, contemplation and its object,
join together, flow into one another, opening a peculiar path of feeling
to the religious concept of expiation and salvation. This locked compassion, locked inside the feeling person, goes—uncognizant of its limits

*   Richard Wagner: *Gesammelte Schriften und Dichtungen,* Vol. X, p. 261.

—to such extremes that, along with the "bliss" to which it treats the "rational creature," it captures, or so it thinks, salvation.

Speaking about such a goal or peak of the "atoning death," Wagner continues:

> This befell all the martyrs and saints who were irresistibly drawn to voluntary suffering in order to luxuriate in the wellspring of compassion until the annihilation of the worldly delusion. Legends report on animals that trustingly joined these saints—perhaps not just for the protection they were assured of, but also urged by a deep inducement of possibly germinating compassion; here wounds and finally also the protective hand were to be licked. In these myths, such as Genovefa's roe and so many others, there lies a meaning that goes beyond the Old Testament.*

However, such reveling in misery as commiseration is promptly and strikingly, if unintentionally, reversed into legend the moment the writer of this "Open Letter" comes back to his practical question and demand, wrathfully threatening to invoke police sanctions against the vivisectors themselves, who previously seemed so lamentable to "that sage." and on whom he now pours his indignant scorn: "Yet there can be only unconditional abolition, not 'feasible limitation,' under 'government supervision,' and 'government supervision' could only be construed as the presence of a properly instructed policeman at every physiological lecture of the professors in question with their 'spectators.' "†

The place of this religion of compassion cannot be designated more drastically than here through its own consistency and application. There can be no sharper proof that compassion, although raised in the same breath to the cardinal hallmark distinguishing man from the animals, and to the intrinsic substance of human dignity, does not have the strength to purify and is in truth nothing but the inner side or correlative of the anger that promptly seized the beholder of the cruel scene, the *tableau vivant*, the frozen genre-moment.

---

*   Ibid., p. 262
†   Ibid., p. 270.

THE RE-EVALUATION

Everything in genre makes an appeal, everything piteously or even seductively courts the favor of the interested spectator. And he, in his avid feeling, which he thinks will redeem the animals and slaves and the —beauteous—slave girls, which he imagines will reknot the torn threads of humanity with his sighs and the flow of his tears—that spectator also has a concealed secret pleasure in the slaveholder's whip and cold gaze, in the vivisector's butcherous hands and knife, and he, the feeling liberator, calls the police. He needs the cruelty in order to feel the suffering. Virtue and vice, those ex-allegories that have acquired a pseudo-life and been exiled into the scenic instant (maimed time), that depend on continually renewed memory and the precious memento to ward off their own destruction—virtue and vice are indissolubly shackled together in genre.

Even the re-evaluation of values, the siding with cruelty against suffering, with the masters against the slaves, with the physiologists against the lambs, with passion against virtue, with evil against good (mind you: genre-evil and genre-good!); even all such disgust and all such turning of the viewer could not pull the two halves asunder, could not really lead out of the world of genre. The beholder remains a beholder, whichever side of the picture his interest may turn to. "But from time to time, grant me the benefit (assuming there are heavenly benefactresses beyond good and evil) of a glimpse, grant me One Glimpse only of something perfect, complete, happy, powerful, triumphant, in which there is still something to fear!"

That was the glimpse, and this is what was glimpsed—the two "counterparts" that belong together.

The fact that the lambs bear a grudge against the great predatory birds is not astonishing: yet there is no reason here to blame the great predatory birds for capturing small lambs. And the lambs tell one another these predatory birds are evil; and if someone is as little of a predatory bird as possible, and actually their counterpart, a lamb—would he not be good—there is nothing to be said against the sincerity of this ideal, even though the predatory birds may gaze a bit scornfully and perhaps say to one another: "We bear them no grudge, those good lambs, we really love them: Nothing is tastier than a tender lamb."

But now more clearly. The reader recalls the " blackest fact in natural history," which the sensitive Darwin so intricately twisted back and forth; it now returns, the very same fact, totally unchanged, merely "re-evaluated": "Let the weak and the failures die out: the first principle of our humanitarianism. And we should even help them to do so. What is more damaging than a vice?—Active compassion for all failures and weak people—Christianity."

What kind of Christianity is that? The man who wrote this, Nietz-sche,* calls his spade a spade: slave morality. It is the Christianity of Uncle Tom, and nothing else—Uncle Tom, the slave whose dying words are: "O, Mas'r George! what a thing 't is to be a Christian!"

It goes on here, for everything recurs in the re-evaluated genre, even that special religion, that totally psychological "religion" in the "Open Letter" to Herr Von Weber:

Christianity is known as the religion of compassion.—Compassion is the opposite of the tonic affects that heighten the energy of vital feeling: compassion is depressive. A man loses energy when compassionating. Compassion further increases and multiplies the energy loss that suffering already causes in life. Suffering, because of compassion, becomes contagious; compassion may quite possibly even result in a complete loss of life and vital energy, a loss that is in an absurd proportion to the quantity of the cause (—the case of the Nazarene's death).†

It is the Wagnerian "sage" of before, it is the Wagnerian saints of legend, who luxuriated in voluntary suffering until the annihilation of all worldly delusion, who offer the effigy of the "Death of the Nazarene" here and who are to be totally condemned.

---

* These last few lines are in *The Antichrist*, no. 2 (Vol. VIII, p. 208); the two earlier quotations are from *Genealogie der Moral, Erste Abhandlung*, nos. 12 and 13 (Vol. VII, pp. 321-22). Quoted from the classic edition of Nietzsche's works put out by the head of the Nietzsche Archive and published by the Kröner Verlag, Leipzig, 1919.

† *Der Antichrist*, no. 7 (Vol. VIII, p. 211).

Something else crops up again: Natural Selection, earlier removed from sight as objective mercilessness and cruelty and seemingly offset and overtoned, now comes into play itself, to be played against compassion:

> Assuming we measure compassion by the value of the reactions it tends to bring forth, its vitally dangerous character appears in a far brighter light. Compassion clashes by and large with the law of evolution, which is the law of selection. It preserves what is ready to perish; it defends the deprived and the doomed; through the plethora of all kinds of failures, which it keeps alive, it gives life itself a somber and dubious aspect. People have dared to call compassion a virtue (in every noble morality it is counted as a weakness); people have even gone further and made it *the* virtue, the ground and source of all virtues—only, to be sure, and this must always be kept sight of, from the viewpoint of a philosophy that was nihilistic, and whose watchword was the negation of life. . . . Nothing is unhealthier, amidst our unhealthy modernity, than Christian compassion. Being a physician here, being ruthless here, wielding the knife here—that is part of us, that is our kind of humanitarianism, that is how we are philosophers, we Hyperboreans!*

But the psychological operation as an aid to Natural Selection, this lifting of the knife to cut genre apart so that the one heretofore so attractive half, the misery-and-commiseration half, may be wiped out *(écrasé)*, and the other half, the cruel half, strangely forlorn, deprived of its counterpart and object, may be exalted and glorified— these things do not yet complete the return of genre in re-evaluation. The Orient also returns, burning Africa, the yellow desert together with its daughters, albeit merely as a "last course" and scherzo, its daughters, "the maidens of the East," who sit there so well-behaved when they are not dancing, "deep, but without thoughts, like small secrets, like beribboned enigmas, like after-dinner nuts—"†

And, above all, the Renaissance returns, that excessive, so frequent-

---

*   *Der Antichrist*, no. 7 (Vol. VIII, pp. 211-13).

†   *Dionysos-Dithyramben: Unter Töchtern der Wüste*, no. 1 (Vol. VIII, p. 442).

ly painted canvas of pleasure and cruelty. The Renaissance particularly appeals to the freethinker, who has cast off moral horror as well as the excuse with which earlier viewers covered their interested delight, namely, that this painting is simply "art" and that the beautiful vices to be regarded in it are studio privileges, artistic license. No indeed, this caution was not deployed by the new, the re-evaluating beholder— which did not prevent the painting from remaining a painting or the Renaissance from remaining a vividly arranged allegory of vice, be it ever so beauteous vice.

> I see a possibility before me of a completely unearthly enchant-
> ment and luring coloration: —It seems to me that this possibility
> glows in all terrors of refined beauty, that an art is operating in it,
> so godly, so devilishly godly, that one may scour millenia in vain
> for a second such possibility; I see a spectacle, so ingenious, so
> marvelously paradoxical at once, that all the deities of Mount
> Olympus would have been stirred to immortal laughter—Cesare
> Borgia as Pope.*

And with the assumed mien of a lunatic's impishness, as though dancing before his idol, the sketcher of this tableau (which portrays the invest- ment of cruelty on the throne of compassion, the triumph of the other half of genre over the half that has turned empty), continues: "Cesare Borgia as Pope . . . Do you understand? . . . Well then! Now that would have been the victory which I yearn for alone today: That would have been the abolition of Christianity!"

Tongue-lashing the spoilers of this phantasmagoria and with a laughter that sounds too bitter and too intentional to be reckoned im- mortal like that of the Olympic gods, the re-evaluation observer turns away. This mirth could do as little with its peal to join together the dis- integrated world of human relations as the weeping of the compassion- ate had done with its flood of tears.

---

* *Der Antichrist*, no. 61 (Vol. VIII, p. 301)

IV

THE MAGIC WORD "EVOLUTION"

It was the naturalist Charles Darwin who discovered the principle of natural selection, which, theoretically, was supposed to have produced or at least determined the myriad formations of species among organisms now sharply distinct from, but co-existing with, one another. This principle, according to repeated observers, has more than an outward analogy to the phenomenon of competition dominating the economic "struggle for survival" in the era of free capitalism. The continual extinction of inferior and less powerful enterprises (and people) causes a likewise continual positive selection of the more powerful and more skillfully "adapted"; and this brutal automatism is always accompanied and encouraged by the justifying hope, nay, persuasion that the victors are actually the fittest, and thus have a native right, as it were, to their victory. Darwin himself, by citing the national economist Malthus,[21] hinted at that analogy, and the quotation plays a crucial part in the naturalist's earliest draft *The Variation of Species and Natural Selection* (sketched in 1839 and published twenty years after).

In these terms, Darwin's theory (without exaggeration the most potent, popular, and effective ideological novelty of the nineteenth century) appears as an enormous confirmation and justification of competitiveness, as a rediscovery and reperusal of this basic phenomenon in latter-day economy—under the vast aegis of natural history. The doctrine offers an imposing picture of nature's eternal warfare, which, however, just as eternally winds up properly in that the victor ever and anon proves his right to win simply by winning; in that such a right is swallowed up in power, which in turn finds its grounds and goals in the best possible "adaptation" to the factors and perils of existence. The spectacle of a vast battlefield strewn with corpses is thereby disguised and overshadowed by admiration for the unerring and expedient choice of those who elude destruction—the senselessness of universal annihilation being camouflaged by the "sense" in the formation of ever more perfect surviving species.

That first draft of Darwin's contained the sentences: "DeCandolle, in an eloquent passage, has declared that all nature is at war, one organism with another, or with external nature. Seeing the contented face of nature, this may at first be well doubted; but reflection will inevitably prove it is true." (*The Foundations of the Origin of the Species*, ed. by Francis Darwin. Cambridge, 1909.)

And later, shifting from the war to its positive effect: "Yearly more [individuals] are bred than survive; the smallest grain in the balance, in the long run, must tell on which death shall fall, and which shall survive. Let this work of selection, on the one hand, and death, on the other, go on for a thousand generations; who would pretend to affirm that it would produce no effect?" (p. 91)

But now the decisive point is the fact that the naturalist Darwin and all his successors (nor could it be otherwise after that starting point) regarded not so much the war as its issue, not so much the destroyed as the survivors, not so much the extinction as the selection; and all these scientists, with a resoluteness quite befitting the process, sided with the victors, which was all the easier since, after all, the victims withdrew from observation and scientific study by their nonexistence.

Let us, for the purpose of this temporary characterization, add a third quotation to the two earlier ones, in order to gain precise knowledge of the progress from death to life, from non-sense to sense. This line is from a letter of Darwin's in 1857: "I think it can be shown that there is . . . an unerring power at work, or *Natural Selection* (the title of my book), which selects exclusively for the good of each organic being" (*The Life and Letters of Charles Darwin*: London, 1887, Vol. II, p. 95).

An unerring power! And selecting exclusively for the good of each being! How remote now lies the field of destruction, how brilliantly the myriads of deaths are rationalized! Truly, Darwin offered the simplest theodicy or justification of God imaginable by—not claiming, but proving, and supporting with thousands of examples, that everywhere in nature, death serves only for the best of life. And he wasn't even out to understand the workings of God.

Now the affinity of Darwin's theory to economic competitiveness may well be historically conclusive; but the justifying and rationalizing of this theory and thought go a great deal further. The struggle for existence and natural selection are principles that do not necessarily merely confirm the living habits of only an "individualistically" organized society. There are other possibilities. Darwin himself, to be sure, at the end of *The Origin of the Species* (p. 633), makes demands on human society—rather peculiar ones—if for no other reason than that he leaps from analysis to postulate, from scientific observation and investigation to political demand, by claiming that human beings must follow the very same law he has been demonstrating for seven hundred pages as obtaining automatically in nature: "There should be open competition for all men; and the most able should not be prevented by laws or customs from succeeding best or having the largest number of offspring." (p. 633)

It would not be necessary or even possible to insert a "should" here if man were ceaselessly at the mercy of that evolution by natural selection and its automatism of wiping out or picking out—but this just in passing, since we are not aiming at a philosophical critique. In any event, to state it once more, Darwin's theory does not necessarily have to wind up with individualism in terms of his own requirements, however individualistic the motives may be. On the contrary, several of his zoological accounts indicate clearly enough how the group, the herd, in short, a society can derive the basis of its superiority and the right to its power from natural selection and nothing else.

"Judging from the habits of savages," he writes in *The Descent of Man* (p. 63), "and of the greater number of the Quadrumana, primeval men, and even their ape-like progenitors, probably lived in society. With strictly social animals, natural selection sometimes acts on the individual, through the preservation of variations which are beneficial to the community."

That is how far his observation goes, acknowledging certain cases of a division of labor in which individual groups of an animal society own and pass properties or weapons useful to the "whole" and not the individual members, one example being the stinger of the worker bee. But now comes the gist, which completely establishes and justifies raising some closed societies over their competitors on the principle of natural selection: "A community which includes a number of well-endowed individuals increases in number, and is victorious over less-favored ones; even though each separate member gains no advantage over the others of the community."

The wording is odd enough. The "even though" sounds vaguely regretful: If the individual cannot gain an advantage over the other individuals, then at least the entire horde or community of these individuals can and should triumph over other communities. Thus the motive of individual competition is really not the only practical way of applying the "struggle for existence" among human beings.

Darwin goes deeper with the self-justification of power, of success, of violence—whether of an individual or an entire society is beside the point. Once again he offers the simplest theodicy. For the doctrine of natural selection slashes right through the knot of the ancient, the basic and cardinal question of theodicy as to how injustice and violence could come into the world. There is no injustice in the world, says Darwin's rationale, since the victors, by being victorious, irrefutably prove that they are the fittest, the strongest, the best "adapted," which means the best.

A LONG HAUL

Once the focus shifts from the battlefield left by natural selection (and that shift, as those few sentences of Darwin's show, takes place quickly and perfectly), we promptly see a very different spectacle, an unbroken chain of animal forms, in which every new species points back to an earlier one; in which no individual remains isolated; in which everything, on the contrary, has an origin and a genesis, a link backwards and (except for man) also forwards—in short, an endless panorama unrolls before us, and its name is: Evolution.

One might almost think that this word itself indicated the long, un-folded picture. Only on rare occasions does a tiny, barely perceptible aperture permit a furtive glance at what Natural Selection (quite properly capitalized) leaves behind on its battlefield during its both ruthless and solicitous advances. Normally, however, such a perspective is closed and locked; the eye and the mind's eye can slide unhindered, up and down, back and forth, across the pictures as they themselves "evolve." The whole of organic nature fits together in a new and quite suggestive fashion in that Darwin's theory, with its immense treasure-trove of personal and other observations, keeps "explaining," connecting, and clarifying the variety of forms in the animal kingdom. Nothing seems to be left of anything exterior that might be alien to this tightly structured whole of development in its autonomous succession and its sliding closure—not the influence or interference of the Creator, nor the interjection or aberration of blind natural chance. Everything joins together quite meekly, once immoderate waste and destruction are declared necessary and hence made indifferent, and are forgotten and covered over.

Even the confusing, nay, apparently abstruse co-existence of such untold, hopelessly scattered organisms sharply delimited in their individualities (mussels, bees, crabs, elephants, beetles, geese, eels, dogs, sparrows, lizards, apes, starfish, human beings)—or, less chaotic, in a cabinet or cage, the hard system of traditional zoology, Linnaeus's system of mammals, birds, amphibians, fishes, insects, worms, and Cuvier's system of vertebrata, mollusca, articulata, and radiata, systems that, precisely by classifying (whatever the principle may be), so clearly preserve the sharp adjacency and the incomprehensibility, even peculiarity of the many and the interchangeable—even this and this first is made to vanish in the evolution panorama.[22] The reader of Darwin's writings will notice something very strange: the unsettling co-existence of so many living forms is never expressly kept in the background, yet it moves into the background of its own accord, or at least is never mentioned in positive terms, even merely as an enigma or a problem of natural philosophy. That phenomenon becomes almost trivial next to the urgent and, here, far more interesting phenomenon of succession and differentiation. Development obscures true simultaneity, although Darwin never ventured so far as to set up the daring construction of a linear, all-comprehensive, graduated sequence of organisms, a structure relativizing every-thing into a mere stage, from protozoa to homo sapiens. Instead, Dar-win's concrete analysis, only for stretches at a time, say, from man back to the ape at most to the fishes, established a kinship and pursued the effect of natural selection, permitting many quite different outcomes of evolutionary lines to exist side by side. This too remains peculiarly in-conspicuous; the suggested analogism and premonition give the *coup de grâce* to that remnant.

Finally, it was the theory itself that was driven with so much pas-sion and precision through the mass of experience, issuing stronger from every successful explanation and becoming strong enough to demand trust, even faith, to require that the incomplete parts of the panorama, where there was still sharp juxtaposition, be regarded with no other feeling than the expectancy that those parts would soon be similarly filled out, very richly and very consistently. The thronging crowd, the peculiar chaos of all genera and species of animals (it is so peculiar that at times we must doubt whether the name common to all of them, "ani-mal," has the strength to encompass that chaos!) had at last been exten-sively and ingeniously distributed by all those methods and generally tucked away in the remoteness of immense evolutionary eras as required by Natural Selection for performing its works; all that remained urgent-ly close was practically man himself and his much-cited "primal progen-itors."

These immeasurable eras, never really subdivided and reckoned, which have nothing to do with any familiar time, whether finite or infinite, but are merely an indefinite, even astonishing expression of the "gradualness" with which variation is piled upon variation until a new and always better species is produced—this vast time spreading tremen-dously everywhere, is needed to allay all differences, convey all limits, and fill all gaps with countless transitions. This time is the final, perhaps most important way to bring the world of organic nature into the pano-rama. It is virtually the cartoon or unrolled canvas on which the forms and products of Natural Selection are registered in sequence.

If an annihilating competition was one side, the back view of Dar-win's theory, if you will, then this panorama of evolution was the other and more pleasant front view. We now have to describe more specifically and hold on to those individual, heretofore briefly designated elements of its formation and the means of its creation.

DARWIN'S INTENTIONS

The agency or act of creation is eliminated, and so nature seems "whole," coherent, not of a settled but at most of a developed diversity; in a word, panoramistic. It is essential to know that this element in Darwin's theory (causing such fierce struggles with churches and theologians by coming more and more to the center of philosophical application, particularly in Germany) did not signify or imply simple "atheism" in Darwin, i.e. in its original form; but rather a far more definite, specific opinion: namely that there are no separate, successive but mutually independent acts of creation.

This is quite purposely termed an "opinion," albeit just provisionally (since our actual goal is not to report on opinions and subjective doctrines); an "opinion," first of all, because Darwin quite surprisingly confesses that his guiding aim, prior to any investigation of facts, was to topple the "dogma" of independent creations. This admission occurs strikingly in *The Descent of Man*, when Darwin revises his earlier feeling about the role of Natural Selection, which he now somewhat modifies as less absolute.

> I may be permitted to say, as some excuse, that I had two distinct objects in view; firstly, to show that species had not been separately created, and secondly, that natural selection had been the chief agent of change, though largely aided by the inherited effects of habit, and slightly by the direct action of the surrounding conditions.

The legitimacy of these prior aims or of the process of entertaining and then demonstrating principles in natural science is so little questioned by this author and so taken for granted that he actually bids his critics to consider not just his results but his intentions as well: "Some of those who admit the principle of evolution, but reject natural selection, seem to forget, when they criticize my book, that I had the above two objects in view.

Yet it is not enough to put the principles over the observations, nay, over their own explanatory value—Darwin goes even further, sacrificing, though within limits, the positive aspects of his detailed results in favor of the negative accomplishment of having subverted a dogma and established a new form of overall viewing. "If I have erred in giving to natural selection great power, which I am very far from admitting, or in having exaggerated its power, which is in itself probable, I have at least, as I hope, done good service in aiding to overthrow the dogma of separate creations." (*Descent of Man*, pp. 61-62).

This testimony is significant. It permits assessing how unbearable that traditional Nature was, sliced up in stages, each premising a new and absolute beginning; how repulsive the awareness of those sharp gaps in natural history, into which an alien and incontestable hand reached to destroy and to bring new things; how urgent the (we must describe it thus) imperialistic gesture that requires closing the gaps, excluding or catching up with anything alien, in short, getting the whole mass of organic forms and millennia under the sway of a single power—natural selection. For what is at work here is by no means the mere general need of thinking man (a need that mild philosophers have at times spoken about) to "explain" as much as possible, and to explain, if possible, by a single paragraph. Instead, Darwin himself and, above all, others after him and in his footsteps hoped for greater successes of "explanation" from a combination of several principles, say, selection allied with the principle of innate organic structural laws, and above all that awful nuisance, the "dogma" of creations, was able to explain just as much and just as little as natural selection (though, to be sure, the empirical foundations of the traditional scientific form of that dogma had multiply proven erroneous). No indeed, it is not a greater explicative value that distinguishes natural selection, but its unifying power, which dissolves every individual thing into unbroken series of variations and then closes it all the more solidly together. An unsurpassable instrument of mastering.

And that too is why natural selection always remains in the twilight between an autonomy and a power device or, speaking scientifically, between an objective law—better, an operative force—and a sheer heuristic principle, a sheer assumption for the sake of the best possible explanation. Half natural force, half tool (if closely examined, both at once), serviceable and yet demanding admiration if not veneration, but at least submission, natural selection accurately performs the task of joining together the previously separated forms of organic nature into an unbroken gliding sequence of changing images and at the same time offering this whole of evolution as its own work to the scientist, a further traveler on the railroad.

Man and Natural Selection

Man himself (this, after all, was the most offensive thing about "Darwinism"), by means of ponderously sought and constructed transitions, enters the line of his zoological progenitors, forgets his different dimensions and relations, and professes (with defiant pride, no less) to have not so much emerged directly from God's hand as very gradually developed from plain, and further back even plainer, beginnings or rather preliminary stages, through the steady, exceedingly slow, yet sure effects of natural selection. Man himself puts shelters under this bizarre gradualness, and he is warmer here (notwithstanding the rigorous technique of this selection, of which, after all, he feels nothing now), warmer than in the position of the free outcast who confronted the rest of nature as a trial, task, issue, and enigma, as an alien abode. Man flees "deep into the warming womb of earth," like Venus into the mountain.

But he remains twofold, for he both lets the row of images pass before him and appears in them at the end. He is the product of natural selection, and it is also his tool. It is far from remaining a purely empirical notion, from virtually vanishing in the long, unrolled surface of evolution—so very far that it even comes forth clearly and expressly and is labeled a "power" and a "being," i.e. a subject. Thus, for instance, the passage on the genesis of the human eye states: "We must suppose that there is a power, represented by natural selection or the survival of the fittest, always intently watching each slight accidental alteration ... and carefully selecting each alteration, under varied circumstances, may in any way, or in any degree, tend to produce a distincter image (namely: in the transparent tissue posited as the original form of the eye)" (*The Origin of Species*). We must suppose, and Darwin did suppose.

He supposed a power having so much subjectivity that it intently watches, selects, picks over, refusing one thing, preserving another. And the situation is even clearer in the already quoted letter of 1857: "Now, suppose there was a being, who did not judge by mere external appearance, but could study the whole internal organisation—who never was capricious—who should go on selecting for one end during millions of generations, who will say what he might not effect!" (*Life and Letters of Charles Darwin*, London, 1887). This being judges, studies, and though rigorously consistent and never capricious (an ideal scientist), it performs its task with both zeal and patience. And yet it is not called a "breeder," which would be only fair, but has the more colorless name of "selection," the name of a constant action rather than of an actor. It is virtually a neuter.

And yet so much bombast is spent on ascribing blindness, dullness, total lack of intelligence to this being, and on constantly recertifying these things so that the being shall not become too powerful or betray the borrowed human properties. It has the blindness of pure empirical "facts." "It is scarcely possible to avoid comparing the eye to a telescope. We know that this instrument has been perfected by the long-continued efforts of the highest human intellects; and we naturally infer that the eye has been shaped by a somewhat analogous process. But may not this inference be presumptuous? Have we any right to assume that the Creator works by intellectual powers like those of man?" (p. 228). And then, after this rhetorical question gets its well-deserved negation: "In living bodies, variation will cause the slight alterations, generation will multiply them almost infinitely, and natural selection will pick out with unerring skill each improvement." Hence: "We should be extremely cautious in concluding that an organ could not have been formed by transitional gradations of some kind." The immensity of alterations upon alterations, gradations upon gradations, and the lavishing of millions of years on this very purpose rush to the aid of, and make up for, the blindness and dullness of that being known as "Natural Selection."

Unerring skill and yet no intellect. A contradiction? Yes, if it is a a contradiction that the godforsaken facts must yield a meaning. If it is a contradiction that such a meaning, locked up in an evenly dark and endless nature (to speak metaphorically), can knock on the cover of its grave and try to spring forth. If, finally, it is a contradiction that evolution is evolution and as remote from providence as from scattered figures of chance.

THE RETURN OF CHANCE

Of chance. Evolution on the whole excludes it, for there is nothing to evolve in chance: it balks. But natural selection, that bizarre shadow of a power which does not so much create as choose among already created things to foster the ones that seem worth fostering and have proven themselves—natural selection for its part cannot fully and definitively swallow balking chance. And so, at the lower edge of the evolutionary panorama, as it were, we see the scraps of unconquered chance—a chaos of irritating aspect. Some of Darwin's contemporary critics felt this to be disturbing and displeasing when they complained that this new "principle" did not "explain" everything, particularly the incipient stages in a line of evolution. For in point of fact, natural selection, in order to pick out and then further develop the "fittest," requires an already existing mass of, albeit quite trivially, distinct cases, exemplars, and characters of a species. Selection itself cannot bring forth these distinctions; but the moment it notices one, the moment its "unerring skill" feels that some minute departure from the norm is worth preserving and improving, natural selection can cut in, take over the minute individual curiosity (occurring "of its own accord" and cast there by chance), hand it down and hand it down again, and gradually cultivate it into a variation, nay, a new species.

Friedrich Albert Lange, the German writer who provided the "materialism" of the nineteenth century with its family tree, cites an anonymous critique of Darwin (in the *Literarisches Centralblatt*), which broaches that very issue:

He prefers to supplant an expedient, but marvelously working transmundane causation with the possibility of happy accidents, and in the progressive evolution of what a happy accident commenced, he finds a substitute for the circumstances that all phenomena of the world are ultimately without sense or purpose, and that the good and the beautiful lie not at the beginning but only at the end, or at least come to light during the process of events.*

These lines, especially because they conservatively culminate in a return to the idea of the expedience of all creation, are a thorn in the side for Lange, who profoundly despises all supernatural "evasions," and he tries to disarm the argument and neutralize chance or accident by turning that leftover of natural selection into an admittedly no less mysterious "law":

> Experience emerges from the preservation of relatively accidental formations; yet these formations may be called accidental only insofar as we cannot indicate a reason for their occurring at that precise moment. On the whole, everything is necessary and is governed by everlasting laws, and hence also the occurrence of these formations, which, adapting and propagating, become the basis of new creations. These laws, to be sure, do not immediately produce the expedience, but they do bring forth a plethora of variations, a wealth of seeds, among which the special case of expedience, of survival may be relatively rare.†

The poignant and yet wrathful appeal, "everlasting laws," must help cover a weak point that is obviously embarrassing to the author—embarrassing because the unifying work of evolution, while dull and blind, ought to be carried out with fully unrestricted power. Still, the evocation of the everlasting and of laws covers this gap rather defectively since, after all, beneath this name, the sight of immoderately scattered masses of basically useless variations is as unsettling as ever.

THE MONOPOLY OF THE GIRAFFE

However, this indissoluble remnant that evolution cannot incorporate appears far more clearly and originally in Darwin's own quarrel (in *The Origin of Species*) with a detractor of his theory, the zoologist George Mivart. This man too, had among other things protested that "natural selection is incompetent to account for incipient stages of useful

---

*   F.A. Lange: *Geschichte des Materialismus und Kritik seiner Bedeutung in der Gegenwart*. Third edition, Vol. II, p. 245. Iserlohn, Germany, 1876.
†   Ibid., p. 274.

structures." Darwin retorts with the example of the giraffe, thoroughly analyzed, and this interpretation, with all its peculiarities, especially the effort to keep reducing the role of chance to negligible point and to make the triumph of selection all the more sublime and glorious, is so informative that the main parts must be quoted here.

George Mivart's example is cited first, in its opposite sense, of course. Thus, Darwin states: "The giraffe, by its lofty stature, much elongated neck, forelegs, head, and tongue, has its whole frame beautifully adapted for browsing on the higher branches of trees. It can thus obtain food beyond the reach of the other Ungulata or hoofed animals inhabiting the same country; and this must be a great advantage to it during dearths."

Then, after a few digressions on analogous examples, the "explanation" is launched:

> So under nature with the nascent giraffe, the individuals which were the highest browsers and were able during dearths to reach even an inch or two above the others, will often have been preserved; for they will have roamed over the whole country in search of food. That the individuals of the same species often differ slightly in the relative lengths of all their parts may be seen in many works of natural history, in which careful measurements are given.

Here, in this unimportant diversity of individuals, merely individuals of the same species, we have chance, the scrap existing before all selection, and cast out by a promiscuously manufacturing nature—and the "power" of selection, greedy for the useful and studying intently, pounces upon that scrap in order to elaborate it. Since all these things are simply trifling individual niceties, the gamble of chance is removed from the higher realm of selection and regarded as harmless, apparently for being self-evident. But why—the question urges itself—are these individual differences, which can be found anywhere, more self-evident, more neutral, more indifferent than those of "variations," much less "species"? After all, under the aegis of selection, which continually mellows and draws together the severe borders of co-existing animal forms by inserting countless and ever finer "transitions" through its singular pacing, there is still a difference, if not in principle then certainly in degree, between a rigorously delineated "species" and a mere variation or deviation.

But let us listen further:

> These slight proportional differences, due to the laws of growth and variation, are not of the slightest use or importance to most species. But it will have been otherwise with the nascent giraffe, considering its probable habits of life; for those individuals which had some one part or several parts of their bodies rather more elongated than usual, would generally have survived. These will have intercrossed and left offspring, either inheriting the same bodily peculiarities, or with a tendency to vary again in the same manner; whilst the individuals, less favored in the same respects, will have been the most liable to perish. By this process long-continued, which exactly corresponds with what I have called unconscious selection by man, combined no doubt in a most important manner with the inherited effects of the increased use of parts, it seems to me almost certain that an ordinary hoofed quadruped might be converted into a giraffe.

According to Darwin, the necks of these "ordinary hoofed quadrupeds" that existed at the start became longer and longer through selection after chance, only coming into play with the slight individual nuances of the body and face formation, offered, among countless others, that nuance of the ever-so-slightly longer neck, which ultimately reached a towering height and stopped its growth to become the specific feature of the giraffe. Mivart then asks: "If natural selection be so potent, and if high browsing be so great an advantage, why has not any other hoofed quadruped a long neck and lofty stature?" Or why are there not at least more animals with long trunks, which can also perform the same task? In his answer, Darwin geographically limits the area for settling this problem to the natural range of the giraffe—a noteworthy thing: The restriction discloses that only the field of a possible immediate competition can also be the field of natural selection. However, the competition for pasturing high branches is as follows:

> In every meadow in England in which trees grow, we see the

lower branches trimmed or planed to an exact level by the browsing of the horses or cattle; and what advantage would it be, for instance, to sheep, if kept there, to acquire slightly longer necks? In every district some one kind of animal will certainly be able to browse higher than the others; and it is almost equally certain that this one kind alone could have its neck elongated for this purpose, through natural selection and the effects of increased use. In S. Africa the competition for browsing on the higher branches of the acacias and other trees must be between giraffe and giraffe, and not with the other ungulate animals.

This reply to Mivart's criticism is explicitly called "not difficult" by Darwin himself—which is amazing, since it actually contains a host of complications. First of all, in order to present the noncompetitiveness of a special advantage gained by selection, Darwin premises a specific coexistence of virtually completed species. At the same time that the giraffe (we must thus assume in analogy to English horses and sheep) evolves its long neck, all other South African species are already so totally individualized and developed that there is no chance for them to compete for the giraffe's elongation. But, to return to the inconspicuous everyday English instance: Under the given conditions, it would of course be of no advantage to the sheep to develop "slightly longer necks"—yet why should this development be slight? Why should natural selection, that otherwise so powerful albeit shadowy force, be adjudged too feeble to let the sheep evolve anything more than *slightly* longer necks? Why, here of all places, is there no possibility for these gentle and humble creatures to significantly change their entire frames along with their necks?

Evidently, the answer to all these questions hinges on the essence of competition. An individual competes with members of its own community, says Darwin—but that's not all. There is also the essential factor that competition does not always boundlessly lead to achieving advantages, to imitating and even outstripping the other members of the community. Sooner or later, the racing stops—namely at the point when a monopoly is reached. The giraffe's long neck is a monopoly, and, in fact, one requiring no defense, but existing "without competition." This is the point at which the otherwise tempered or veiled phenomenon of the acute adjacency of the species emerges openly—as a relative final stage of evolution. Notwithstanding all the changeability, all the diversity of transitions in which natural selection so greatly and so luxuriously excels, there is a point (with every consideration of a specific and special line of evolution) at which sheep are so decidedly sheep, antelopes so decidedly antelopes, that there is absolutely no prospect of the former competing with horses in English meadows, or the latter with giraffes in South Africa; rather, an attentive natural selection can see no prospect of letting them compete any further and developing new advantages. The process of competition, in which the "species" still capable of all sorts of possible variations chase one another as they vary, comes to rest in a dispensed monopoly.

Thus once again we can clearly see the "national-economic" framework of Darwin's natural history—the machinery, so to speak, of the mobile panorama of evolution. The exposé seems prophetic in that, quite similarly, the age of free capitalistic competition surges towards an age of stable monopolies, the earlier age being both terminated by and captured in the later one. The chance emergence of a minute physiognomical difference offered natural selection the first inducement and object of its operations, on which it pounced, in order to "evolve" it. By the same token, all its "work with life and death" ends with the other, perhaps even more tremendous chance of the simultaneity of "completed" species—only, of course, when one views a limited area populated by certain animals. The "ordinary hoofed quadrupeds" from which the giraffe sprang either lagged behind or developed in a different direction, toward other advantages and monopolies. The species were born.

But *when* this stop-signal resounds, and *what* peculiar frozen ensemble of completed shapes we get to see at that point (and only at the point, since previously, after all, during the "journey," everything was steadily involved in modifications and transitions), are again a matter of chance. Chance is the beginning, chance is the end of evolution.

THE EXTERMINATED TRANSITIONS

The sharp borders becoming visible between the panorama figures in the moment of halting remained hidden during the imaginary voyage, or, more precisely, they were constantly shifting and dissolving. Nevertheless, their so plain existence at the end is a further disturbing and unsettling factor in the unwinding of the tableaux. The audience's astonishment at seeing that rigid adjacency of peculiar shapes the very second the performance is done, the unrolling panorama arrested, challenged the theoretician Darwin to ask: "Why, if species have descended from other species by fine gradations, do we not everywhere see innumerable transitional forms? Why is not all nature in confusion, instead of the species being, as we see them, well defined?" This question is the first of four in the chapter entitled "Difficulties of the Theory" in *The Origin of the Species*. The effectively ineffaceable contours of the species, which make up their individuality, have to constitute an enigma if everything boils down to gliding transitions, progress by tiny degrees, imperceptibly tiny degrees, the further and further, more and more intense reduction of distances, the removal of empty places, in short the "in between," which is indispensable if one wishes to travel from one to the other. The transition is—in the panorama of evolution—more important than the final result, the precisely delimited species; the originating is more important than what has originated; the journey or the traveling more important than the destination or the stations. The "well defined," the sharp and contoured, is the strange, repulsive, defiant thing requiring justification and "explanation" more urgently than anything else.

Here is the explanation:

> As natural selection acts solely by the preservation of profitable modifications, each new form will tend in a fully-stocked country to take the place of, and finally to exterminate, its own less improved parent-form and other less-favored forms with which it comes into competition. Thus extinction and natural selection go hand in hand. Hence, if we look at each species as descended from some unknown form, both the parent and all the transitional varieties will generally have been exterminated by the very process of the formation and perfection of the new form.

This is once again the phenomenon of advanced competition, in the course of which the better always wipes out the good; and many tiny starts or enterprises, unable to compete, are put out of business, as it were, destroyed in their independence and—to employ economic jargon that seems quite fitting here—"swallowed up" as soon as a form (a business) of the same "species" (branch) has become superior, that is to say, most fittingly "adapted" itself, thereby dominating the area (the market). The annihilation of transitional varieties can all the more aptly be described as an absorbing or "swallowing-up" in that its trend is preserved and brought to the goal in the organization with the greatest usefulness, with which the individual evolution always terminates.

A definition of the species, a specific form, an individuality are thus derived in two ways within the panorama: By the nonexistence of intermediary forms, which results from the paradox of competition, the specific and defined species must really be reversed at a certain point, rather than continuing as before, and must terminate its work with the triumph of the most powerful, i.e. with the demolition of the small individuals and species.

> In travelling from north to south over a continent, we generally meet at succesive intervals with closely allied or representative species, evidently filling nearly the same place in the natural economy of the land. These representative species often meet and interlock; and as the one becomes rarer and rarer, the other becomes more and more frequent, till the one replaces the other. But if we compare these species where they intermingle, they are generally as absolutely distinct from each other in every detail of structure as are specimens taken from the metropolis inhabited by each. By my theory these allied species are descended from a common parent; and during the process of modification, each has become adapted to the conditions of life of its own region, and has supplanted and exterminated its original parent-form and all the transitional varieties between its past and present states.

That is how great the power of the new monopoly is in abolishing all competition. Yet now comes a new difficulty, ensuing from the observation of the "conditions of life" (the conditions of the market—to continue exposing the "machinery" of the panorama!): "But in the intermediate region, having intermediate conditions of life, why do we not now find closely-linked intermediate varieties?"—"This difficulty," Darwin sincerely adds, "for a long time quite confounded me. But I think it can be in large part explained" (pp. 209-10). Indeed, if the monopoly form appears legitimized in its widespread destruction by the very fact that it has best adapted to the given conditions, then the borders of its "metropolis" would have to coincide exactly with those of its specific conditions of life. The reckoning, that is to say, the legitimation reckoning, apparently does not quite work out. For the adjacent market is likewise conquered and cornered by the powerfully developed and ever-spreading final form, even though that market was previously held by another variety of the same branch, which seemed to have all the necessary prerequisites for abiding forever. The occupation could be called unlawful if the best adaptation provided rights and not merely power. Nevertheless, Darwin explains the issue:

> I may illustrate what I mean by supposing three varieties of sheep to be kept, one adapted to an extensive mountainous region; a second to a comparatively narrow, hilly tract; and a third to the wide plains at the base; and that the inhabitants are all trying with equal steadiness and skill to improve their stocks by selection: the chances in this case will be strongly in favor of the great holders on the mountains or on the plains, improving their breeds more quickly than the small holders on the intermediate narrow, hilly tract; and consequently the improved mountain or plain breed will soon take the place of the less improved hill breed; and thus the two breeds, which originally existed in greater numbers, will come into close contact with each other, without the interposition of the supplanted, intermediate hill variety.

Hence, if adaptation itself, in the second stage of its operations, that of monopoly and retrograde extinction of the formerly competing transitions, has not driven the varieties out to the borders of both their forms and regions, then the sheer mass, the dense weight of sheer number (accumulated capital) provides the *coup de grâce* for supplanting and totally extinguishing the less fortunate intermediate varieties, though the latter may be better prepared for and adapted to their hilly tract. Thus vanishes the very last, feeble legitimation of power—its selection of the fittest; he who has the power uses it even beyond the borders of his fitness. And the struggle for survival is forthwith decided.

Not even civilization prevents such a spread of attained power, which destroys "transitions" and sharpens borders. Nor can civilization in any way hinder it, since it itself is, after all, nothing but a "natural" evolutionary stage—the highest, to be sure, but what difference does that make!

> At some future period, not very distant as measured by centuries, the civilised races of man will almost certainly exterminate, and replace, the savage races throughout the world. At the same time the anthropomorphous apes, as Professor Schaaffhausen has remarked, will no doubt be exterminated. The break between man and his nearest allies will then be wider, for it will intervene between man in a more civilised state, as we may hope, even than the Caucasian, and some ape as low as a baboon, instead of as now between the negro or Australian and the gorilla. (*Descent of Man*, pp. 159-60).

Hence, far from breaking the automatism of power, civilization, simultaneously and stirringly labeled "ennoblement" or "improvement," and rendered a mere attribute of the more highly evolved state, stoutly keeps operating with extinction and extermination as if indeed civilization were not itself; since the "civilised races" have gained the upper hand, they are really for this reason more savage than the savages. This paradox lies concealed in Darwin's theory of transitions.

REPLACEMENT OF ETERNITY

"To sum up, I believe that species come to be tolerably well-defined objects, and do not at any one period present an inextricable chaos of varying and intermediate links" (*Origin of the Species*, p. 213). Not at any one period, if, namely, the procession is halted, the unfurling of the evolution panorama is stopped, i.e. a specific relative state of the results of competition, a specific existing set of already developed species are viewed. The art of explication has reached such a peak here that the distinctness and the sharp outlines of the forms are still and all conceded as being "tolerably well" defined; whereas the gliding change and the excess of the "intermediate" is shielded from an ultimate turbulent mixture in chaos and reduced to an endurable degree that can be viewed overall with no confusion whatsoever. The borders between the individualized species thus abide in the middle between confusing haziness and disturbing sharpness. For this very reason, the famous saying *Natura non facit saltum,* Nature makes no leaps, can generally be deemed correct in the panorama albeit "somewhat exaggerated": "For natural selection acts only by taking advantage of slight successive variations; she can never take a great and sudden leap, but must advance by short and sure, though slow steps" (*Origin of the Species,* p. 244).

For this peculiar gait, natural selection, understandably, requires an extraordinary amount of time. The vast eras, the millions of years (as already stated) are the cartoon on which evolution paints. The less hope there is that it will lead from its own realm into another with its short steps, the more tremendously the other realm must extend backwards. By now, it is secure against intervention from above, the finger of God; by now, chance, dangerously interfering from below, is scarcely noticed; by now, the internal borders have been wiped away by "transitions," and the whole thing is happily saved from chaos. Now, the "millions of years" ultimately constitute a type of surrogate for vanished eternity, which was why the conception of them was so extraordinarily satisfying to nineteenth-century contemporaries, nay, imbued them with an appreciative pride. Friedrich Albert Lange, in *History of Materialism,* emphatically steps forward (several important passages in his work demonstrate this) as a pioneer and prophet of those millions of years and as a passionate preacher against the aversion to close intercourse with them.

> One can find the condition of the earth's crust and the continuation of the processes taking place upon it relatively stable compared with the theory of the revolutions of the earth, with which the. . . . timidity about huge numbers is often enough connected. If, however, we assume sufficiently larger periods, then a change, a waxing and waning, are not merely probable but can be proven with the most rigorous scientific arguments.*

* F.A. Lange: *Geschichte des Materialismus.* Vol. II, p. 223.

Thus all we need, according to this opinion, is the assumption, so that the walls of nature may yield and space expand into enormous reaches. We just have to overcome our timidity, the dead point, as it were—and the strictest proofs will promptly be at hand. Timidity is the price of admission we must pay in order to gain by losing ourselves in contemplating the space of time as which this panorama internally presents itself.

Lange wonders next whence that timidity stems, and he instantly finds that the "reason for this queer phenomenon can only . . . [reside] in our senses being deadened by habituation to the concept of eternity." This resolute explanation is doubtless as stunning as it is difficult to accept. After all, one may object, should not such habituation to the concept of eternity do the very reverse, i.e. facilitate the use of large numbers, which would thus no longer be terrifying? But no, we do not get off that easily. Lange's psychology is a lot trickier. "Although the concept of an absolute eternity embraces so much that anything the unbridled imagination might conceive would be nothing more than the most ordinary measure of time—nevertheless, that concept is so current with us that the man assuming an eternal existence of the earth and humanity seems quite modest compared with another who, in order to go back to man's origin from the simplest organic cell, would posit a period trillions of times greater than the transition from diluvial to present-day man." Until now, one could lightly construe Lange as saying that the fault for that timidity about millions and trillions of years lies not so much with the concept of reality as actually with the pedagogics of the "theologians," namely the way of making the inconceivable concept conceivable—a very inadequate way, to be sure.

But Lange, in an obscure fashion, has a much more basic intention. He continues:

> Here, sensuality is everywhere at odds with logic. What we can, to a certain degree, visualize, strikes us as easily excessive and improbable, whereas we play with the most enormous ideas as soon as we have reduced them to the form of a totally abstract concept. Six thousand years on the one side—eternity on the other; we are accustomed to that. Anything in between seems at first

strange, then bold, then grandiose, and then phantastic; and yet all such predicates merely belong to the sphere of emotions; cold logic has nothing to do with them.*

Here it appears as if the fault no longer lies with that "deadening habituation" to the concept of eternity, but actually with the well-nigh medieval relish for glib "abstract concepts," which impede blowing up the empirical concept all too greatly. The truth is that the millions of years, far from being in the middle "between" the six thousand years (which make up history, according to Hegel) and eternity, are as sharply sundered from eternity as those six thousand, not one iota less; furthermore, this confusion is not a fight between sensuality and logic, for actually the logic of "abstract concepts" is merely bolstered by the sensuality that refuses to absorb millions or trillions of years. Now this mysterious "explanation" may bear upon the anxiety of getting too close to eternity with numbers, or rather the poverty of the senses, which takes any fantastic, hence inconceivable figure for as good as eternity and thus punitively out of the empirical context—yet one thing is clear: The whole convoluted matter, having been thoroughly twisted for a while, is abruptly cut off by Lange's remark that all such predicates belong to the sphere of emotions and that cold logic has nothing to do with them. A remark that, by the bye, did not prevent people from sinking with true voluptuousness into the newly opened bath of huge reaches of time. Furthermore, and above all, it is established that this queer new homeland of cold logic was destined to expel or devour eternity—to such an extent that the previously scorned attribute of eternity itself passed into it, and this new empirical eternity was paid all honors of worship that the age was capable of.

"What is man's whole life and striving," says the book that had the largest edition of any products in that era, Ludwig Büchner's *Kraft und Stoff*[23]—"what is man's whole life and striving in the face of that eternal, irresistible march of nature, which is borne only by iron necessity or relentless law? The brief flicker of an ephemera flitting over the sea of eternity and infinity?"†

---

* Ibid., pp. 223-24
† Ludwig Büchner: *Kraft und Stoff*, p. 150. Popular edition. Leipzig, 1894.

THE NOBLE APE AND THE CRUDE BARBARIAN

Still, the ephemera did flit *over* the sea. In rigorously grasped "evolution," however, in the slow succession of short but sure steps, in the line of the insensibly merging forms of organic life, the ephemera or—to get out of materialist poetry—man himself is included. At the end, of course. For, writes Darwin (in *The Descent of Man*, p. 620): "He who is not content to look, like a savage, at the phenomena of nature as disconnected, cannot any longer believe that man is the work of a separate act of creation."

However, the direction in which the origin of man is contemplated is, in a certain way, different from the direction of viewing all other stages of evolution or products of natural selection. For everywhere else, and to as great a degree as possible, the "slight" beginnings of a specific peculiarity were sought, in order then, from this point, following the short steps, to glide along the countless gradations and finally reach the "completed" variety. Here however, in the case of man, the direction is exactly opposite. We first tarry extensively with the formed peculiarities of man, especially those that are usually adduced as explicit features distinguishing him from the entire world of animals; and then we turn our gazes backwards with the aim of rediscovering those same characteristics (notwithstanding all lofty opinion about the ineffaceable special position of man) to as great a degree as possible, albeit on a less perfect level, in the foregoing stations of the natural voyage, at least among the apes, and in some ways among the birds and even the insects.

Both Darwin and his successors waged a large-scale battle against privileges—namely, against all kinds of human privileges. The struggle was utterly thorough, and in the end there was not much reason left for pride in being human. Neither the essential hairlessness of man, nor his upright walk, nor the absence of a tail, nor the faculty of speech, nor the aptitude for inventing tools, nor the power of moral discrimination, nor the sense of beauty retains the character of an exclusive possession or talent of mankind. Instead, everything has previous stages, everything already appears, at least sketchily, among the higher and sometimes even less high-ranking animals.

It is as if this place in the evolution panorama were not so much further *de*veloped as altogether *en*veloped. A spontaneous caution, supported by or even identical with the drive to polemicize against privileges, hinders the presenters of this panorama in letting the machinery keep operating and the tableaux keep unfolding. For Truth, Justice, Beauty, God (if we may go along with Darwin's thinking to the extent of mentioning all these names in one breath) would quickly destroy the fine uniformity of the unrolled painting, virtually punch holes in it or open unexpected issues from the tempered interior of the natural time-space, if we were to achieve the objective significance of those concepts, a significance surpassing and indeed guiding and determining any mere faculty or power. For this precise reason, the end of evolution is rolled up so that it may not elude us and lead us into a pathless jungle.

We have seen . . . that man bears in his bodily structure clear traces of his descent from some lower form; but it may be urged that, as man differs so greatly in his mortal power from all other animals, there must be some error in this conclusion. No doubt the difference in this respect is enormous, even if we compare the mind of one of the lowest savages, who has no words to express any number higher than four, and who uses hardly any abstract terms for common objects or for the affections, with that of the most highly organised ape. The difference would, no doubt, still remain immense, even if one of the higher apes had been improved or civilised as much as a dog has been in comparison with its parent-form, the wolf or jackal. The Fuegians rank amongst the lowest barbarians; but I was continually struck with surprise how closely the three natives on board H.M.S. "Beagle," who had lived some years in England, and could talk a little English, resembled us in disposition and in most of our mental faculties. If no organic being excepting man had possessed any mental power, or if his powers had been of a wholly different nature from those of the lower animals, then we should never have been able to convince ourselves that our high faculties had been gradually developed. But it can be shown that there is no fundamental difference of this kind. We must also admit that there is a much wider interval in mental power between one of the lowest fishes, as a lamprey or lancelet, and one of the higher apes, than between an ape and man;

yet this interval is filled up by numberless gradations. (*The Descent of Man*, pp. 65-66).

Thus, if the reader will permit this translation into bathos, there really is not that much difference between man and the rest of the animal kingdom. Between him and the higher apes, there are not even as many transitions or tiny steps of evolution as between those apes and the lower fishes—what, then, can be so amazing or absurd about the thesis that the "mental faculties" of man developed as gradually as the ape's prehensile grip from the fish's fin! A shove from behind makes the tableaux squeeze together.

Now in the mid 1830's, when Darwin had set out on his world voyage aboard H.M.S. *Beagle*, thereby launching his career, he had returned those above-mentioned Fuegians to their homeland after they, brought along from Cook's earlier circumnavigation, had spent several years getting to know, perhaps even absorbing, English civilization. One is struck with surprise to learn that these Fuegians are also human beings, a thought urging itself upon us, especially when we hear them "talk a little English." For even these lowest barbarians, who behave so strangely under the eyes of the purely observing naturalist, seem extraordinarily remote from a civilized Englishman. But *that* is merely the perspective of the Englishman himself standing in the line of evolution—at its extreme end—the painted Englishman, as it were, who, considering his position, cannot cast very far-reaching gazes or achieve any sort of criteria. The man however who is able to have the entire panorama, from the lower fishes up to this Englishman, unwind before his eyes, will soon realize that this perspective is a figment, and that the gap between the Englishman and the Fuegian, no matter how odd the latter may appear, is, in fact, highly insignificant.

Nor is the difference slight in moral disposition between a barbarian, such as the man described by the old navigator Byron, who dashed his child on the rocks for dropping a basket of sea-urchins, and a Howard or Clarkson; and in intellect, between a savage who uses hardly any abstract terms, and a Newton or Shakespeare. Differences of this kind between the highest men of the highest races and the lowest savages, are connected by the finest gradations.

Therefore it is possible that they might pass and be developed into each other.

My object in this chapter is to show that there is no fundamental differences between man and the higher mammals in their mental faculties (*The Descent of Man*, p. 66).

What is happening cannot be more glaringly visible than at this point. Dashing a child on the rocks to punish carelessness (let us, for a moment, disregard the doer of this deed, the "barbarian") is, in terms of a totally innerwordly moral law, as different from Howard's establishing healthy prisons and other humane help for inmates as vice is from virtue. Between the two of them, consequently, there is, under the eye of valid morality, absolutely no mediation, but only the most acute differentiation, no "evolution," but only a weighing judgment. Taking this aspect as a foil, virtue and vice, good and evil, turn out to have lost their unconditional distinction, though not at all "relativized," but merely gulped into the evolutionary phases attached to their forms, the barbarian and the civilized man, whereby the barbarian contains in himself evil as part of his "lower" stage, and the civilized man has good as the accessory of a "higher" stage of development. Both, the lower and the higher, are also once again *en*veloped in the now merely one-dimensional distinction between the earlier and the later, a distinction fully corresponding to the series of evolutionary tableaux.

Vice and virtue are pulled so far apart from one another and, under the heading of the "moral disposition of man," simultaneously united and apprehended. The barbarian who dashes his child on the rocks, shockingly, and Howard, the noble philanthropist and prison-reformer who travels the length and breadth of Europe—from this anecdotal genre picture, the still unresolved moral decision peeps forth clearly enough. Yet evil is chained to its place (very remote, incidentally) and good is chained to the other place (close by and ogled with satisfied pride), and neither will ever be released from this imprisonment. Carefully divorced from one another and widely distributed, the moral opposites can no longer prevent the gap between them from being filled in. (In the past, it was a sharp and deep split, whose abyss was measureless; but with the widening of the split, a bottom has come into sight and even considerably risen.) The gap fills in with countless gradations, with sheer transition and gradualness, that is to say, with time.

The "moral disposition," however, in which the moral law was captured or coated (without this precaution, the end of the panorama would have inevitably slipped away or even torn apart), can now be sought and found further back than in the barbarian and the gruesome scene of his cruelty. And likewise, these earlier forms of moral disposition in the animal kingdom are presented as genre scenes usually poignant; nor can they be otherwise, since good has been tugged away from evil and then reconnected with it through "imperceptible gradations," which, by the way, always remain pallid.

The *en*velopment (of both morality and intelligence) is *de*velopment (if this apt and accurate paradox be allowed) already includes genre as a place and form and not merely, say, as an illustration; indeed the scene, immersed in the fluid medium of poignancy or horror, is actually the fashion in which morality crops up within "evolution." The dog licking the hand of his truculent operator has already been mentioned (see "Vivisection," p. 63). There are other touching scenes in Darwin:

> As Whewell has well asked, "Who that reads the touching instances of maternal affection, related so often of the women of all nations, and of the females of all animals, can doubt that the principle of action is the same in the two cases?" We see maternal affection exhibited in the most trifling details: thus Rengger observed an American monkey (a Cebus) carefully driving away the flies which plagued her infant; and Duvaucel saw a Hylobates washing the faces of her young ones in a stream (*Descent of Man*, p. 70).

It is obvious that here, as one can assume from the remorse demanded of the vivisector, the moral disposition within the animal mind is already perfectly, indeed abashingly developed, and, on the basis of this insight, we can scarcely fancy how it is to become any greater or "higher." In this point, however, the theory corrects the presented genre, which challenges us to express boundless, will-less, and tearful amazement. This is simply known as instinct, and it is confronted by the later product known as the conscience. "The following sentence," writes Darwin (in *The Origin of Man*, p. 99), "seems to me in a high degree probable —namely that any animal whatever, endowed with well-marked social instincts, the parental and filial affections being here included, would inevitably acquire a moral sense or conscience, as soon as its intellectual powers had become as well, or nearly as well developed, as in man."

Thus instinct seamlessly merges into intellect and conscience, and the pallid intermediate stage or transitional form betrays all the signs of the treatment of man's possibilities: "Many of the faculties, which have been of inestimable service to man for his progressive advancement, such as the powers of the imagination, wonder, curiosity, an undefined sense of beauty, a tendency to imitation, and the love of excitement or novelty, could hardly fail to lead to capricious changes of customs and fashions" (*Descent of Man*, pp. 94-95). In all these psychological attributes, we all too plainly recognize stunned phantasy, perception, knowledge, language and, in the "undefined sense of beauty," the defined sense of beauty (which constitutes its more advanced stage). In short, this singular, incipient man proves to be a completed man, virtually stripped and shorn in order to run around "savagely." Between him and "cultivated" man—to repeat it yet anew—there is no other kinship than that of the gradual advancement of all faculties, which is occasionally termed the "improvement" or "ennoblement" of the crude. Howard is nobler than the barbarian who kills his child, Newton or Shakespeare nobler than the three Fuegians who shipped along on the *Beagle*, and they, in turn, are a wee bit nobler than their stay-at-home fellow tribesmen—because of their experience and education in London.

It seems (to insert an historical comparison) as if all this involves the old sense and concept of "culture" used by the Enlightenment philosophers, by Kant—culture, which helps man out of the crudeness of beginning; and *humanitas*, which elaborates the humaneness of human beings. But the essence was lost: the element of the demand, mission, and purpose of all history, of the future. Instead, everything is empirical; and culture, though in various degrees of perfection, has already become a fact. The noble and the higher have been transformed into a mobile scene, an admirable monument to Howard or Newton; and all this floats aimlessly along with an evolution that has no other inherent meaning than the one expressed in its name. Hence, the historical comparison at

the start of this paragraph says basically very little, since this "enlightenment" is not one that keeps operating, but is at best made available and
displayed for contemplation.

Neither enlightenment nor Christianity causes any cut, break, or
upheaval in this entity, which blithely keeps on rolling by and away; instead, everything disintegrates into the "finest gradations" and into a
device of ennoblement, improvement, recognizable long since.

> It is not improbable that after long practice virtuous tendencies
> may be inherited. With the more civilised races, the conviction of
> the existence of an all-seeing Deity has had a potent influence on
> the advance of morality. . . . Nevertheless the first foundation or
> origin of the moral sense lies in the social instincts, including sym-
> pathy; and these instincts no doubt were primarily gained, as in
> the case of the lower animals, through natural selection (*Descent
> of Man*, pp. 626-27).

How deeply enveloped morality and ennobling faith are, how greatly
they occur here as attached attributes of an albeit "higher" stage of evolution, how widely estranged they are from all demand and consequence
—these things are nowhere more explicit than in that thoughtless justification for the real imperialism of perfect civilization, a justification
already cited in a different context: "At some future period, not very
distant as measured by centuries, the civilised races of man will almost
certainly exterminate, and replace, the savage races throughout the
world" (*Descent of Man*, p. 159).

But with such a prognosis, how does the civilization of the civilized
differ from the savagery of the savages? That question is quite remote,
and cannot even arise, because all laws and all demands that might be
subsumed under the name of civilization are here expelled or rather enveloped and pressed flat into attributes carried by those forms occurring
at the end of the series of images in the evolution panorama. Civilization
itself, though highly and proudly extolled, has lost its sting. Precisely
speaking, it is no longer mentioned, being replaced by "civilised races,"
and here we have its transformation into an attribute of the race.

The end of the panorama is so throughly rolled up that at times an
earlier stage seems to have a higher value than a later one, and the track-

er of nobility prefers abiding with apes rather than savages. Such a singular return to the older (always, of course, anecdotal) images confirms in an extreme manner the work of envelopment into development. The conclusion of Darwin's *Descent of Man* offers a characteristic example for this:

> The astonishment which I felt on first seeing a party of Fuegians on a wild and broken shore will never be forgotten by me, for the reflection at once rushed into my mind—such were our ancestors. These men were absolutely naked and bedaubed with paint, their long hair was tangled, their mouths frothed with excitement, and their expression was wild, startled, and distrustful. They possessed hardly any arts, and like wild animals lived on what they could catch; they had no government, and were merciless to every one not of their own small tribe. He who has seen a savage in his native land will not feel much shame, if forced to acknowledge that the blood of some more humble creature flows in his veins. For my own part I would as soon be descended from that heroic little monkey, who braved his dreaded enemy in order to save the life of his keeper, or from that old baboon, who descending from the mountains, carried away in triumph his young comrade from a crowd of astonished dogs—as from a savage who delights to torture his enemies, offers up bloody sacrifices, practises infanticide without remorse, treats his wives like slaves, knows no decency, and is haunted by the grossest superstitions.

This distribution of good and evil genre scenes, of touched wonder and indignant horror, makes it easier for everyone to befriend the old baboon, but without having to forfeit the power and privilege of his own sublime vantage point, which leaves that of the Fuegians so far below; and thus the loftier observer can blithely close the panorama in which he himself is now so fully captured.

Anton von Werner's Panorama of the Battle of Sedan, woodcut by Wilhelm Geissler.
Picture Archive, Stiftung Preussischer Kulturbesitz

"Nothing can be done here . . . with the subordination, sketching, or suggestiveness permitted in easel pictures," says Anton
von Werner. (8)

The Evening at Sedan, September 1, 1870, diorama from Anton von Werner: *Erlebnisse und Eindrücke 1870-1890* (Berlin 1915)

The pictures on exhibition . . . flickered with the . . . supernatural lighting that had once accompanied an Assumption, a Crucifixion or the dawn of Judgment Day. (9)

Bismarck meets Napoleon III, diorama from Anton von Werner: *Erlebnisse und Eindrücke 1870-1890* (Berlin 1915)

The Armistice Negotiations in Donchery, diorama from Anton von Werner: *Erlebnisse und Eindrücke 1870-1890* (Berlin 1915)

The dioramas were erected in such a way as to be brightly illuminated from above while the viewer stood in an absolutely darkened room at the exact horizon level of the painting. (10)

Machine-Factory (1873) by Paul Meyerheim. Märkisches Museum, Berlin, German Democratic Republic

"*The shiny steel moves up and down,*
It animates all parts behind
A single goal. The huge construction
Always obeys the master's mind." (22)

Wheel with wings, book illustration by Hans Kraemer: *Das Neunzehnte Jahrhundert in Wort und Bild. Politische und Kulturgeschichte,* (four volumes) Berlin, Leipzig, n.d.

. . . a kind of organic engine, making the wheel roll over the level ground. (22)

Allegory of Telegraphy (1863) study by Hans Canon. Staatliche Kunsthalle Karlsruhe

Allegory of Steam Power (1863) study by Hans Canon. Staatliche Kunsthalle Karlsruhe
Karlsruhe

"But just as the muscle of the human body would be a lifeless mass of flesh without the nerve drawing through it, so too the flying muscles, which Watt's and Stephenson's inventions have brought to mankind, would be only half as powerful if the guiding thought, the nerves of telegraph wires, did not pulsate through them and control them." (24)

Velarium (original missing; photography) by Anton von Werner. Archiv Berlinische Galerie, West Berlin.

. . . the attribute "brazen" or "iron," in regard to the natural as well as the human and historical, pops up wherever irrefutable validity, utmost energy and necessity have to be made evident. (25)

Arlberg Bridge, woodcut, artist unknown. Archiv Berlinische Galerie, West Berlin.

The violently and thoroughly altered landscape of the nineteenth century has remained visible until today . . . (27)

Telegraph Building of the City of New York, artist unknown. *Les Capitales du Monde,* Paris (Librarie Hachette et Cie) 1892, p. 75

Transmitting, receiving, current, circuit, damaging or interrupting the circuit, pressing the Morse key—all these things . . . combine into a picture of a psychophysical telegraphy. (26)

Algerian Women in their chambers (1834) by Eugène Delacroix. Musée du Louvre, Paris

. . . in the wealth of glistening African color the Frenchman . . . found the simple outline of antiquity, the Homeric era, the same ancient world that was kept in rigorous custody in the halls and cabinets of the Academy of Paris. (40)

Visit at the Harem, woodcut, artist unknown. Private Collection, Berlin

In 1856, the very first African railroad was opened, the Alexandria-Cairo Line. (42)

Climbing a Pyramid, photogravure, artist unknown. *Im Fluge durch die Welt,* edited by John L. Stoddard, Chicago (The Werner Company) n.d.

The subjugation of the free Orient could apparently not be driven any further . . . (44)

Captured Gypsies (1886) woodcut by Eduard Schultz-Briesen. *Deutsche Malerei der Gegenwart auf der Jubiläumsausstellung der königlichen Akademie der Künste zu Berlin 1886,* Munich (Hanfstaengl) 1886

. . . that unsettled, roving, and generally unsafe life, every last detail of which seemed opposed to a bourgeoisie that, in property and security, was locked up against all chance. (50)

Attempts to reconstruct the Venus of Milo, photographs, artist unknown. Archaeological Institute of Heidelberg University

. . . to round out the depicted instant . . . into a complete scenic event. (55)

The Virgin in the Nile River (1865) by Frederico Faruffini. Galeria Nazionale d'Arte Moderna, Rome

Art . . . experienced the return of beauty—this time, however, not as its demanding law but as a piece in its store of figures. (56)

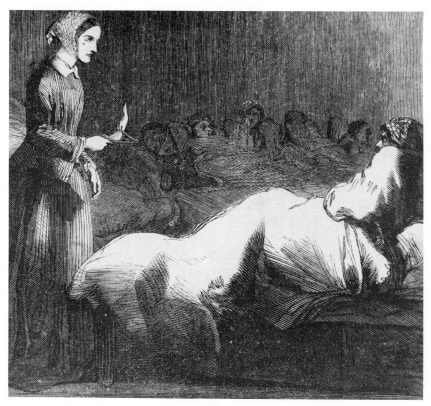

Florence Nightingale, woodcut, artist unknown. Bildarchiv Stiftung Preussischer Kulturbesitz, Berlin

Humanity per se, rather than being an issue for all human beings, became the special mission and function of the sex known as the tender or weaker one . . . (69)

Nach der Natur photographirt.)
Sollen Thiere wie dieses lebendig zerschnitten werden dürfen?

Photographed from Nature.
SHOULD ANIMALS LIKE THIS BE CUT APART ALIVE?

Freundlos!
Friendless!

The Torture Chambers of Science by Ernst von Weber. Berlin and Leipzig 1879

. . . a picture of the organism as a system of reactive mechanisms, each one able to be determined and measured by experiment. (63)

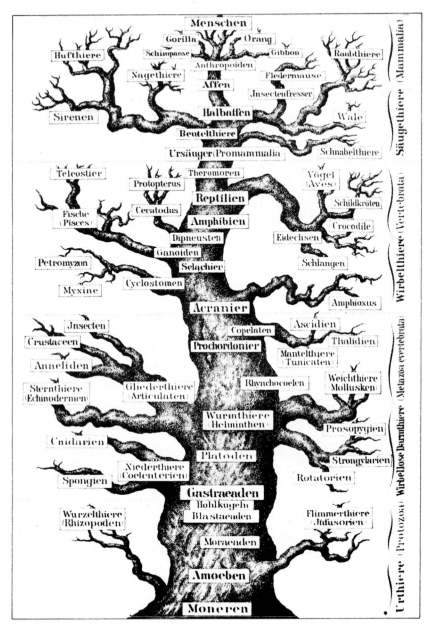

The Origin of Mankind, artist unknown. E. Heckel: *Keimesgeschichte des Menschen,* Leipzig 1910, plate 20

Darwin's theory was without exaggeration the most powerful, popular and influential ideological innovation of the 19th Century. (79)

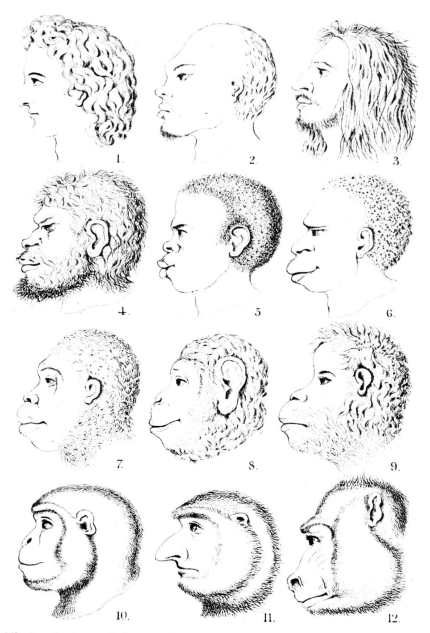

The Family Group of the Katarrhinen, frontispiece, artist unknown. E. Heckel: *Die natürliche Schöpfungsgeschichte* (*The Natural History of Creation*), Berlin 1902

. . . a society can derive the basis of its superiority and the right to its power from natural selection . . . (81)

Charles R. Darwin, painting by J. Collier. © National Portrait Gallery, London.

"There should be open competition for all men; and the most able should not be prevented by laws or customs from succeeding best or having the largest number of offspring." (81)

The Expression of Emotions on Man and on Animals, illustration, artist unknown. Charles Darwin: *Collected Works,* German edition translated by J. B. Carus, Vol. 7, Stuttgart, 1877, (3rd edition)

The agency or act of creation is eliminated and so nature seems "whole," coherent, not of a settled but at most of a developed diversity; in a word: "panoramistic." (85)

Cannibalism in New Zealand, photogravure, artist unknown. *Leipziger illustrierte Zeitung No. 9107,* November 1883, p. 445

. . . civilization . . . itself is, after all, nothing but a "natural" evolutionary stage—the highest, to be sure, but what difference does that make! (98)

Man of Pliocene by Gabriel Max. E. Heckel: *Natürliche Schöpfungsgeschichte,* 10th improved edition, Berlin 1902, also published in *Kunst unserer Zeit (Art of our Times)* Vol. 1894, Munich, 1894

Now, the "millions of years" ultimately constitute a type of surrogate for vanished eternity, which was why the conception . . . was so extraordinarily satisfying . . . (99)

Man in the State of the Future, frontispiece, artist unknown. F. E. Bilz: *Das neue Naturheilverfahren* (*The New Form of Natural Medical Treatment*), Vol. 4, Leipzig, n.d.

. . . the "true, good and beautiful," the inscription of theaters and of a *Weltanschauung,* stuck together, forming a single sublime amalgam that adhered all the more indissolubly to its place. (111)

Foundry with Sculpture of Bavaria (1854) by Wilhelm von Kaulbach. Bayerische Staatsgemäldesammlung

. . . a new awareness of culture itself, a culturalism that scarcely admitted essential distinctions . . . (121)

The Game of the Naiads (1886) by Arnold Böcklin. Kunsthalle Basel

Thus Büchner describes the tiniest particles of matter as "the unwrought goods of which the entire universe with all its wonders and beauties" is constructed. (115)

Awakening of the Sea (1897) by Hans Thoma, Staatliche Kunsthalle Karlsruhe

. . . the endlessly repeated catchword and demand of "idealizing" . . . (119)

The Walhalla Building near Regensburg (built between 1830 and 1842) by Leo von Klenze. Kunsthalle Hamburg

It is the diversely filled panorama temple of such a *Weltanschauung,* in whose interior not so much an operative being as a sum of notions, nay, the semblance of notions, is worshipped. (166)

The Studio of the Painter Hans Makart in Vienna, artist unknown. G. Hirth: *Das deutsche Zimmer seit der Renaissance (The German Room since the Rennaissance)* Munich, 1880, p. 272

Palms and other plants . . . created a greenish twilight mingling and enhancing the tones: the ardent colors of the imported Orient, of Persian carpets, pillows and cushions . . . (136)

Arcade Space (Passage Pommeraye in Nantes) by Benois. Johann Friedrich Geist: *Passagen im 19. Jahrhundert,* Munich (Prestel) 1969, plate no. 169; (photograph: Archive Geist, Berlin)

Light, whether we throw ourselves against it or exclude it, always enters human experience, knowledge, use, love, and enjoyment only insofar and in such a manner as the historical constellation permits . . . (138)

The Palace of Electricity at the Paris World Exhibition. Hans Kraemer, *Das 19. Jahrhundert in Wort und Bild. Politische und Kulturgeschichte* (four volumes) Berlin and Leipzig, n.d., Vol. 4, p. 66

. . . illumination was one of the most intrinsic motifs, one of the noblest purposes of the century. (177)

Building the Great Star on the Palace of Electricity by Hans Kraemer. Ibid., Vol. 4, p. 68

. . . the want of illumination became an outstanding literary token of industrial misery . . . (177)

Street Lanterns. N. H. Schilling, *Handbuch für Steinkohlengasbeleuchtung* (*Handbook for Gaslight Illumination*), Munich 1879

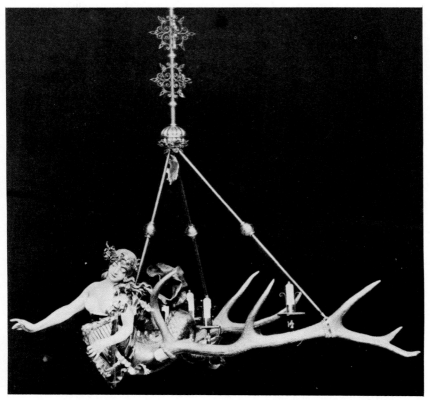

Gas Lamp in form of a Woman, artist unknown. *Zeitschrift des Kunstgewerbsvereins,* Munich 1882, plate 24

The mere chemical substance of gas, the naked pipe sticking out of the wall or pulling down from the ceiling, was underworldly, virtually proletarian. (179)

The Electrical Spark photogravure by Reinhold Begas. *Zur Jubelfeier 1696-1896 der koenigl. Akademischen Hochschule für bildende Künste,* Berlin, p. 118 (Catalogue to the festival celebrating the bicentennial of the royal academy of art in Berlin in 1896)

So much light, so much reflection, so much inwardness. (181)

V

THE HIGHER

Nothing of the "Higher" was lost in that panorama of "evolution." Everything: morality, beauty, faith, reason, and even that much-lauded compassion, which Lange called "the loveliest blossom of earthly organisms," had been so properly gathered and given a place for everyone's joy and pleasure. It all seemed to have been made the most intimate possession of evolved homo sapiens and, at the same time, spread out before him as a painting of his own noble character. Nothing now dwelt beyond the stars. And even if the oft-used generic name, the "Higher," still pointed upwards, it involved no obligation, but merely a highly delicious transfiguration. People could feel warm and cozy in their new skin, clothing, and aura, in this patina of "ennoblement"; and nobleness itself or "civilization" did not suffer from its contact with humbler nature, from which human culture, as it was now known, had after all grown or evolved. All those "ideal goods," once sharply distinguished, but now rendered homogeneous and available, floated along. The "True, Good, and Beautiful," the inscription of theaters and of a *Weltanschauung*, stuck together, forming a single sublime amalgam that adhered all the more indissolubly to its place.

"Art, literature, science, ethics, all these loftiest revelations of the human spirit, are . . . virtually a frail and precious plant, that sprang up tardily and was fecundated by the long labors of generations—the ideal did not come to light as a whole and all at once, it unveiled itself bit by bit."* Nevertheless, Ludwig Büchner's catalogue of ideal goods leaves out religion or faith in God, which did occur in Darwin, albeit psychologized. But this gap is of trifling significance, for what sort of upheaval can it indicate once religion too joined the stock of ideals! Of course, the nineteenth century had the sharpest conflicts between those who ranked faith among the ideals and the others who, for scientific reasons, wanted to exclude it as delusion and "conceptual fancy." Both sides, however, the "religious" and the "materialist," did come to terms in erecting and venerating the "Higher," whether or not counting religion, among other things, as part of it.

SOLACE IN THE DUST

The circulation of immortal matter, whose praises were sung in the "scientific" epics of the so-called materialists, has little left of that wrathful satisfaction of Hamlet's when contemplating Yorick's skull and the dust of his bones. These new "materialists" had an easier time digesting the ineluctable decay of all living things, since their atoms, the signs of death, recombined willingly for all that, into all higher things. "The same atom that helps convey the proud gait of a ruler or hero today, may lie as dirt at his feet tomorrow. The same atom gravitating in the brain of a sheep today, may help a thinker or poet in his intellectual labors tomorrow. The same atom that helps form refuse or dung today, may join its fellow atoms in swaying as a fragrant flush on flowercups tomorrow."† This allegorical atom, however empirical, however scientific it may have been meant to be,[24] seems exactly like the dust that Hamlet found in the churchyard:

> As thus: Alexander died, Alexander was buried, Alexander returneth to dust; the dust is earth; of earth we make loam; and why of that loam whereto he was converted might they not stop a beer barrel?
>
> *Imperious Caesar, dead and turned to clay,*
> *Might stop a hole to keep the wind away.*

---

*   Ludwig Büchner: *Kraft und Stoff*, p. 222. Popular edition, Leipzig, 1894.
†   Ibid., p. 13.

> *O, that that earth which kept the world in awe*
> *Should patch a wall t'expel the winter's flaw!*
> [Hamlet, V, i]

This sounds almost the same and yet quite different. Here everything was dull dust, and the churchyard the place where the greatest dust crumbles and mixes with the smallest and quite ordinary dust. The world is a corpse, and you can patch up a beer barrel with Alexander's carrion. That was a true allegory of the ephemeral, for the decayed dust is the material of death, and death the keen harvest, goal, and substance of all history.

The "materialist" claimed these verses as state's, or king's, evidence:

> With these words, a product of deepest emotion, the great Briton, already three centuries ago, indicated a scientific truth which, despite its lucidity and simplicity, despite its indisputability, does not appear to have gained the universal recognition it so richly deserves. Matter per se is immortal, indestructible; not a mote of sand in the universe can be lost, not a mote of sand can be added. . . . It was thus fully justified of the British poet with his daring imagination to pursue the matter that once helped form Great Caesar's body, pursue it to the point at which, as earth or clay, it patches up a hole in the wall.*

What a singular reversal! The bitterest lament at the transience of earthly grandeur—so bitter as to scarcely be called a lament—has turned into a rather cheering universal and indeed "scientific" truth. The despairing contemplation on the mortality of all human life has been forsaken for the immortality of dust. The horrifying allegorical tokens of the cemetary, bones and dust, have been converted into an indestructible mythological substance whose cult shall now make up for all losses that Hamlet perceived in a single flash. As Büchner then says plainly enough: "Nor is truth bleak or cheerless, for the nature of true knowledge is such that whatever it may seem to destroy or pillage on the one side, it more than replaces on the other."† Such a truth is certainly a fine haven and a reassurance.

* Ibid., pp. 10-11.
† Ibid., p. 71.

Furthermore, that dust is prettified into a "mote of dust"; the sign of the boundless universal decay coagulates into a microscopic thing that has virtually drawn the loving gaze of the scientific observer and now takes it along everywhere. And that icy thunder-bolt of Hamlet's despair, which shed a terrifying light on universal destruction, on the laughably absurd end of human greatness, now appears, virtually warmed over, as "the deepest emotion of the great Briton," as the personal sentiment of the poetic genius.

No, Ludwig Büchner's atoms are of a milder kidney. While previously fashioned of loam or mire, they always soar upwards again to higher purposes, and neither the poets and thinkers nor the swaying flowercups are perturbed that their noble meaning and aspect conceal the matter that lay on the street yesterday. Death always dons new clothing here, and the sweetest and most sublime living garment at that. Everything, the greatest and the smallest, no longer ultimately turns to dust here; instead, dust (or atoms) turns into everything, the greatest and/or the smallest. Downfall and decay are no longer the unhappy end and substance of history, but merely the beginning of nature, for the lower is transformed into the Higher and is unable to pull it down. Matter keeps redecorating or repainting itself, so that at last only the images of ennoblement are visible. Dead "matter" appears if at all then behind veils, at times—like the grinning skull in the studios of contemporary painters, more as a prop of decorative opulence than as a caustic memento.

Here, nature constitutes the interior of civilization, and science zealously investigates it; but civilization, the upshot of evolution, for that very reason abides in its Higher place. Far from making everything equal in death, matter, though all living things commence or are born in it, leaves all privileges fully unscathed: power ("ruler or hero"), intellect ("poet and thinker"), and beauty ("flush on flowercups"). The proof of "matter" or the material element does not unmask, disabuse, or judge; but perhaps out of a feeling of inferiority and a definite need for transfiguration, it buds forth that consistent higher sphere in which faith, compassion, morality, and delight in beauty, with no distinction as to origin and goal, with no stringent meaning in human existence, cohere into a single mass of movable goods, the whole forming a lugubrious cloud in which the material man walks along, safe and secure. Thus Büchner describes the tiniest particles of matter as "the unwrought goods of which the entire universe with all its wonders and beauties" is constructed. This aura of wonders and beauties, this sphere, hovering strangely halfway up and chockfull of all ideal things, this comforting ownership of civilization, regarded as a whole—in short, the "Higher" —is the new object of worship that so-called materialism brought to light in defiance of its own name.

Matter itself, although, as just indicated, merely the "unwrought goods" of all Higher things, radiates gently in the reflection of that aura; its stolid face, usually presented with such wrath, receives nobler lineaments from all the Higher things that owe it their construction. That is how matter is praised by its apologist Büchner. It is, in his eyes, not dead and lifeless, not formless, not raw, but infinitely "fine," not worthless, but the universal "matrix and progenetrix of the very highest importance"; it is "not devoid of feeling, spirit, or thought, but full of the finest emotion"; altogether it is "not unprogressing or eternally the same and unchanging, but, through ever higher and increased complication of its organic relations, it forever keeps producing greater vital and spiritual energy."*

Previously, the splendor and sublimity of ideals, the true, the good, the beautiful, appeared as the garb in which matter, never unclad, so agreeably presented itself; but now matter wore a costume from the very outset, thereby demonstrating its real dignity: "We must, in the future, reject an attitude towards things no longer compatible with the present-day state of science and refrain from looking upon matter as the ragged beggar in which guise it has heretofore appeared to the uneducated mind; instead, one must regard it in its true shape or apparel, in that rich and magnificent gown in which modern science has invested it."† To be sure, this urgent appeal, in accordance with the author's intention, does utilize a poetic metaphor, and, were we to investigate the historical motives and intentions of "materialism," we would scarcely see more in it than some period coloring, worthy, for all that, of a cas-

* Ibid., p. 45.
† Ibid., p. 47.

ual, fleeting smile. Here, however, where the goal is neither intellectual history nor comprehending materialism as a "trend" or "direction" of thought, the metaphor has a greater meaning.

The identification of the true shape of matter with its investment in a magnificent gown shows quite clearly that in this era the mythical tale about the veiled image of Saïs has lost its effect. Reality does not conceal an intrinsically naked Truth under its many envelopes; instead, Truth goes about in a luxurious garment as "higher Truth," while mere reality itself remains naked, i.e. both miserable and homely. The art of dressing, of disguise, must be practiced by all whose calling is to raise matter or material or reality to the realm of a Higher truth or of the Higher per se. To put it banally: Clothes do not just make the man, they also make ideals.

The Artist and the Model

Most of all, however, the Higher is administered, exhibited, and protected by artists. Just like matter in that other area, "reality" or rather the individual real thing, so gray and lusterless per se, is here bedizened and illuminated by being brought into the studio, where the artist is prepared with light as well as the higher garb of color. Reality has become a model.

In these terms, it makes no difference whether art is "realistic" or "idealistic," whether it displays shapes of nature or "imagination." Makart[25] was lauded by contemporaries for restoring poetic invention to art. Few words are needed here to make clear that his "realm of the imagination" is a realm of accumulated sets and costumes, waiting in the studio for the entrance of "reality" in order to give its corpse a singular, opulent life. In this storehouse, the artist, of course, is king, with the absolute freedom of riding roughshod over those elements according to his sovereign whim.

> As free as the ancients with their gods and legends, he does as he likes with his cupids, beauteous damsels, genies, and bacchantes, and by dint of the native privilege of universal art, he draws into his kingdom of imagination the vastness of Nature with her diversity of plants, flowers, and fruits, and all civilization with its

wealth of splendid goods and jewels, brilliant stuffs, emblems, escutcheons, masks, and other things.*

The man who seems to be a lord and master here over so much accumulated jetsam, as it were, promptly, by virtue of his loftiest ambition, finds himself in the midst of the wreckage, similarly costumed and merely gazing forth strangely as from a grave that reaches to his throat. "The studio on Gusshausgasse . . . thanks to the master's lavish love of splendor and art, became more and more of a picturesque museum, which offered to Makart's imagination the convenient use of an apparatus of aids and examples, and in which his own existence and the brilliant social life he surrounded himself with were transformed into an artwork of shimmering colors."†

Into this arsenal of natural and cultural objects, which also includes the master, reality enters, thereby literally gaining a Higher life. "The glorification of beauty, the urge to garb all reality with the magic of beauty and transform the world into a grand festival of blossoming life and seductive charm, such is the fundamental principle of Makart's historical painting."**

If the artist's fantasy is to be understood as a higher art of costuming here, his studio as the apparatus or armory of ennoblement, then there is no "realist," no matter how staunch and no matter how resentful of Makart's freewheeling imagination, who would be found wanting in the "Higher." This is already vouchsafed by the definition of realism, apparently a convention taken for granted in that epoch. We find the definition in a literary critic, Julian Schmidt, when he discusses the novelist Friedrich Spielhagen: "In regard to his characterizations, he is a realist, i.e. in purely technical terms, he works from models. All latter-day writers do it: The idea of sketching expressive physiognomies according to universal, indeterminable ideals, with a flick of the wrist, as it were, has long since been abandoned."‡ The definition contains the re-

---

* Carl von Lützow: Hans Makart. "Ein Beitrag zu seiner Characteristik," *Zeitschrift für bildende Künste*, Vol. XXI (1886), p. 192.
† Ibid., p. 214.
** Ibid., p. 215.
‡ Julian Schmidt: *Neue Bilder aus dem Geistigen Leben unserer Zeit*, p. 188. Third series. Leipzig, 1873.

course to "the Higher" in the negative, so to speak. For working from models means having models available. The artist therefore does not delve into a reality that he must first investigate and familiarize himself with; he has already demolished this unfamiliar reality into a mass of possible models in order to pull these ruins piecemeal into the precincts of his own illumination, into his studio.

Hence, the reality of the models—if we are permitted to speak of a reality here—is thoroughly different from that simple "nature" which, by the older rules of art, had to be imitated. Perhaps these models for the realist are the leftover natural specimens whose sharp peculiarities and individual features, the "characters" of their physiques and physiognomies, were copied by the classicist artists—copied, of course, in order to be transferred to the empty schemata of their busts and statues. Such leftover specimens, however, in contrast to their earlier role, are taken as straightforward reality and, in the literal sense, as the "contents" of art.

Once again the artist working from models does not fully sacrifice himself to them; he has a qualm: the models are not yet art. This quality is all that justifies and salvages his own dominion, art itself. Thus the model exists in a singular twilight. It is alienated from life (if we may use that term for the reality still to be investigated); but it is not a mere sample, a mere penmanship, that one puts into a general schema in order to give that schema definite features. The model ranks as perfectly real, but not as valid for ruling in art and giving it the law. For the realist, it is the only possible substance of art—"all latter-day writers do it"—yet it does remain a "mere" model, from which the artist works, and which he utilizes for another purpose.

This indefinite light that the model enters, by which it is saved from its dismal fate of being a mere model—this very light is "the Higher." Illuminated and costumed in its glow, the model enters art, and in this lighting and costuming, in this higher, more or less overbearing employment of the gray and naked, albeit solely real model, art—in the nineteenth century—proves its worth.

Hence the definition of the realist would scarcely have required the cautiously mediating qualification that was so often and so hastily applied to it and that Julian Schmidt promptly added to the previously quoted sentences: "Not that the writer could depict his models without further ado; even the portraitist cannot do so, much less the narrator, whose characters must be in constant flux. A model is useful for the imaginative writer who can independently re-create."

An Apparatus for Idealizing

The same dubious relationship of and to the model is evinced in the endlessly repeated catchword and demand of "idealizing." The thing to be idealized is quite clear: the model, as the substratum of art, which, in turn, consists uniquely in idealizing. Yet whither the idealization—in other words, what ideal this art, by using models, is to aspire to—the answer to that question is always and inevitably lacking. The ideal is simply the ideal or else the Higher, and it appears uniquely in the procedure of idealization, in catching up with and dressing up the model; for instance, regarding color in painting, in the disposition or arrangement of the color "bouquet."

"For the creation of a sensual splendor of color," wrote Wolfgang Kirchbach in 1888, "any juxtaposition is possible, and the bouquet of a master of painterly technique is far from being tied to the conditions of the bouquet, by which one generally juxtaposes materials according to so-called good taste."* Whatever greater freedom of disposing and arranging is thus conceded to the master, in theory his activity is not distinguished from that of good taste, except that good taste virtually decorates into nothingness, whereas the artist dresses models in color, that is, idealizes them through painting. The same author, who so emphatically recommends not being too cautious or finicky in the coloring further stretches the liberation from rules and definite ideals with his advice, a few pages later, to bank on natural seeing, which, unassisted, renders to art the service of idealizing.

> It was disastrous misconstruing the demand for idealization as a desire for idealizing color as well. Such a striving will always put artists on the wrong scent. In point of fact, the human eye, insofar as it really sees colors, is the most marvelous idealization apparatus that Nature has created among the sensory organs. A chaos of

---

* Wolfgang Kirchbach in the periodical *Kunst für Alle* (1888), p. 134.

light and ether waves is idealized by the color camera of the eye into a visible phenomenon known as "Nature," and the more finely we, as painters and seeing laymen, feel this visible phenomenon in detail and as a whole, the more beautiful the color is. . . . That is why our painterly realism, insofar as it is technical fidelity toward Nature, is actually the only possible and correct route to total artistic beauty.*

However small the distance to the model may seem to have become—it still remains a model, that is to say, it persists in itself and is neither revealed nor fathomed by any scrutinizing or penetrating gaze. The eye itself, the organ of that penetrating seeing and fathoming, takes no initiative, does not get into action; it remains a stable apparatus, an apparatus for idealization (just as there are apparatuses for galvanizing), a space, instrument, illuminator, and costumer in one, making everything within reach and range "beautiful." The eye replaces the studio here. The smooth wall or skin of the model offers no chink for penetrating, no hook for latching onto; nor does the eye, for its part, make any move to tackle this model-reality; instead, it confidently waits for whatever is brought into its sphere and ceaselessly idealizes it: It puts a second, smooth, glowing, higher skin or garb on the model.

SECULAR TEMPLES

The thing that was, in effect, the studio for the artist (or the eye as a natural, always available, and automatically operating studio) was known as something else not only to the countless professional or dilettantish interpreters of art, but also to the venerators of the omnipotence of science, especially the "materialists," and it was known to them, more theoretically and yearningly, as a temple. The *disjecta membra* of the knowledge of nature are garbed with higher signification by such a language that strives for "emotional values"—radiolaria and protozoa, celestial bodies and atoms, thus covered as "models" with a beautiful skin, are united in a "Temple of Nature" that inspires reverence.

Likewise the mass of cultural goods, which had disintegrated into a new wilderness, was coated by the notion of *Kultur* as a special, a

* Ibid., p. 138.

higher realm. A specific brand of such signs of culture can still be seen and touched everywhere: the erratically sprouting throng of monuments scattered through towns and countries. Monuments to events and, above all, to historic personalities, in myriad proportions and relations and therefore without proportion or relation, were meant to manifest historicism and traditionalism and tenanted that separate realm of *Kultur*. Heroes, princes, scientists, inventors, poets, and even saints, brought out on the streets and squares, stepped out of both the past and the controversy of opinions and judgments about this or that historic figure; and they became subjects of local or national pride, but more than anything, the substance of a new awareness of culture itself, a culturalism that scarcely admitted essential distinctions, much less oppositions, of historical importance.[26] This sprouting, confusing pluralism of figures could, of course, be harmonized only by a definite overall principle of unity, which at the same time had to represent a growing power: the principle of nation. This principle and feeling united the monuments rather early in a veritable erected temple whose form was Grecian, whose name was Germanic, and whose mastermind was a Bavarian king: "Walhalla" in Regensburg.[27] Here, according to the speech delivered by Bavarian state minister von Schenk at the cornerstone ceremonies in 1830, "the wanderer is encircled by the effigies and names of the great men that our glorious Fatherland, the heart of Europe, has brought forth in all public positions, in all branches of science and scholarship."* It was the first temple to overshadow the lower wilderness of traditions, the first purely secular mountain sanctuary, encompassing many figures and standing in the Higher. Later on, gigantic statues, either the virtually heraldic national symbol, Germania, or the historic founders of the Reich, Armin and Bismarck, performed the same task in the same places.[28]

In the field of natural science, however, it was the hazier glow of an asserted "*Weltanschauung*," a world-view, that had to unite its elements or pieces. The expectations and urgent demands made upon it are expressed so precisely in the name that Haeckel bestowed upon the "Higher" consequence and unity of materialism: a "monistic *Weltan-*

---

* *Donaustauf und Walhalla. Geschildert von Adalbert Müller. Siebente, mit den kurzgefassten Biographien der Walhalla-Genossen vermehrte Auflage*, p. 16. Regensburg, Germany, 1846.

schauung." That unity, to be sought in the world through research or action, is poured upon it here. Advanced by the subjective need for certainty felt by the scientist, who became the secular priest and prophet, this unity is manifest not just in the title "*Weltanschauung*" itself, but properly and potently in the epithet "monistic." What seems to be the most objective and reliable thing in the world—viewing the world—now totally becomes the subjective ideal coating on all things, on all patchwork, the treasure-house of the Higher. Even matter is transfigured when lit up and dressed up by the monistic world-view and brought into its temple. "The goddess of Truth dwells in the temple of Nature," says Haeckel in *The Enigmas of the World*,* "in the verdant forest, on the blue ocean, on the snow-clad mountain peaks." And all these temples to nature and beauty are overtowered by and amalgamated in that "Temple of the Highest," as identified by Ludwig Büchner: "The brain is the Temple of the Highest."† It is the diversely filled panorama temple of such a *Weltanschauung*, in whose interior not so much an operative being as a sum of notions, nay, the semblance of notions is worshipped.

Above all, Darwin's theory of evolution fully achieves, in Wilhelm Bölsche, the state and character of an expressly proclaimed world-view. The individually interpreted results of research, shone upon solely by the light of the theory of natural selection, willingly join together here in the foregoing picture of the whole, the "world-picture." With the fixed gaze on the panorama of life as a whole, each study in the string of biological investigations is given—in Bölsche's mild, persuasive, intimately ingratiating presentation—not merely its scientific place, but also its consecration. In Bölsche's panorama temple, however (we may recall those specially constructed cupolas in which the illusionistic cycloramas were exhibited to swarms of visitors), it is not just the spell of exact science that has its effect; here, at the same time, there is unveiling of mysteries.

A twilight of knowledge and mystery was already shining on the

---

* Ernst Haeckel: *Die Welträthsel. Gemeinverständliche Studien über Monistische Philosophie*, p. 135. Popular edition. 66-77 thousand. Bonn, 1903.

† L. Büchner: *Kraft und Stoff*, p. 104. The sentence forms the motto to a chapter and was taken by Büchner from a writer named Huschke.

figure of the high priest of "evolution," as Bölsche had portrayed him:
Fifteen years after Darwin's death, Bölsche's life story of him appeared
in the series of popular biographies at the Voigtländer publishing house.
Darwin's portrait, down to the very last feature, resembles the notion
of the priest required by that temple: pure and noble, with "hoary"
hair, a patriarch, gentle, nay, suffering, with a touch of the poet about
him, a compassionate friend to all living things. "He abhorred blood,"
says the biographer, and relates the poignant anecdote I have already
mentioned. "At an advanced age, when mildness in all directions lay
upon him like a transfiguration and a serious complaint prevented any
passionate involvement in anything, he could be provoked to a towering
rage by some animal torture. . . . His family saw him coming home pale
and ill because he, the man of peace, had had a dreadful row in the open
street with draymen who had been beating their animals."* But even this
commiseration is not expressed in moral precepts; instead, it occurs in a
biographical sketch for which, rather than rigorous emulation, pleasant
feelings of mellow veneration are expected from the beholder. In this
way, and through the repeated delineation of his illness as an essential
feature rather than a fate, Bölsche's portrait of Darwin even has a reminiscence of the Man of Sorrows. He calls him the "silent sufferer of
Down," a martyr with a tormented compassion for the sufferings of the
world.

The scholar is thus transfigured into a priest and almost a savior,
and likewise the nature he investigated seems colored and coated by a
mood of redemption. The steady evocation of gigantic dimensions of
time, the appeal to the "millions," "trillions," "myriads" of years (enormous numbers, drifting away and so deliciously breath-taking), especially because of the "poetic" delivery, triggered a kind of amazed and
prideful reverence. Yet the strange poetry of the mysteries of nature is
fully the means for such self-transfiguration of the panorama universe.

New Mysteries

The oddest thing about the evolution panorama that Bölsche unrolls
in *Love Life in Nature* (*Liebesleben in der Natur*) is that this panorama

* Wilhelm Bölsche: *Charles Darwin. Ein Lebensbild*, p. 22. Leipzig, 1898.

as a whole, and also the individual biological pictures, the countless portrayals of lower and higher animal life and of the human act of procreation, all constantly sparkle in the brightness of a specific "beauty." Nature in all its elements seems permeated with strangely precious colors or materials, arranged in a glittering collection of noble artistic values, whose individual pieces resemble the materials of exquisite handicraft. Gold, silver, and purple are so singularly distributed over the anatomical and biological processes or parts of the body.

An early section in Bölsche's book* is entitled "The Silver Love Isle of the Herrings"—referring to and transfiguring the mass spawning of herrings on the North European coasts. The idea of the perfect development of the human character comes to Bölsche under the outlined, shapeless, material aegis of gold: He fills the human spirit with the "ideal image of a man who is physically as beautiful as can be, spiritually as sublime as can be, ethically as golden as can be." The human body itself floats like a "silver blossom on the Lake of Walpurgis." The path taken by the sperm cell during copulation is a path through a "purple shaft." The landscape into which such material values unite with the other tokens (likewise frozen into solid jewelry) of a luxuriant southern nature, with a green expanse, a blue ocean, and solar luster that is always fetched down, now descriptive, now symbolic—this landscape comes directly from Böcklin. "I would like to take you away," the book commences, "to a lovely place. And there I would like to tell you stories. . . . East of San Remo, in the paradise of the Riviera, looms Capo Verde, a brown craggy cliff, jutting out into the free ocean. Strata of stone, themselves once the ground of the sea millions of years ago, break like a fantastic fortress out of the soft, green coastal picture." The blue Mediterranean is no more absent than the dazzling white wreath of foam or the lustrous sunlight. And even those specters of Böcklin's mythologism, which merely redoubles the landscape mood, haunt this picture: "Tender, white hands of foam" are ascribed to the sea for sensualizing the geology.

Not that Bölsche renders all his objects mild and charming (the

---

*   Wilhelm Bölsche: *Das Liebesleben in der Natur. Eine Entwicklungsgeschichte der Liebe*, cf. p. vii. First series. 13-14 thousand, 1903. Leipzig, 1898-1902.

gamble and sensation of his book was precisely his finding ways of articulating, indeed "narrating," the things most "ticklish" to the bourgeois). In fact, he does not fail to attribute demonic qualities to the sexual drive. However, the demonic appears here in an "aesthetic" guise, as an element in the world of the things of taste. "Heated blood," "ardent energy," "spring tempests"—such phrases bring the demonic into play. Moreover, the dark powers receive a reflection from the artistic creations that they destroy (according to the imagery), and this reflection justifies them anew: "There is simply the energy which, when it demolishes the temple, knows that is alone can rebuild that temple." Completely captured in the semiornamental canon of symbols that the early Jugendstil devised, the demonic nature of the drive appears in a sentence like this one: "And then once again we shall be perfectly powerless; indeed, we shall join the wild laughter when the wreaths fall, when the flowers become poor, bleeding hearts." Just as doom and fortune equally or in one are presented there (say, in Jan Toorop's drawings) in the figure of a garden, so too the flowers of love in Bölsche's poetic natural science, the blossoming "new men," or even the intertwining feelings of lovers are pictured as gardens: "emotional sowings and sweet gardens of faith for pure souls!"

Bölsche himself, in his foreword, signalized his language and method expressly as aesthetic. Yet this procedural awareness is so unfit for making the already cited motifs and phrases appear as a random, merely "methodical" trimming or artistic device and hence immaterial to the overall character of the enterprise, that the latter merely stands out in a much sharper light. The author explains his procedure with the following lines: "I am of the opinion that the bridge from the rigorous discipline, in which one accumulates certain facts half or wholly true, to the world operative thinking, which seeks the whole, passes over art. And in fact, all the devices of art: even humor." Incidentally, he uses the same argument for justifying his intimately ingratiating tone of storytelling, which he characterizes as a "Biedermeier style of tempered coziness," like consistently addressing the reader with the intimate pronoun *Du*. The basic conviction of a central role for art already makes clear that we are dealing with more than a merely skillful technique for a popular discussion of ticklish matters. Bölsche's peculiar effect and achievement reside precisely in this aesthetic method: Now at times is may be meant as a technique of dressing up, enveloping, or costuming technical knowledge, which could also be transmitted undisguised but without loss of substance; yet the centaurian character of such a "world-view" emerges all the more distinctly when showing itself to be a singular compound of science and art.

This combination itself, however, is possible only if, on the one hand, the labor of knowledge is premised as relatively terminated or at least theoretically terminable (which is why Bölsche would take over only "assured results"), and if, on the other hand, art is understood as a special precinct lovingly looked after and promising a kind of earthly Ascension. This realm of art, having projected its glow upon all stations of the panorama of evolution, reveals itself at the end of the process as a clearly painted vision of mankind's future in total purity. In that realm, the element of the Ascension or liberation from the heaviness and wildness of an existence of sensual drives and the element of the fulfillment of earthly happiness meet halfway. What was just recently "indecent" turns out to be "natural," and the clinging veil of "holiness" is quickly thrown over the natural.

> A luminous future world of a better Hellenism cleansed of its cinders: where ethics and nudity, a pure hallowing of art and a hot fragrance of the springtime of love could rest side by side on a common flowery meadow without disturbing one another, while the white temple, with its sacred curtain before the deepest mysteries of life and of thought, looms silently into the azure. . . . When shall we emerge from the deep shadowy vale of our aberrations and reach thine Isle of the Blest?

The picture of such harmony of sensual happiness and spiritual peace (the intention is to overcome or at least overpaint that anxiety-ridden choice of Schiller's) can scarcely show itself more clearly as resulting from a handicraft arrangement of costly materials. The attributes of hallowing and holiness, occurring at every mention of either the realm of art or the ultimately and necessarily unexplained biological processes, adhere totally to the individual piece in the thus assembled apotheosis: the word "holy" is applied only and precisely to the curtain in the temple, and not even to the temple itself, much less to a congregation gathering there, for the temple is devoid of both gods and men. The sole things brought into it are the "mysteries of life and of thought," or more precisely of thinking life or of a science brought to life. But the holy curtain veiling those mysteries actually signifies nothing else than that the mere title "holy" itself functions as a curtain or mantle against cynicism. Bölsche's justification is announced in the table of contents with the sentence "What should be holy for us": "It is not that the mystery of procreation should be dragged out into the street. As little as the mystery of a Beethoven symphony can be shared among, and enjoyed by, any but a few in a secluded and solemn hallowing of mood and place . . . so too this utterly profound mystery of mankind will never lose its holy solitude." Thus the sheer naming of what is universally natural as "holy" acts in tandem with the adducement of set pieces from the sphere of worship, set pieces in the pseudo-freedom of those flowery meadows or May forests, and this alliance is meant to expel any sense of guilt and the morality of concealment.

It is the paradise or future age of a reformed life that Bölsche has blueprinted. This writer's intimacy with his readers, the Biedermeier tone of storytelling which he speaks about in the foreword, the constant *"Du"* with which he hopes to gain the good will of his audience—this entire atmosphere of a community of noble minds that he creates can rank as anticipating the paradisal state, as being a first step towards reformation, which does however lead right into the midst of the "luminous future world." The costume identifying this new community of saints is nudity. For eyes long weaned from the sight of naked people, nudity itself was, in effect, a costume. It is the last and perhaps most cunning way of bedizening and "idealizing" the full-scale human models produced by that century. The recollection of Greek life set the stylistic character. Photographs of "normally" beautiful bodies, such as were published later, after the turn of the century, for justifying the clothing reform, are usually combined with pictures of Hellenic deities. Those are not simply naked people, any more than the sight of them is exhausted by grasping the immediate aim to give examples of ideal bodies. The concept of "noble nudity" itself truly seems to reclothe such figures like a costume or thick veil, warding off importunate sensual gazes and removing all allurements. In this way, the "holy curtain" virtually amounts to a garment, producing, albeit invisibly, an atmosphere of artistic life, in which, singularly mixed with conquered and therefore still present modesty, far removed from the paradisal naïveté and unembarrassedness to be achieved, the newly won freedom evinces itself precisely in the arrangement of gestures, postures, and half-concealed lineaments. From the midst of that more massive costume world of the waning century, from the midst of those twice-curving corsets, those heavy folded and pleated skirts, those braidings, trimmings, fur linings, in short, everything that the protagonists of reformed clothing condemned as unendurable corruption and crippling in an almost museum-like mustiness—from that cast-off sumptuousness, no pure, untouched Nature emerges as fresh as on the first day. On the contrary: These naked figures reveal, down to the very last trait, their thoroughly historical formation and their definite embarrassment. For one thing, the steady comparisons of the reform goals with ancient or even pre-Raphaelite artworks incessantly brought to mind that this paradise could be aspired to only by way of art and as a realm of art. Furthermore, added attributes, like pipes of Pan or animal skins, as well as prospects with ideal landscapes or sparsely distributed floral embroideries, plus the bare ensemble of bright cloths dropping down in a few large folds, give the photographed samples of reform-nature their style—plain Jugendstil. But even if all this were to be omitted or removed, the signature of the epoch would be imprinted with all sufficient clarity in the well-arranged composure of the postures, in the measured rigor of parallel body outlines, in the deliberate "ideality" of the stretching neck, in the compressed lips of the ever averted face, throning proudly, as it were, over the body, to which both laughter and weeping seem alien. "Were the least shadow of an impure thought to steal up," Bölsche says in describing a painting by Fidus, "the lotus petals would fold over her in defiant haste."* Such lotus petals are always at hand here, they seem to be one with the skin. Nakedness is a costume here, freedom a mask. A mask, to be sure, that cannot be taken off, for it is one with the face itself.

---

*   Ibid., Third series, p. 10.

Bölsche's life panorama, to which the uncatastrophic transition from picture to picture lent itself, as to all panoramas, and in which the illusion was kept awake by intimate speech, thus passed into another realm, not the art of living but an artificial life. The illusionistic vastness contracted into the small field of a flowery meadow, formed only of noble materials but still "plainly natural," with the paradise of a reformed life unfolding on its quiet, self-illuminated expanse. The figures of the nineteenth century shifted and changed into figures of Jugendstil. This art-light of Bölsche's, however, the sun of a lovelier future and a reformed present, is merely the final, deeply expectant stage of the history of light in the nineteenth century, the light in the panorama.

VI

INSIDE THE HOME

From a rigorously scientific viewpoint, the future was by no means as bright as Bölsche had ultimately painted it; in fact, it was quite dark. One of the logical consequences of the law of energy preservation was the insight that the sun does not shine eternally but is gradually exhausted. Although especially the popular presentations (here forming the sole basis) never tired of rhapsodizing about its life-giving, nay, life-permitting importance, sunshine became, for physics, merely a form of heat release, someday to reach an end.

The cosmos of Kant and Laplace, fashioned of nebula masses by gravitation (and nineteenth century physics did remain true to this cosmogony), kept to the lightless and heatless realm of pure mechanics; it was cold and dark. Light remained an element shooting in from the outside, from a source of its own. But now it entered the cosmos, explained by that conversion of energy during the attraction of such enormous masses. In the same instant, light was traced back to deeper causes, a phenomenon elucidated and encompassed by more general processes. It was captured, so to speak, in the endless interior of the "whole of nature." It was born in a knowable and even calculable way and will perish in the same way. Actually it was a mere interruption of darkness, and night was in a certain sense the more comprehensive, more permanent condition of the universe, whose past lies as much in night as its future.

The observation in 1862 of a celestial body (almost imperceptible because of its darkness) near Sirius, and the surmisal of other dark stars simply on the basis of gravitational relationships, were welcomed as substaniating what followed anyway from the principle of energy: that light comes to an end. These dark stars ominously revealed the future and the real character of this new sky. "Extinct suns!" cries Helmholtz in one of his popular lectures: "Extinct suns! The fact that they exist lends new weight to our reasons for concluding that our sun too is a body that gradually expends its immanent store of heat and thus will some day be extinguished."* The horror that even the cool scientist finds in this unnerving picture impels him to find possibilities of solace; but the conjectures he comes up with are involved and difficult to carry through. It was as if people were trying to grope their way out of this murky, cavernous universe. "This is a thought to which we can yield only with reluctance; it seems to us like an infraction of the beneficent creative power that we usually find operating in all conditions, especially those relating to living creatures."

The virtually balking introduction itself evinces the striving to propitiate, since indeed the previous blind "natural energy" or "work energy" suddenly floats up here as if from a childhood memory, but transmuted into a friendlier "creative power."

> Who can say, after seventeen million years (that is the time left, according to physical calculations, for the heat supply of the sun), to what level of perfection our descendants will have developed in their marvelous capacity, common to all organisms, for adjusting to the conditions of life? . . . Indeed, if earth and sun were to turn numb and moveless, who can say what new worlds will be prepared to welcome life.

But even if someone thus took it upon himself to sacrifice, on a trial basis, the usual lofty concept of man's organic structure and imagine far loftier and more refined living creatures, this "who-knows?" metaphysics remained unsatisfactory. For such a scientific fantasy had something of the occult about it and was unable to replace the lost eternity of light. The last haven was the certitude of preserving energy in what-

---

*   H. Helmholtz: "Über die Entstehung des Planetensystems" (lecture given in Heidelberg and Cologne in 1871) Published in *Populäre wissenschaftliche Vorträge*, no. III, p. 134. Brunswick, 1876.

ever metamorphoses, even though life, and perhaps even the definite form of the human individual might be regarded as something "energy-like", which could thus be transmuted but not totally annihilated. Yet, for all such speculations, scientists remained—inevitably, to be sure—inside the one, the same universe, inside the familiar night of nature.

HIGHLIGHTS

Though the world was basically dark from this high vantage point, though light itself had become transitory, and though there was no real solace or escape from this imprisonment, there was nevertheless something of a surrogate in the smaller and smallest of human life, the inside of the home. Some dispersed light, itself a tangible, clung to the things people dealt with. And here it seemed all the more familiar and homey.

"The September sun once again whisked shyly through the vast hall of the castle mill, then it took the last, warm sparklet of radiance from the strange objects on the deep stone sill of the corner window, and vanished in the bed of snowy clouds rising indolently but steadfastly along the heavens."* This still life opens Eugenie Marlitt's novel *In the Home of the Councilor of Commerce (Im Hause des Kommerzienrates)*.[29] The setting of the sun is the first event in a plot that is truly anything but uneventful—"setting," however, may be too heavy a word for a being so well integrated in the milieu as to whisk like a lady's maid and vanish in bed like a maiden. Its visible part, however, is that sparklet of radiation that only just now lay rather independently on the "strange objects" (the authoress loved playing the myopic and identifying things little by little), the sparklet which is then taken along by its own sun like a forgotten cap. The "strange objects," incidentally, are next discerned: a physician's "tweeze," "that collection of instruments whose sharp, cold sparkle terrifies the eye and sends a shudder through the human nervous system." Thus we have a different sparkling after the more amiable sparklet has been removed. Only now does the still life disclose its ominous, fateful nature; and the teeming life of the novel, all acrackle with the demonics of "promoterism" and speculation, commences quite fittingly in twilight.

* Eugenie Marlitt's collected novels and novellas, Vol. V, p. 5.

Later, to be sure, more such highlights flit through the densely cluttered interiors of the councilor's home; always split off from the invisible light sources, they linger in both good places and bad. Thus, for instance, the old tower, in which the freshly ennobled Kommerzien- rat has luxuriously settled in together with his strongbox, is first des- cribed as follows: "No trace of fresh mortar was left on the walls by renovating human hands; no new stone had been inserted, and yet none seemed to be wanting; only the mighty window cavities of the tower, once shielded by decayed wooden shutters, yawned wide open, and the stone frames glittered so singularly as if a secluded sunbeam were weav- ing a mysterious golden web in the profound darkness."* This poetic foreboding is not so inaccurate in regard to the dark interior, even though the gold spun there may not glitter: The Kommerzienrat draws aside a heavy Gobelin curtain and shows his safe to the freshly arrived heroine. The contents of the safe, namely the heiress's stockholdings, were what was concealed in the darkness behind the yawning window cavities and what the secluded sunbeam indicated, not by way of trans- figurement, but as a tempting glow.

Even in the friendly home of "Aunt Diakonus," the simple counter- setting to that tower, the foil in the same park (in that thoroughly peaceful little cottage of the vicar's widow, which her nephew pur- chased for her, not with stock dividends but with his savings of non- interest-bearing fees for medical services)—even here the light appears in no other guise than secluded, captured, and reified: "The groups of plants on the two high, wide windows were an exquisite embellishment, the azalea and palm species, the magnificent rubber trees, warmly and powerfully gilded by the sunlight breaking through the clear network curtains. The goldfish in the glass bowl and the warbler in the brass cage, those foster-children of lonesome women, were not lacking eith- er."† By gilding palms and rubber trees, and quite powerfully at that, the light seems to function here as a compensating justice, and the flash- ing gold of the fishes in the glass bowl is the finer wealth, but, for all that, a wealth too. The pious old lady, diversely surrounded by the

*   Ibid., p. 71.
†   Ibid., p. 90.

scattered golden brilliance, holds it together as zealously as the Kommerzienrat holds on to his capital. Here is the secret of the countless genially
illuminated *gemütlich* cottages in literature and painting; they contain
the property of good people, and this way of gilding existence abides,
its pieces are never removed by any timidly whisking sun from the
homey gazes of aging dwellers.

It is, incidentally, the same gilding that Anton von Werner took
literally when making the painted trumpets of the military band in the
Sedan panorama flash with such crafty illusionism. And one may assume
that, likewise, the admittedly really "gilded trumpet," casting such an
enigmatic (later so often derided) spell for decades, especially on the
untold throngs of female readers—that this inalienable attribute of
Scheffel's *Trumpeter of Säckingen* owes its enormous heart-moving
power to its glitter and its blare alike—both being actually the same:

> *What a lovely sight he was,*
> *Standing gracefully in snow,*
> *Leaning up against his mount:*
> *Here and there a sunbeam flashing*
> *On the man and on his trumpet—*
> *With the gloomy firs behind him.*[30]

That is how young Werner appears at his very first entrance, enframed
by the darkness of the Black Forest (the same in which subsequently
thirty-eight tunnels were bored) and covered with highlights that stay
with this free minstrel until the happy end: insignia of natural nobility,
to which the end also adds a nobility granted by human authority,
namely the papal nobility. However, Werner's misfortune, resulting
from the social gap between the homeless minstrel and his beloved, a
baron's daughter, is properly manifested only in the doubled highlight:

> *So he blew;—was that a teardrop*
> *Glittering upon the trumpet,*
> *Or was that a raindrop merely?*

Instead (as one might conjecture today) of competing with the sparkle
of the metal, this covert sign of feeling raises the brilliance and thereby
the Trumpeter's unminted wealth to a realm of fable.

A Digression

Wherever art and goodness were thus not rewarded by natural gilding, and the cells of gamblers and speculators were not designated by the glow of a secluded ray, the scene was dominated by a wan pallor, almost a variety of the night—for instance the interiors of homes, the basement and rear buildings as well as the crammed, heavily furnished floor-throughs of the rich. For not even the white outdoor light penetrated the rooms. Help was actually provided either by the dense walls of creepers growing between balcony columns; or the hosts of palms and other plants on window-sills and in winter gardens, oriels, and balustrades; and finally, the thick envelope of the fourfold window-coverings, from the blinds to the portières. All these things created a greenish twilight mingling and enhancing the tones: the ardent colors of the imported Orient, of Persian carpets[31], pillows, and cushions; the iridescent brillance of damasks and taffeta frocks; the matt shimmer of statues; and the ivory or alabaster cheeks and limbs of women.

Ever since the wane of the century—ever since Ibsen first pierced the bourgeois home with a "draft of air" as an irritant announcing liberation—and ever since, especially along with Jugendstil, the sun itself, a moral, salubrious, and aesthetic remedy, was cited in every way, as revealed in the poetic slogans "Sunshine, you final human happiness" (Otto Ernst) and "Have sunlight in your heart!" (Cäsar Fleischlen), or in the watchword "The house in the sun" (Carl Larsson);[32] and ever since, last but not least, in our day, the especially hygenic cult of sunlight, in residential architecture and in photography as in canoeing, skiing, and swimming, reached an unequalled popularity to establish itself in all minds as one of the most precious and most intrinsic, ergo proudest acquisitions in the modern era—ever since all these things happened, it has become difficult to really perceive and properly depict the inherent nature of those twilit interiors. The sharp and often cheap abuse that has since been hurled at this scarcely bygone sphere would be of no service whatsoever. The German word *Muff* (musty odor), packing its own punch, is the most widespread term of reproof. It seems to express the thorough spring-cleaning of that interior world, delapidated into rubbish and decayed into mustiness.

The turn-of-the-century movement, to which today's modernistic self-assurance owes all its motives and arguments, united its programs and objectives under the title of "reform" (of clothing, society, and life itself), a title that could easily describe the true nature of the entire epoch. Nevertheless, the recent and present champions of these achievements are not seldom of the deeply rooted opinion that they truly and irrevocably live in a totally "new" time, and that no vestige or spell of the "transcended" era of indoor gardens and portières could possibly occupy any space between the glass and concrete of their homes, under the blazing sunlight that is captured everywhere. These "transcenders," were they simply to take the trouble of peering more closely at some nineteenth-century documents, would frequently enough be disabused. To put it more cordially: Not everyone whom one now hears ridiculing the bygone bourgeous milieu has, withal, stopped being such a "bourgeois" himself.

May the reader, however, excuse these somewhat excited remarks, which have almost unexpectedly stolen into the even and peaceful course of this investigation: They are of some use to him in shooing away, for the moment at least, an all-too-premature sarcastic and amused smile that may have been about to cross his features at the first quick sketch of the twilit interior; and those remarks may well have brought the smiler to other objects of his pleasure. It is easy to deride the past anyway, and one must regard it as a waste of humor, whereas a joke usually gains brilliance from spareness. But after smoothing the path for a more detailed approach, we must first say a word about the attitude of our undertaking. After all, our goal is not to terminate that previous mockery with a "fairer appreciation," which, weighing intelligently, would separate the good and the bad sides, rejecting the latter and bringing in the former as safe property Such conduct would probably ill defend itself against being "reactionary," whether this harsh rebuke came from a legitimate or an unauthorized source. The goal is to investigate the image twisted by modern scorn, present it once again in clearer strokes and articulate in terse concepts (certainly neglecting a great deal) what that image means when taken as a whole figure—and we hope that this will contribute to a more thorough "transcending."

Ardor and Shimmer

Light, whether we throw ourselves against it or exclude it, always enters human experience, knowledge, use, love, and enjoyment only insofar and in such a manner as the historical constellation permits; for we always know nature itself, in all its power and permanence, only as something historical.

Here, consequently, the diffuse pallor of the north, all that is allowed to penetrate the dwelling, is toned down by curtains and nettings to filter through the diverse, usually barely translucent green of the leaves on indoor plants. "It is fortunate," said a lady during the 1890s, and many contemporaries no doubt still recall similar utterances, "that we have a northern exposure, otherwise our things might discolor." This down-to-earth standpoint of a conscientious *Hausfrau* is noteworthy for two reasons: the weight of the practical argument against the sun, irrefutable as long as the "things," namely the rugs, wallpaper, and various hued slipcovers, maintain their indoor dominion, in short, as long as this interior forms an Oriental ensemble; and second, the view of the sun itself as an intruder "discoloring" the things by robbing them of their (to use an authentic word) "ardent" hues. The sun would be the wrong light, not just for the things, but for the whole interior. The latter is not twilit because the sun is locked out, but the sun remains locked out because the interior is twilit by its very nature. Still, it is not deprived of the matt brilliance and the wan shimmer cleaving to textiles, statues, human shapes, and costumes.

The German Renaissance, say, utilized and imitated in the bourgeois home's cultivation of art as of the 1870s, did not owe its renown merely to the need of the new ruling stratum to aggrandize itself, like a sixteenth-century prince, by visibly promoting the arts; nor merely to the national motive of choosing, among numerous familiar and tested possibilities, and with a kind of fierce resoluteness, a style that could already be considered and proclaimed a historical possession. No, the German Renaissance truly and outstandingly proved its worth by making that precept of a twilight interior a reality. The Munich publisher Georg Hirth, who for many years was a great success at publishing more and more volumes with model decorations, furnishings, and clothes, and who made himself the prophet of this renascence of the Renaissance, does cite the most positive examples for those other motives, especially the national one: ". . . If the conviction has now become universal," he writes, "that we are to seek our salvation in the German Renaissance of the sixteenth and seventeenth centuries, then we really ought to succeed in mastering the misshapen moloch of poor style and taste";* and "by solidifying a sterling national taste, we hope once again to become masters of our own market."† Yet the national decorative style contains the Orient, and that is about the first thing with which Hirth characterizes it: for the Renaissance, in regard to ornamentation, was expanded by absorbing Oriental surface patterns into engraving and carpet weaving, embroidery and marquetry. This re-counter with the Orient was merely the signal announcing the effective power of decoration itself and its primary categories—color, mood, harmony, and inner glow.

For the glow or the inherent shimmering light of the interior, it was of utmost importance to bar all direct, sharply gleaming reflection, which reverberated clear external images. "The metallic glow . . . if its effect is to be decoratively colorful, must never become a mirror, for the random mirror is barbaric and styleless."** The wording is harsh, the condemning definitive. Such mirroring is barbaric and styleless because it would sharply cut off the snugly glowing twilight, because it would slash through the gliding color transitions, and because, more than anything, it would rudely demolish the certitude of the inner light preserved in the textiles and playing above them. Such destruction would be wrought by the sight of the reflex, which would let the other, the outer light mysteriously tumble in and bounce back unabsorbed. Thus the first requirement for making brilliance decorative (according to Hirth's instructions, virtually leaking out from the esotery of the decorating mystique) is to break up the reflexes.

By making the brilliance "matt" (i.e. smashing the neutral light reflections to such an extent that they yield no more sharp coher-

---

* Georg Hirth: *Das deutsche Zimmer der Renaissance. Anregungen zu häuslicher Kunstpflege.* p. 9. Munich, 1880.

† Ibid., p. 32.

** Ibid., p. 54.

ent mirror images and can be individually distinguished only by a microscope), we promote the more intimate fusion with the local color; this, essentially, is the basis for the splendid effect of the old pewter, the waxed or oiled wooden furniture, the satins, velvets, and brocades, etc.*

The polished black grand piano is therefore always gauche, as are the broad, radiantly golden picture frames, which not only Hirth advised replacing with dark, say brown or even red-velvet, frames.

The gamut of brilliances in Hirth's work is served up for the taste-conscious reader's enjoyment in a reproduction that does not stand for any specific kind of interior, but is simply called a "decoration": "Decoration by Alexander Pollak, Imperial-Royal Court Decorator in Vienna."† This, aside from a two-page spread devoted to Makart's studio, is the most conspicuous, most subtly executed reproduction in the entire book. One sees a cluttered and hence unusable, fully deserted arrangement of practical and ornamental articles, eerily showing the autocracy of the niceties of brilliance and color or the "values." With unmistakable refinement (whose analogy could be discerned at best in today's combinations of properly worked materials, glass, metals, and woods), an obtuse, warming, and enveloping carpet and Gobelin are joined with the "smashed reflections' of the waxed table and chair; a piece of brown, woolly bearskin juts out, as though casually suspended, between the fairly blank edge of the table and the shinier bronze bust; and further back, a heavy, most likely deep-red Oriental cover is pushed together into enormous bulges; while the patinated, open-worked spherical surface of what seems to be a coal-pan shines up from the floor, the gamut heightens forwards to the dull white glow of a pewter jug and to the final and most daring accent of a naked sword. There can be no doubt as to the mastery of the game that the decorator knew how to play with all this cultural jetsam.

The values of ardor and shimmer, however, were not just used insofar as they adhered to objects—they were also captured for themselves, registered and treated in a doctrine of the elements of "practical

*   Ibid., p. 76.
†   Ibid., p. 125.

aesthetics." Gottfried Semper, the architect and teacher of the art industry, produced a literary masterpiece entitled *Style in the Technical and Tectonic Arts or Practical Aesthetics.** Here, more specifically when designating textile art as the true "ultimate art," he describes or (perhaps more accurately) defines the chief fabrics according to their make and character and with all their differences. He is, incidentally, always guided by the intention of pinpointing and establishing the materials and purposes as accurately as humanly possible in order to have these (as he terms it) virtually natural basic elements serve as the foundation for constructing aesthetics, developing each specific "style," and forming taste.

It is particularly interesting to mention this early and thus far unsurpassed theoretician of a "material-specific" art practice; for the, of course, differently oriented and also simplified motto of "material-specificity" is and has been used for a long time as a robust "counter-example" to polemically condemn the previous century's art industry. It is true that Semper also sharply criticized the industrial art of his day; but it is not fair to alienate him from his historical sphere by setting him up as a lone prophet and mere forerunner of an abstract modernity. His impact on his era was evinced in positive and negative things, in emulation as in controversy and hostility; and no one would ever dream of localizing Semper's Dresden Theater anywhere but in the nineteenth century.

The element of brilliance or mattness, more generally of the absorbing or reflecting relationship to light, plays an outstanding role throughout Semper's descriptions or definitions of fabrics. Thus, regarding the (medieval) birth of brocade, he calls the first major step in the development of the "silk style" the "system of assimilation": "The shine of the silk was made the basis of the shinier gold thread, and either the pattern of gold was emphasized on a silk ground or, vice versa, the silk pattern was grounded with gold." Putting the trait of shininess more emphatically at the center, he adds: "Such a system of toning down and harmonizing color shine with something shinier could not fail to have

---

*   Gottfried Semper. *Der Stil in den technischen und tektonischen Künsten oder Praktische Ästhetik.* Two volumes: first edition, Frankfurt, 1860-63; second edition, Munich, 1878. The quotations are from the latter.

its splendidly earnest effect."* Detached from this, but quite similarly regarded under the aspect of the adhering light, satin appears as the next special form of the silk style: "This fabric has, to a certain extent, no texture, but consists of satin-stitches placed incessantly next to one another and interlocking, so that the silk thread may remain unbent and unbroken for as long as possible and blend its shine with the shine of the parallel neighboring threads into the utterly smooth surface and the highly brilliant effect of light and shadow. The miraculous qualities of this fabric were recognized early, and it was employed solidly at times, but more often in league with matt parts as a shiny contrast and ground."†

The peculiar light relationship is joined, in the characterization of material, by the peculiar color, which, no less than the light relationship, is considered part of the nature of the fabric. Thus, in regard to satin: "The fiery red, the cochineal extracted from the juice of the kermes insect or the gall-nuts it produces on leaves, is the very specific color, the color par excellence, of satin, and this fact is quite in keeping with the artistic taste." Satin is followed in Semper's treatise by velvet, and his way of relating them sounds almost like an idealistic construction applied to materials:

> The contrast to satin is velvet, and yet velvet, like satin, is a happy result of knowledgeable technical exploitation of the peculiarities of the fibrous material in question, namely silk. Just as silk threads, viewed lengthwise, are the most shining tissue (aside from metal threads), so too a surface is absolutely lusterless (i.e. light-absorbing or rather preventing the separation of the light rays into absorbed and reflected light) if formed by an infinite number of bias-cut silk threads standing next to one another, this being the case with close-cropped satin.

And now the joint homeland of these intensely colored light-carriers, of these so differentiated elements of the interior: "The Orient, the old seat of all silk manufacture, was likewise the seat of velvet manufacture, and all poets and chroniclers trace velvet there, giving it Oriental pro-

---

*   Ibid., Vol. I, p. 151.
†   Ibid., Vol. I, p. 155.

duction names. Calif Haroun-al-Rashid's gifts to Charlemagne supposedly included some velvet fabrics." What is here a historical note becomes
a ubiquitously realized grand vision everywhere else. The Orient itself,
whether Turkish, Egyptian, Arabic, or even Moorish, with the splendor
of carpets and the shine of silken fabrics, enters the bourgeois home—
this is the place of luxury and all dreams. The internal light, captured
and preserved in the ensemble of "decoration" fabrics, radiates seductively in the home; and the intoxication of the heavy, richly folded
textiles, luxuriating in "thick dyes," matt, shining, and iridescent, can
still be perceived in Semper's sober catalogue of materials.

It is as if all these things were announcing that nervous, sensitive
flair for the different lures of the costly stuffs, an awareness that subsequently, in the *fin de siècle*, was developed into a vice (and also
accompanied by the sweet consciousness of vice), as we can see in
Dorian Gray, in Stefan George's *Carpet of Life* (*Teppich des Lebens*),
and in Rilke's partiality for old brocades and lace. This attitude becomes
even more intense if one observes, as in Semper, that parts of the living
landscape are placed in an intimate relation to the textile art product—
"As the satin flowers of spring loom on the velvet carpet of the fresh
lawn, so too must green be the chief color of velvet, which serves as the
ground for a rich embroidery or a shinier silk fabric."* How many
artificial gardens of later ointment-drunk princes in poetry and painting
are anticipated here!

Still, this is not yet "applied art," it is not a view of nature as preserved in applied art, for no other reason than that these "flowers,"
Semper's "satin flowers of spring," were taken so literally in the panorama world that an entire industry of artificial flowers and "Makart
nosegays" (consisting of real, dried grasses) manufactured them and
marketed them to the textile-craving homeowners and costume-wearing
women. This industry had already begun during the 1820's in Germany
(and previously in France), steadily increasing its output and volume.
It still exists today, though its charms may be plainer, its market smaller,
its products less popular. The people who once delighted in artificial
flowers never took them as a pure substitute for genuine flowers. In-

---

* Ibid., Vol. I, p. 162.

stead, the natural model, by being imitated, seemed to be ennobled, and the imitation, moreover, was superior to the cruder natural product by its permanence and shininess.

More than anything, however, the pleasure in fabrics, solidly cropping up in Semper's descriptions, is distinguished from the later and still extant cult of material sensations in the following ways: Those fabrics normally served to "clothe" both walls, floors, and furnishings, as well as people; they were in any event subordinate to the art of arrangement, interior design, and drapery; whereas later, at the end of the century, in the epoch of actual "commercial art," which belongs to Jugendstil, those fabrics were expelled into the isolation of unattached, has-been values or elements of taste.

THE TROUBLESOME WINDOW

The peculiar indoor light, the varied gradation of the matt shine, the ardor of the colors and the unified "mood" they strive for, caused the windows—those sharp interruptions of the "covering" and gateways for outdoor light—to be a lasting nuisance, or at least a knotty problem for the decorators. The paradox of the window, the modern, fully transparent window, which both opens up to, and admits, and yet then again locks off the outside, was a constant source of anxiety. All the essential writers dealing with interior design during the final decades of that century perceive this anxiety and try to make it bearable without ever quite managing to resolve it.

Thus: "Our usual large windows," writes Cornelius Gurlitt (in his chats, dedicated to his fiancée and entitled *In the Bourgeois Home* [*Im Bürgerhaus*], "deprive the space of its inner calm, relate it too closely to the outside world." As a remedy (according to Gurlitt's historical explanation), people hit upon "the idea of hanging a sheer, lightweight fabric over the window, a textile mellowing the severe architectural lines of the window with the deeper shadows in the wide folds, without earnestly hindering the ingress of light, and the fabric was white because in that period colorlessness appeared to be the highest revelation of taste." But then the curtain promptly seems as paradoxical as the window itself:

Why do people spend a deal of money on crystal-clear panes if they then reverse the effect with the tight loops of the tulle and the lines of an ornament? Why do people strain to make the demarcation between the interior space and the exterior world barely discernible if they then intend to emphasize that boundary so conspicuously? Is it really so advantageous to have a fairly unhampered view through the curtain while keeping off the outside gaze that one would put up with the great expenditure?

These unanswerable questions bring his reflections to an end, and the author seeks and finds comfort only in the nostalgic longing for the crown glass of our forebears, who needed no curtains: "The entire room is twilit, snug. We feel alone here, whether with our thoughts or our friends. Whatever is happening outside is far away. Not even the drifting of clouds can be detected through the greenish mingling of light." Here we have the real motive behind the much-derided penchant for crown panes, which were then, according to Gurlitt, reintroduced by people of distinction and by innkeepers; it was no randomly nostalgic "historicism" that made them seem so desirable, but the necessity, comprehensible under those circumstances, of also drawing the troublesome window into the interior and yet letting it remain a window.

Now Gurlitt is quite aware that crown glass is not in place everywhere—he recommends it mainly for bedrooms and dining rooms, where people do not care to look out. And finally he returns to the singular curtain with the sighing sentence: "But the curtain *is* with us, and we must talk about its employment." The curtain, after all, because of its paradoxical task, was contrary not to reason alone, but also, because of its obnoxious whiteness, to the color-craving of the tenant, who would like to envelop himself inside his home. Colorful threads and cream-colored undercurtains are supposed to help mitigate the whiteness. Using heavier textiles seems dubious since they might go too far in negating the sense of the window. But now, at last, though fraught with some embarrassment, comes the solution to the window problem, a solution that remained valid throughtout the era: "Any halfway experienced man knows how harsh the difference is between the brightness of the entering daylight and the solid objects delimiting it, how greatly the effect of color is thereby disturbed. A gradation of ever thicker curtains from the uncovered glass surface to the heavy, opaque fabric is the best way to increase awareness of the color of that fabric."* Here we thus have the well-known system of multiple coverings, from the curtain to the portière, a system deduced from the "harmony" of the colorful envelope, which tolerates no sharp interruption, or at best a sliding transition—if need be, until the transparent glass itself.

Yet there is an unsatisfactory remainder, which Georg Hirth classically formulated: "The broad, white surface [of the curtain] is actually quite unattractive, but one must put up with it as a necessary evil."† At this point, the reckoning does not work out, for even "in the bourgeois home," indoor light is contingent on outdoor light. Otherwise, the burghers might indeed be quite in the dark.

POLYCHROMY

Even when threatened by the window, the fabrics thus offer the only salvation. Semper, so rigorous about observing the ends in art and so averse to all illusionism, emphasizes this historically decisive prepotency of fabrics (and emphasizes it unconsciously) in two ways: In his highly peculiar division of textile art according to ends, the chapter entitled "The Cover" takes up the most space; and, obviously corresponding to this, the first volume (running to 490 pages) is devoted to textile art alone, the second one, however (576 pages), to ceramics, tectonics, stereotomy, and metallotechny together. These outer and seeming disproportions may surprise the modern reader, but they express Semper's basic operative thought, characteristic for the entire epoch in so many ways: namely, that wickerwork and weaving, the cover and the carpet, are the true genetic and essential element of architecture.

Like no other, Gottfried Semper's little book marks the entrance of color into architectural theory and practice and rings out classicism insofar as the latter's chief aims, taken for granted and beyond discussion, resided in the white wall and the white solid statue. That book, *The Four Elements of Architecture (Die Vier Elemente der Baukunst)*,

---

*   Cornelius Gurlitt: *Im Bürgerhaus*, p. 166 ff. Dresden, 1888.

†   Ibid., p. 173. *Das deutsche Zimmer der Renaissance*, p. 293.

contains the following lines, which do not so much explain as quite accurately characterize, at one swoop, the dominion of decoration, the principle of covering and clothing all surfaces and objects that would otherwise be "naked" and empty. Of the four elements, hearth, roof, enclosure, embankment or terrace, he interprets enclosure first and with utmost passion:

> Now what primordial technology was developed for the enclosure? None other than the art of the wall-finishers, i.e. the mat-makers and carpet-weavers. . . . The use of pole wickerwork for separating off one's property, of mats and rugs for foot-coverings, for shielding against sunshine and cold, and for the internal spatial division of homes, usually long preceded the brick wall, especially under favorable climatic conditions. The brick wall entered the area of wall-finishers as an intrusion of masonry, which had first developed on terrace walls and was subject to very different stylistic circumstances.*

In support of this, we are reminded that the German words *Wand* (wall) and *Gewand* (garment) are cognate, a kinship dwelt on by Max von Pettenkofer with a different goal, when he presents the primary demands of hygiene in clothing and dwelling:

> One's clothes and one's home intersect, as it were, in certain ways. A cloak and a tent are quite germane. The wide, heavy bicycle cloak that used to be so popular might be called a tent that one carries about, and the tent a stationary cloak in which one wraps oneself, into which one slips one's entire body, just as one slips an arm into the sleeve of a coat. The hat is the roof of one's clothing, and the roof the headgear of the house.†

We must not, of course, so underrate the nineteenth century, and above all Pettenkofer, by viewing this clothing house as merely a strifling shell, simply a vessel for *Muff*. After all, Pettenkofer in particular, an advocate of hygiene, devoted practical energy and eloquence alike to propagating

---

* Semper: *Die vier Elemente der Baukunst*, p. 56-57. Brunswick, 1851.
† Max von Pettenkofer: *Populäre Vorträge*. No. 1, third printing, p. 39. Brunswick, 1876.

ventilation, the constant "intercourse with the ambient atmosphere"; and as surely as his precept was frequently, indeed generally flouted, it is equally certain that the precept and recognition of hygiene originated in the nineteenth century, not the twentieth. Thus we are all the more struck by Pettenkofer's testimony to that cognation of *Wand* (wall) and *Gewand* (garment). Semper's theory, to be sure, expresses far more, namely the priority of the tent over the brick house—and the consequences are weighty.

For as soon as this priority of wickerwork over brick is established and historically justified, Semper still has to deal with a question of greater interest to and, in practice, greater import for, the era. Just what has become and is to become of the carpet wall once the brick wall has been invented and has replaced it? This is Semper's answer:

> As the wickerwork came first, so too it subsequently maintained, in reality or merely as an ideal, the full momentum of its quondam significance, the true essence of the wall, after the lightweight matt walls were transformed into solid walls of earth-brick, fire-brick or broadstone.—The carpet remained the wall, the visible confinement of space. The walls behind it, often very powerful, were necessary for other purposes having no bearing on space, for safe support, greater durability, and the like.—Wherever these side purposes were not also intended, the carpets remained the sole original separations; and even when solid walls were required, they formed only the internal, invisible skeleton, concealed behind the true and legitimate representatives of the wall, the colorfully woven carpets.*

This singular theory, delivered earnestly and resolutely, bolstered by a sovereign and out-of-the-ordinary education as well as personal studies, may be considered the purest expression of that attitude toward the house and its design which sees walls per se as bare and skeletons and structures per se as naked and unworthy, and which therefore aims ubiquitously at covering, concealing, coating, decorating—an attitude which, later and today, was and is accused of fundamental "hypocrisy."

And if, as in Semper, such oppressively numerous and such sublime

---

*   *Die vier Elemente der Baukunst*, p. 57-58.

historical examples are cited for transfering the rug motif to other ways of treating the wall (plastering, paneling, painting, polychromy in general), then we cannot be satisfied with the modern axiom of honesty (at least as a standard for criticizing the nineteenth century) with its purely moral argument, which, after all, subjugates the shaping spirit to the material and its demands.

> Painting and sculpture on wood, stucco, fired clay, metal, or stone, were and are, in the latest unconscious tradition, mere replicas of the particolored embroideries and lattices in ancient carpet walls. The entire system of Oriental polychromy, closely intergrown and to a certain degree one with the panelling and covering in the oldest architecture, hence also the arts of painting and relief sculpture, issued from the looms and dyeing vats of the industrious Assyrians or their precursors in the inventions of prehistoric times.*

Though covering and architecture may "to a certain degree be one," though this principle of unity may operate powerfully on and in houses throughout the panorama world, as a lasting compulsion for coloring all surrounding surfaces—still, the previously mentioned moral argument, so vigorously opposed to decoration and costume, especially during the early reform movement, can be, at best, indirectly useful for the purpose of historical understanding. How comprehensive the principle of decorating was, how vastly all white nature was affected by it, is trenchantly shown in Semper's brief chapter significantly entitled "Your Skin, the Most Natural Cover," which touches, albeit cursorily, upon "the so peculiar historical phenomenon of painting or tattooing the skin." If the skin itself is a "cover," it follows that the converse is equally valid: real covers are a kind of skin and thus have nothing hypocritically attached.

The thinnest and finest skin to cover a wall or masonry is painting, the color glaze, and this supplied the curious energy for that fight about the polychomy of ancient temples, a fight that raged bitterly for decades. Semper's well-founded opinion, borne out by his research in Greece and Sicily, was that the ancient buildings, even those of Parian marble (whose dazzling white had, after all, excited the full enthusiasm

*   Ibid., p. 59.

of the classicists), had actually been treated with color, just like the statues of deities. This opinion marked an upheaval whose effect cannot be exaggerated, an upheaval not only in classical studies, but also in the sense of space and building. The historical circumstances of that controversy would confuse us here.[33] It suffices to say that architecture henceforth, even when one viewed the classical models, was presented in colors, more precisely, it was glazed, coated, lined; that a stone wall as such really looked naked; and that nakedness was unendurable.

The interior in particular was thus covered by a decorative skin, but without forfeiting its festive structural basis. It was only much later, with Jugendstil, that the interior, like the "home" itself, became an organic envelope and skin, while decoration became the essence, remolding architecture. Here, however, decoration was still a "coating."

THE INNER ORIENT

The "entire Oriental system of polychromy" which Semper adulated made its entrance—or rather, with the principle of color above all, color at any price, something else, nearly incognito, merely felt and then translated and absorbed into the more general need for a color "mood" —the Orient properly came indoors.

The priority of color was emphatically proclaimed by the major theoreticians of decorating and the advocates of "cultivating art in the home." "Color is something indispensable, something primary, form is accessory, secondary," wrote Georg Hirth, "for everything we see is color; . . . color is felt, form must be understood. Hence there cannot be the least doubt that color is the first and absolute prerequisite for all interior design. That is why chromatics must be at the fore of any teaching, any self-instruction in these matters."* Likewise Jacob Falke in his studies on decorating:

> It is color more than anything else that makes up the character of a home, and by using color we can produce this character however we will. With color we can make a room seem narrower or wider, lower or higher. If we wish to turn a room serious or cheerful, bare or rich, plain or luxurious, if we wish to give it a snug and

*   *Das deutsche Zimmer der Renaissance*, p. 33.

cozy, a poetic, a cold or warm mood, if we wish to create a dreamy, peaceful nook, a place of solitude and tranquil meditation or a place of pleasure and socializing—our first and last device will be color. Color is a fairy, a sorcerer, bringing good and bad, joy and sunshine, sadness and gloom, but never indifferent or permitting an indifferent treatment.*

Thus color, as the chief element and means of "mood," that is to say, of the final coating, drawn from emotional introspection and now manufacturable, crawls or floats over all surfaces, bodies, corners, and edges, over floors, ceilings, and walls, brooking no free space, no interruption, no aperture. It is virtually a compulsion to shut off everything around with color, like the compulsion of some more or less well-off people to hermetically lock up all doors and windows at night and then keep checking them.

An unparalleled hatred pursued the color known as the foe of all true colors, namely of polychromy and "mood" colors, the noncolor and trouble-maker in the kingdom of harmony—white. Semper the forerunner's struggle against the archeologists' conception of white marble temples in antiquity was waged fiercely here, in practice and daily life, on all fronts. Jacob Falke calls white the negation of color, and his book gives the clearest indications of how the color waves licked at, and finally washed over, that final vestige of blank white or even merely pallor and light.

> Today, thank goodness, we are coming back from the love of gray and white to a healthier color, and thus we are faced with the question of light or dark. Dark chambers making the impression of gloom and graves, we can reject without further ado; color should be preserved as that which it is, as color, but not appear black. For this very reason, we must speak out against very bright walls: On them too, color is not effective, and the character we wish to give a room, whether it be earnest or cheerful, quietly cozy or splendidly rich, cannot thus achieve utterance. . . . The light wall also has the disadvantage that all the adornment of vases, pictures, figures, and other *objets d'art* that we wish to install there

*   Jacob Falke: *Die Kunst im Hause*, p. 180. Vienna, 1871.

and do not care to do without, are harsh and fitful against it: the decorations do not fuse with the ground into an overall effect; the dark objects make holes and spots on the wall, the light ones do not stand out or "get moving" as the painter puts it.*

These lines are articulate enough. The primacy of color in practical instruction is matched in the general philosophy of decorating by the primacy of what is here called first the "character" of a room and then, more indicatively, the "overall effect." An extremely odd reversal: Any specific use or purpose of either the total space or the individual objects within it, any distinction of practical and decorative things, indeed any structure and formal character of doors or furnishings is subordinated to this all-encompassing, all-enveloping overall effect that tolerates no interruption, nothing "harsh and fitful." The last thing, which usually comes involuntarily by itself, the "effect" of the whole, when all details are finished and installed in terms of their respective functions—this last thing ranks here as the first.

White, however, signifies the invasion of naked and sharp material. Whatever is white—"merely" or "still" white—is unfinished, namely uncoated, and must be incorporated or colored. White, as it were, is a ray from the outside, an element of the world, also a vestigial sign of feudal sovereignty, absolute monarchy, embarrassing and injurious to the burgher, who does not care to throne or rule visibly, but would rather withdraw (into that very inner "overall effect"). The criticism of white, of mirrors and shiny gold frames, contains the historical critique of both the Rococo and the Empire, which, in their social styles are lumped together as "rigid ceremony" by these art writers and theoreticians. The ceremonial is given the same attributes as white, both, to bourgeois viewers, are "dead" and "cold." The traditional Biedermeier room stove, a thick, fluted, white-glazed column, was anathema to all the late-nineteenth-century authors who dealt with this object because the stove, as the heat-giver *par excellence*, ought to have a "warm" color, say brown or green. Such color warmth is in turn merely the correlative to the compulsory predominance of the overall effect—coating all bare-

* Ibid., p. 224.

ness, resolving all "harshness," blurring all boundaries, radiating out of itself in a diverse matt and twilit glow.

This overall effect, as I have already stated, had to subdue the harshness of bodies, namely furniture.

> We have before us a four-doored buffet, whose basic color mood is golden-brown. At close view, the eye is taken up with the streaks and mirrors of the panels, which have a veneer of German or Hungarian ash; we move a step or two away, and now the individual fields, separated by inserted veins, by delicate strips and moldings, stand out in over a thousand different colors, inlaid and exposed ornaments emerge fully in their connections; let us station ourselves at the opposite wall of the room: now the natural grain of the wood is barely perceptible, and likewise the minor ornamentation recedes, giving way to the impression made on us by the entire tectonic structure of the buffet, with the lights and shadows of its vertical and horizontal divisions, with its protruding moldings and powerful columns. Thus we see how various authorities of color interruption follow one another on a huge visual field of a basic monochrome mood: whatever our position may be, we always find a harmony of the parts, brought forth by the wise subordination of the small to the large. And one should not fancy that this is primarily a matter of form rather than color: the noblest form is thwarted if that which is to remain subordinate pushes forward with an importunate color, breaking through its given framework.*

The dominion of mood halts in no wise at the tectonics of the piece. Edges, moldings, and columns blur into lights and shadows, the massive structural elements evaporate into color nuances.

Clearly, the testing, circling, and gliding gaze, sucking up satisfaction, is at work here—the gaze that wishes to glide and refuses to be held down. And by taking one, two, five, or ten steps back from the object, possibly even squinting like the painter at his easel, testing the mood values, the beholder (who is, after all, the user as well) extinguishes the thinglike substance, extension, construction, and weight of

---

*   *Das deutsche Zimmer der Renaissance*, p. 66.

this practical item in order to integrate the latter completely into his inner world alone. Color and mood impose and efface the material forms, making the purpose, structure, and spatial quality into necessary evils that are fastened to the higher, the artistic impression.

HORROR VACUI

The paradox of the interior, however, is that, despite such extinction or even negation of thinglike forms, despite their demotion to a mere substratum of the coating color, the indoor space fills up with more and more quite physical, even unwieldy decorative objects. More and more flotsam is washed up on its shore, more and more jetsam is drawn into its vacuum, seemingly losing their character of floatsam and jetsam (leaving it outside as they become solid property) merely to figure as nuances and color values in the mood harmony. All objects thereby become subjective, and the room ultimately teems, after the example of the artist's studio, not merely with fabrics, but also with pictures, easels, vases, weapons, trophies, animal skins, stuffed eagles and peacocks, dried plants, picturesquely strewn crockery, and books. In Makart's studio, which was, after all, praised as a museum, everything was so purposefully arranged and harmonized for the viewer's gliding gaze that almost none of the countless Old German or Oriental chairs was free for sitting. Or so it appears in Angerer's photograph, reproduced on a centerfold spread in Hirth's book *The German Room*.

Jacob Falke (for the special case of wall decoration, but also for universal application) came up with a name for the driving motive of this filling, a motive eerily driving ever onward beyond all moderation: "If we now ask . . . about the manner and drawing of the decoration, about the further ornamental or pictorial adornment of the wall, we will probably agree that simply painting colors on can in no wise satisfy artistic demands. Whether the wall be white or red, we will be seized with a *horror vacui*, the surface gapes at us with its emptiness; it has need of ornament"* *Horror vacui*, the horror of emptiness or the fear of a vacuum.

The interior per se is always empty. However, the objects of im-

* *Die Kunst im Hause*, p. 226.

mediate use are unable to fill out this specific vacuum, since they are really just repetitions or prolongations of the outer world, which is ruled by use and usefulness, appraisable and utilizable things, wares in general. The inner void, to be sure, cannot draw in anything but things or wares, obtained and brought by horror, by fear; but, the moment they arrive and are decoratively placed, they gain a new, an inner significance, which thickly coats their immediate concrete value, enshrouding them in oblivion. Taste, however, born from the fear of the vacuum and active in preparing for the gliding gaze, in arranging and producing transitions and nuances, until, without sharp white or absolute black, it achieves the harmony of the colorful overall effect or of mood—such taste ultimately deludes itself into imagining that *it* has created, that *it* has begotten such an interior, in which things crowd in the warmth, in the color, and in the matt glow.

Delusion is the work of fear, it warrants pleasure. Far from deceiving himself on this point, the lover and promoter of interior decorating in *The German Room* actually sings the praises of delusion:

> There are hours and days in which the outside world with its frustrations is thoroughly soured for us, in which, afflicted and weary of life, we see human activities as gray in gray. In such stricken moods, only a fortunate few can be helped over these trials and tribulations by a powerful faith in God; we human beings, after all, forever keep seeking sensory impressions to help whisk away dreary thoughts. One man finds salvation on mountain tops and in forest depths, the next in the harmony of tones, the third in the creations of visual art. To be sure, the relief we thus obtain, like our life, may merely be based on a fortunate change of delusions; yet this is no empty delusion if we thereby gain new strength and new hope. Indeed, this faculty for delusion, if I may say so, constitutes, for civilized man, an insurance against the inclemencies of fate, as necessary as insurance against the perils of fire and impoverishment. In this magic circle, in which a good education can bring us and our own efforts can make us feel at home, the artistic design of our domesticity should, to a certain degree, form the center, the warming heart.*

*   *Das deutsche Zimmer der Renaissance*, p. 2.

Delusion as insurance against destiny, the peace and quiet of delusion:
Here, the art of decoration, putting its polychrome coating on everything, finds its ultimate rationale.

THE WHISKING GIRL

The space between the color-coated walls was governed by the dim
pallor of northern light, which made the ubiquitously arranged fabrics
—satin, velvet, and silk costumes—emerge in their own glow. Nowhere
was the space opened outward or upward—even illusionistically; yet it
was stuffed with now voluminous, now fragile, but always transportable
objects and furnishings that might ever be rearranged and that represented power and property—a property that was mighty but also movable, and consisted, in the economic sense, of mobile goods.

It was amidst the pieces of that property that girls and ladies
spent their time, adapting themselves to the variable disposition, at best
"whisking" (how often that verb, *huschen* in German, was employed in
the novels and biographies of the time!). That ghostly "whisking" or
"stealing," though meant teasingly and affectionately, must be applauded
as highly skillful behavior among so many objects. Above all, however,
it is the most accurate term for a way of moving, nay, existing—a way
that, like a permanent flight from persecution, luring with modesty,
eluding any intervention as interference, escaping almost but not altogether unseeingly, dissolved the body well-nigh into mere wafting
breath .

This whisking girl (not, incidentally, the only female tenant of the
interior) resembled, when she was good, the dove, the butterfly, or even
(not infrequently in Frau Marlitt) the wild bumblebee [idiomatic, in
German, for a romp, a hoyden. Trans], and, when she was bad, the slith-
ering serpent. She was the familiar "brownie," the fleeing something
in between the solid possessions, the gracious wind that whooshed
through the large rooms, that was not, or not yet, a possession or a piece
of the property, but that would never flutter away completely. A captured or leftover shadow, rambling about, quite in keeping with the wan
light, and nevertheless usually looked upon by one and all with an enigmatic, amorous benevolence.

NOBLE PALLOR

Still, the whisking girl is not the mistress in this light; that role is assumed by the statuesque beauty whose marble whiteness and alabaster complexion are so often dwelt upon. There is something uncanny about these being the formulas of sublimest praise for female loveliness.

Friedrich Spielhagen, the author of countless "contemporary novels," at least impressively employed the term "noble pallor" for this woman, even if he did not invent it. Ferdinande is the melodious name of a woman in one of his most famous books, *The Storm Tide;* she is a figure oscillating between the bourgeois world and the other one, which really belongs to her, the world of wandering artistry, the hoard of all passions. The father is a "Forty-eighter," a supporter of the Revolution of 1848, a democrat rigid in his principles and fiercely hating the Prussian ruling caste of officers and officials. And in her, this revolutionary heritage has achieved a new state, as it were: she practices a calling, that of sculpture. Living in a studio, always surrounded by statues, she has, in Spielhagen's words, a "noble pallor and aristocratic beauty." And this lofty hallmark of pallor is equally that of the goddess venerated and desired in the twilight of the bourgeois home with its splendid crimson and dark-hued decoration. This goddess too sheds a light of her own, now a mild, now a radiant glow.

The theoreticians of decorating also took precautionary measures in the same direction, for , as Georg Hirth said, it was only fair "to regard the dwellers as a staffage to the furnishings of the room."* For now the dark coloring of walls and fabrics proved even more advantageous. Jacob Falke writes: "To lovely and interesting faces the light- colored wall is a disadvantage; only the dark wall permits them to exert their full effect. This is the same reason why the painter has his portraits emerge from a dark and not a light background."† No vehement motion, no lively gesture or language ruffles this outshining picture of wan beauty, and every turn of its head is merely a transition to a new aspect in profile or *en face*. Scarcely any distinction is left between the living

---

*   Ibid., p. 94.
†   *Die Kunst im Hause,* p. 224.

woman and the truly marble or alabaster statue shining from the darkness; and it is very bizarre that classicism, otherwise banned, found a secret refuge here, from which to exert its power—torso of antiquity, densely and "polychromatically" enveloped, concealed almost as something forbidden and infinitely fascinating. The charm is not that of life. It is not the statue that has been aroused to life, but rather life that has congealed into a statue; and the fact that it walks about is enchantment.

The peculiar transplant of classicism here is nowhere more apparent than in that "sanctuary of love" which Spielhagen's Melitta (in *Problematical Natures*), a lady of the manor and a society woman, brilliant and self-confident, has put up in a remote nook of her park: a Swiss Chalet ringed by lofty, soughing trees and containing, as a graven image and sole witness of her secret passion for the lower-born private tutor, the Venus de Milo, white and shimmering. In the depths of the forest—we can smell the fragrance of rotting leaves—the Swiss cottage is itself the traditional setting of pure nature, and here the statue thrones as a pale icon of lust.

It is the pallor of not just the antique statue but also of death that constitutes the attractive beauty of the mistress in the bourgeois chambers. Gabriel Max, a luminary of Munich painting under Ludwig II and one of the most intriguing figures of the time, who could never depict his fill of suffering women (and also, incidentally, dealt with spiritism), painted *The Resurrection of Jairus's Daughter* in 1875. This opus is described by Pecht in *The History of Art in Munich during the Nineteenth Century*:

> One of the finest and most touching of these pictures, *The Resurrection of Jairus's Daughter*, [shows] Christ sitting pensively in the front, a dark shape, while full light streams upon the infinitely darling daughter lying on the bed and awakening to life. Both figures are equally successful, but the whole is so striking that when the picture was shown in the German Room at the Paris World's Fair of 1878, it drew more attention than any other work.*

The brief account is inaccurate in at least one point. The girl's awaken-

* Friedrich Pecht: *Geschichte der Müchener Kunst im 19. Jahrhundert*, p. 329. Munich, 1888.

ing to life is not noticeable; swathed in white cloths, which of course leave the arms, head, and throat bare, she lies with closed eyes, and her right hand rests limp and lifeless in the left hand of the dark exorcist or hypnotist, Christ, sitting on the edge of the bed. Outlines of a thick, cavernous stone wall are visible behind the generously arranged white sheet—the event seems to be taking place in a tomb. Most strangely of all, however, the light is not falling upon the daughter (as Pecht thought), but actually emanating from her, the dead girl. Only a feeble glimmer is "falling" upon the ascetic, emaciated, black-bearded countenance of the resurrector. The daughter glows rather than the supernatural light of salvation falling into the darkness of death.

It need scarcely be remarked that this is no "religious," or at least no Christian, portrayal. However, the noble pallor is at the height of its power, and the female pulchritude on the verge of putrescence. It makes no difference that, as Pecht sophisticatedly observed, the master took the "wise precaution" of always depicting his suffering women as "young and beautiful." On the contrary, the charm of such youth and beauty arises precisely from the cadaverousness of their bearers. At this point, we should not hold back Pecht's surprising and perhaps revealing judgment on the painter Gabriel Max: One must own, he wrote, that for all his unilateral tendencies, no other artist of today so sharply articulates the modern sensibility.

If death is behind the ideal pallor and beauty of the lady honored in the home, then it is a special category of corpse that takes the lead in this sphere. I hesitate to name it because of its dreadful and netherwordly, and at times even cynically comical, street-ballad tinge—yet there can be no doubt as to the eerily suggestive role of this figure throughout the epoch: the body found floating on water.

We know those countless genre scenes that capture and constitute the shipwreck in literature and painting—and also, as can be seen in some memoirs, true experience as well. However, this apocalyptic area, so intrinsic to the nineteenth century, contains not merely the element of catastrophe, the dissolution and destruction of all order and security, both technological and sociological, i.e. absolute danger, but also and always an element of bliss and enjoyment. Seldom is there a lack of a senseless or lifeless female figure, whose limp and lovely shape, more distinct than normal in the soaked garment, is held by a powerful rescuer or rescue-seeker. They form the sublime couple in the highly significant shipwreck scene: the tough, storm-swept hero and the lovely wave-washed corpse.

Horror is the unnoticed undertow of the compassion which feasts on genre—but which, capturing death itself and nourishing the emotions, creates the pale beauty as its object. Pallor—not frailty or sickliness or emaciation or other such solid physical properties—pallor, lightless, yet feebly glowing itself, is the alluring sign that death has given this beauty.

> A snow-white garment came floating by, and the waves were tearing and rending it to take it hence, but the long, blond braids on the pale female head had entwined themselves in the tangled roots of the waterside trees and were holding the dead woman fast, for him, so that he might once again gaze into the wide, staring eyes.*

HUGIDEO

Well sheltered and unrecognized, something came seething along which in the *fin de siècle* erupted as an open flirting with "vice." There is a tale that one can dub the classical paraphrase of noble pallor, and that unites all the scattered elements with concise brevity and uncanny accuracy. Like its main character, an anchorite out of spurned love, it has the bizarre name of *Hugideo*. Its author is Joseph Viktor von Scheffel.†

The story is told in a chatty, sentimental, archaic German, which, in tandem with the portrayal of the familiar Black Forest landscape and the historical, archeological trappings (a salmon fisher tells about "the Battle of Nations on the Catalonian Plain, where the Alemanni on Attila's left wing with the Franks and Gepidae wag'd war against the legions of Aëtius"), makes up the muddled but quite harmless surface. Its locale is the so-called "Stump of Istein," the spur of the Black Forest, near the Rhine. "Nowadays, incidentally, a good drop of wine can be

---

*   Eugenie Marlitt: *Im Hause des Kommerzienrates*, p. 168.

†   *Hugideo* was written in 1857 and published that same year in *Westermanns Monatshefte*, but did not come out in book form until 1883. In Vol. 3, pp. 7-17 of *Gesammelte Werke*, edited by Johannes Proelss, Stuttgart, 1908.

found there," writes Scheffel at the beginning, winking and full of *Lebenslust* as though among friends at the neighborhood beerhall.

However, the landscape does not remain all that familiar. It is transformed by the arrival of Hugideo, the lonesome wayfarer. It shows an inside, an interior, namely a shadowy cavern in the face of the mountain, and here the enigmatic stranger installs himself, turning that cavern into a "stone cell." Here he brings—along with furnishings—a snow-white marble bust. "And this bust was the effigy of a young and beauteous Roman maiden, one of those heads the sight of which, a millenium and a half later, seem'd to the old master Wolfgang of Frankfurt like a passage from Homer: —the hair knotted at the nape in a loose pleat, the countenance free, noble, and grand, a golden coronet encircling the brow." Classicism has once again been shifted—like the marble image to the stone cave—and the chronicle style hopelessly ensnarls the reader's historical ideas by having the "old master Wolfgang," costumed as a member of a guild, shilly-shallying unsteadily in the twilight of memory and prophesy. The pale effigy is set up in a specially hewn niche accessible only to Hugideo, and it is venerated there by him as his most priceless possession.

Otherwise, the man's only occupation is burying corpses. Incessantly the Rhine washes them up on the bend of the river, the bodies of people who have drowned or been drowned; incessantly, Hugideo, with the aid of that salmon fisher, digs graves. This gruesome intercourse, to be sure, is treated more benignly by Scheffel. There is something downright cozy about the Rhine personified as a decent element: "But for its northward wandering towards the cheery fields of wine in the Rhineland, the river does not take along the corpses of the uplands, and in the silent bight at the Stump of Istein, it gingerly washes them ashore." This "gingerliness" is significant, for it hinders destruction by rotting and is the only thing enabling the beauty to leave the dead clamminess. For the moment, of course, the cadavers are all—conspicuously—male: unfortunate fisherman, slain warriors. However, once the campaign of the Huns is over (with all its circumstances and incidents, which are peripheral here) and the salmon fisher who took part in it has returned— only now comes a female corpse. But first, a foretoken: Hugideo takes his marble bust from the niche to clean it—

and as he stood before it and fix'd his gaze upon it as though en-
deavoring to submerge fully into the splendor of the lineaments,
he suddenly felt as if this head were gazing back at him full of silent majesty and with inspired eyes, a blissful thrill flash'd through
the heart of the lonesome wight, and he press'd a kiss on the stony
brow. The bust slipt from the rim of the wall and plung'd down-
ward, struck the edge of the rock without shattering, whirr'd into
the waters of the Rhine, and sank.

The woman thus thrown by the kiss does come back, however—as a
real corpse.

In the bight of the Rhine, on the white, shimmering sand of the
shore, lay the washed-up body of a maiden, the white Roman tunic
soak'd with water and hugging the slender limbs, the hair surging
in braids over the proud neck, the brow encircl'd by a golden coronet. Under the left breast a small rip gap'd in her garment,
as though left by the thrust of a cutting weapon. "Odd," quoth
Nebi the fisher, "how this pale maid resembleth the marble bust
that thou didst put up there, on the mountain."

A small rip does indeed gape, but no blood, no grime dims the most perfect pallor.

And he bore her up to his retreat and plac'd her gingerly on the
stone-hewn bench of the cell and sat down opposite her and held
a wordless wake, and from the ivy entwining the rock he wove
two wreaths and adorn'd the head of the cadaver with one and his
own head with the other and fill'd a beaker of wine for himself and
nodded to her as he drain'd it, and he left her no more.

The further plot is not of essential interest here—the beauteous corpse
is interred, Hugideo stabs himself, and the fisher buries him at her side.
"Today," goes the final paragraph, now in modern German, "a tunnel
has pierced the mountain not far from that burial place on the shore,
and the locomotive zooms right through the Istein."

A gravedigger has celebrated a wedding with a corpse in a cave—
but this is barely noticable in the leisurely narrative. Scheffel's faithful

biographer Johannes Proelss, who throughly researched all the connections between "experience and creation," observed that the idea of the hermit gazing at the snow-white bust came to the author "from the world of his own feelings": The death of his lovely sister (she had suddenly contracted typhus amidst preparations for a huge artist's festival in Munich, to be celebrated in costumes of the Rubens period) was allegedly an effective cause in that the brother's sorrow was distilled in a poetic image. Furthermore, as is often the case, "the torment of unrequited love" added to the inventiveness. One can see that the world of the author's feelings (at least those accessible to the biographer) did not suffice to make that Gothic genre more intelligible, or even to interpret what is happening in the clutter of historical trappings. *Hugideo* rightfully deserves the designation of *An Antient Tale* on the title page —not, however, because of the antiquarian chroniclers' tone, nor even because it takes place in the fifth century, but because the glaze of sentimentality lets a shimmer through of "antient," namely vanished human penchants. But examining this is not our task here. We have made the acquaintance of the primal images of nobly pallid beauty—in a cave.

VII

AT NIGHT

Light itself (let us return to it from the glow and from the luminescent pallor) does not even make an immediate appearance when it is to be sought, captured, and depicted in art, particularly in painting. To the extent that painting gets involved with light (which of course, it does constantly and not reluctantly), it does not so much track it down as handle it like a diversely applicable means of composing and arranging. First of all, painting has to deal with a slew of dark bodies and fabrics—those models previously discussed. The painter picks out what he considers worthwhile and then doles out brightness and darkness, placing accents with "natural" or "mystical" illumination, and groups things in this fashion. Painting is, as I have already said, to a large degree the art of illumination.

> *No one can ever paint pure light;*
> *Just paint things in its rays so bright,*
> *And then the solid masses' sight*
> *Will make us grasp the essence of light.*

This homily by Emanuel Geibel* puts it into unsurpassable words and virtually justifies the procedure once and for all.

It seems to be a universal truism that one cannot paint "pure light," and yet it is not so, for the event of light has—in totally different historical frameworks—been painted often enough; Rembrandt, not to men-

---

* *Juniuslieder, Stuttgart and Tübingen*, first published in 1848. Seventh edition, 1851.

tion Grünewald, did nothing else. Granted, this was a different light from the kind acting on, and graspable on, solid masses. However, the essence of light, insofar as it is graspable only on solid masses, is simply illumination. The effect is here the essence of the cause—but that would be a paradox solely if nature presented itself in one eternally consistent way, if it did not have a history and, although permanent and constant, nevertheless make leaps.

Illumination was now to be found both in the open landscape and in art. A sunset, an Alpine glow, were nothing but "light effects," with tourists and mountaineers absorbed in the sight of them. But still, each such illumination phenomenon (and how else could these "spectacles of nature" be as attractive as they truly were) concealed a supernatural vestige. When the "solid masses" of the Dolomites turned a flickering red at sundown, all eyes fixed upon them— knowing, of course, that these "solid masses" would not dissolve, expecting no salvation from them, and yet spellbound by the dazzling spectacle of a seeming transfigurement, which, still and all, was totally natural. They were sprinkled in between day and night—those few moments in which the memory of the transfiguring light of Assumption could be aroused, and the admiration for the fairy world of alpenglow, a light effect with which nature was stranger than theater, contained the enduring sorrow for the lost rays of salvation.

Something of this grief, transmuted of course into pleasant poignancy, can even be detected in the explanation that Helmholtz, the rigorous scientist, offered for the effect of afterglow. At the same time, to be sure, his explanation would seem to indicate a kind of quiet alliance with natural illumination, which still "transfigured" (how ambivalent that word became!) wherever day only signified misery. This is the passage: "A natural model for the artistic harmony that a careful and proper light of airmasses can produce in a painting is to be found in the illumination of a setting sun, which can pour out a sea of light and colors on the poorest area and thereby harmoniously transfigure it."*

---

*   *Populäre wissenschaftliche Vorträge*, no. III, p. 94. Brunswick, 1876.

HARMONY IN THE EYE

Illumination is transfiguration inside the lightless masses, which are nature discolored. Every painter handling the art of lighting tried to use its glow for restoring to his carefully ordered objects and models what had been lost; and yet he kept proving the inevitable impotence of his venture precisely because he illuminated only by grace of his own authority, having total freedom in selecting and distributing the dark and light parts. "In the transfer to a painting, numerous influential circumstances are left fully to the artist's choosing so that he may reach his decisions according to individual preference or the requisites of his subject." No more rigorous necessity guides him than his individual preference, that is, his taste, or at best the requisites of the subject matter, which means, in turn, the freely selected theme or motif; and this, of course, was exactly what formed the basis of the artist's glory.

Now as for the relationship of lighting in art to lighting in nature —this problem vividly occupied the physicist and physiologist Helmholtz. It is strange and significant that this outstanding man, who was, and ought to be, ranked as one of the stars of science in the "scientific age," was led to some of his most outstanding works by analyzing the methods and effects of art, both painting and music. "I came to studying art by a circuitous and well-nigh untrodden route, namely the physiology of the senses, and thus for those who are long since well known and well versed in the lovely land of art, I can only liken myself to a wayfarer who has made his entrance at the frontier over a steep and stony mountain, and has thereby reached a vantage point or two offering a fine overview."* The courtesy and modesty of this remark divulge an ambition of this science, namely to deal with beauty, at least from the "frontier."

The general relationship between nature and art is not explored by Helmholtz, but simply taken for granted: It is the relationship between the crude and the noble, whereby on the one side, however, crude nature contains noble things, but merely scattered; and on the other

* Ibid., p. 57.

side, art, which picks out and arranges these scattered noble things, must, in so doing, observe the illusion of naturalness. For solely

> the uncultivated beholder normally demands nothing but decep-
> tive fidelity to nature. . . . . A beholder, however, who has cultivated
> a finer taste in artworks, will, consciously or unconsciously, make
> greater and other demands. He will regard a faithful copy of na-
> ture as at most an *objet d'art*. Satisfying him will necessitate an
> artistic choice, arrangement, and even idealization of the rendered
> objects. . . . If, however, the artist has to depict only such idealized
> types, whether of human beings or other natural objects, in a selec-
> tive disposition, should the painting then not be at least a truly
> perfect and directly faithful portrayal of how they would appear
> were they somewhere and sometime to enter life?*

It is singular enough: What the scientist is trying to, and actually does, accomplish for the "lovely land of art" is nothing other than preparing the proper devices for illusion. The selection and the changing, even self-willed utilization of these devices are left to the artists themselves, and Helmholtz is utterly tolerant here; he is generous enough to allow both Rembrandt and Fra Angelico their respective characteristic "man-ners of illumination." The painter can, like Rembrandt, "exaggerate the gradations of light in order to obtain a powerful relief," but he can also, like your Fra Angelico and his modern epigoni, "reduce those grada-tions in order to mute the earthly shadows in renderings of sacred themes." Fully in accordance with individual preference or the requisites of the subject—one might add yet again. In this way, the authentic light pouring from outside into Rembrandt's pictures and the uniformly bright heaven of Fra Angelico (who does not yet know or need to know light, either mundane or transmundane) are thrown together in a single stock of employable illuminations, as though there had always been the same "masses" to be lit up in one way or another. Thus natural science created that dark and chaotic but therefore uniform arsenal of natural objects and illusion devices, which it then willingly forsook, leaving the field to the artist as the freely selecting arranger. It was a field of ruins, with pieces, masses, bodies or even torsos, statues, fabrics,

*   Ibid., p. 60.

and characters jumbled about every which way. Indeed, with such preliminary work, Helmholtz is right in concluding about the lighting possibilities now available: "As a result, a great diversity is given in what
the artists call the 'style' or 'manner,' to wit, in their purely painterly
elements."* Diversity is, namely, the precise consequence of "style" becoming mere "manner." Yet, in having a manner and a lighting, in selecting, ordering, and illuminating their subjects from that blind field of
ruins when they paint, all the artists of that era are in agreement, and the
diversity makes up their constant "style."

The work of arranging took place in the studio. Here too—in fact
here more than anywhere else—space is dominated by the wan light of
the northern sky. When, in 1902 and 1903, Oskar Messter temporarily
wanted to shoot his films in sunlight, he combed half of Berlin looking
for a glass-covered studio with a southern exposure; and not finding any,
he had to resolve to build his own—the very first. He constructed it on
Friedrichstrasse.† The significance of this item is in no wise lessened by
the fact that the advanced movie industry returned to the artificially lit
studio around 1920 after working with either sunlight or sun lamps. One
can safely assume that the Berlin studios inspected by Messter the film
pioneer included spaces belonging not just to photographers, but also
painters, perhaps sculptors, for in point of lighting there was no distinction whatsoever.

This assumption is borne out by the general instructions offered to
architects in the *German Manual of Building*** under number XIX,
"Workshops for Artists," which focused on designing painters' studios:
"The light for painting is a calm light with an even coloring and intensity, obtained from northern light without the interference of reflexes."
The term "light for painting" is of course rather specific here—it refers
to a light advantageous for the painter's canvas and easel. This is to be
distinguished, according to the architect's craft, from the illumination
of the painter's object, the model.

For the disposition of the painter's space, a suitable daytime illum-

---

*   Ibid., p. 88.
†   Cf. Oskar Messter: *Mien Weg mit dem Film*, p. 57. Berlin-Schöneberg, 1936.
**   *Deutsches Bauhandbuch.* Vol. II: *Baukunde des Architekten*, Part 2, p. 1090.
Berlin, 1884.

ination is of cardinal importance. This illumination is to be created (a) for the act of painting, (b) for the illumination of the models. One easily overlooks the fact that any consideration of this latter illumination requirement, if present, can greatly complicate the issue and make its solution contingent in a very high degree on the painter's artistic direction and personal needs.

In contrast to the easel and the canvas, the models "must be potentially subject to extremely disparate illuminations through reflex light, overhead light, sidelight, and backlight." However, even these disparate possibilities, for which the builder of such an artist's studio must take steps, are merely varieties of diffuse, i.e. principally northern light. They are, as is apparent here, provided for and kept at hand from the very outset in order to put inherently gray, lightless, and unsubstantial bodies, i.e. the model," in a specific place of light; and this place, along with the illuminated model, is quite unearthly to the painting observer, is so isolated as to be in a different light from the man who looks over and who, of course, has regulated the light beforehand.

The arguments for this general and total exclusion of direct sunlight occur in that already cited lecture of Helmholtz's: "Direct illumination from the sun or from a flame makes the shadows hard and gives them sharp outlines."* Hard and sharp shadows, however, (one may thus continue), would obfuscate the intrinsic solid condition and formation of the "masses" and bodies in their massiveness and extension; indeed, perhaps even destroy their materiality and confuse the dimensions of mobile things.

Here too, as in the phenomenon of pallor, there may be a vestigial motif of lost classicism insofar as the old academic art room, with its plaster casts of antique works, paid much heed to the soft harmony of light and shadow. Still, "illumination" was no art there, or more precisely, did not belong to art, being, instead, a purely technical measure that could be left to the janitor; and the sheer possibility of having the element of light disturb the strict canon of formal beauty was quite remote. The art adept who most faithfully upheld this ideal of all-around soft "modeling" until late in the century, yet who drew the artist's dig-

---

*   Populäre wissenschaftliche Vorträge, no. III, p. 65.

nity and posture from the janitor's task by operating freely and high-handedly with the white and bluish haze on the studio skylight, was the photographer. Helmholtz, too, thinks of him, although actually speaking about painting: "Illumination from a stretch of the sky, restricted by a window or trees, etc. brings out the shadows more or less, as wished, depending on the kind of object. You will have observed how important this is to photographers, who must delimit their light with all sorts of shades and curtains in order to achieve well-modeled portraits."* In support of what was said before about classicism in the photographer's studio and what was so precisely referred to in the concept of the "well-modeled portrait," we may mention in passing that a 1930 textbook for professional photographers advises beginners to first study the requirements and possibilities of "posing and arranging" on plaster figures so as to avoid awkwardness with a living model.

Modeling a portrait or body may still be the sole and dominant purpose of all art of lighting for photographers, but in no way for painters. The diversity of manners, admired by the physicist with the slight archness of the art layman and available at will to the Master in the lovely land of art, demands and supplies more and quite different possibilities. The genre picture and the landscape (just think of the painters of the Orient, especially the desert) often had to deal with more vehemently illuminated masses or an even greater darkness than could be seen in the studio under the glow of that stretch of the vast heavens.

"A gallery may show a desert picture with a procession of white-enshrouded Bedouins and dusky Negroes passing through the burning sunshine; right next to it a bluish moonlit night with the moon reflected in water, and clumps of trees and human shapes barely perceptible in the darkness."† For a while it seemed as if those sharply contrasted illuminations and degrees of brightness could not bear even the least comparison to those of reality, and as if therefore the painter, strive as he might, would always have to fall woefully short of his illusionistic goals. For Helmholtz calculated that those Bedouin garments in the picture could, at the very outside, show perhaps one-twentieth of the brightness they

---

*   Ibid., p. 65.
†   Ibid., p. 75.

would have "in reality," and that, vice versa, the moonlit white marble surfaces in the picture are still ten or twenty thousand times brighter than they would be under a "real" full moon. That was how scientific reckoning set about analyzing painterly illusion as a perfectly hopeless enterprise from start to finish.

In this dilemma, however, illusion was aided from two sides. On the one hand, physiology demonstrated that the human eye itself is prey to a beneficial illusion about physical "reality," in that it can passively endure absolute brightnesses only for a moment at a time, but otherwise grows accustomed to a given illumination and adjusts to the proportions of light and dark, toning down harshness and brightening up gloom. "That is exactly why the painter can generally produce an apparently equally large difference for the beholder of his painting despite the divergent intensity of light in the gallery, if he merely gives his colors the same proportion of brightnesses as reality shows."* Thus the painter, having barely realized his impotence toward optical "reality," was given his first consolation by physiology of the senses, which revealed the more intimate world of the eye, a world that fends off or assimilates all unbearable sharpnesses of physical reality, a world that thereby constitutes a sort of interior or covered glass house in which life is gentler and mellower.

The second consolation, however, fully making a virtue of necessity, came to the painter from the basic relationship between nature and art, already briefly characterized earlier: Picking noble things from the crude chaos of "nature," the painter would have to be faithless to this chief mission of his and endanger the harmony of his arrangement if he carried the lighting illusionism too far. The fact that he seems restrained even with a strong illumination in a picture makes up a good deal of his noble superiority. For, as Helmholtz finally puts it, "we may thus actually describe the natural lifelikeness of a beautiful painting as an ennobled fidelity to nature." The world of the eye, through this organ's inuring, tiring, and recovering, forms a consonant sphere that is gentle toward the crasser outer world, an invisible cavern, as it were, which man takes along everywhere. And even more, it is the glory of art to

* Ibid., p. 76.

distribute the relations and proportions of brightnesses in keeping with their bodies and masses, but not admit any sharp ray or dense darkness from outside. A painting "renders all that is essential to the impression and achieves a total liveliness of the viewing, but without injuring or fatiguing the eye with the harsh lights of reality."* Thus, so far as the painter may venture into the burning of the tropical sun, that "harsh light of reality" will never penetrate, either destructively or conciliatorily, since it is always transmuted into illumination.

In this respect, even the freest landscape in a picture is enclosed in a sort of studio, if this term may be used figuratively. This, in any event, is the reason for that strange uniformity in German painting of the nineteenth century, which, for all the "diversity of manners," for all the widely divergent efforts, remained in that figurative but decisive studio, either in a Rembrandt-like "chiaroscuro" (Lenbach as well as Gabriel Max) or in the Dutch open-air manner, or even the Oriental color splendor à la Delacroix, or in the totally muted cold stone air of Feuerbach, or even the scarcely light-frayed, actually "gilded" rooms of Fritz von Uhde (for whom the term "Impressionist" is barely adequate). This uniformity was not a defect to be removed with a bit of good will, but a historical doom and dungeon. The grip of the panorama allowed no other light to enter.

Helmholtz's science, however, and the physiology of the senses in general, rendered that age the important service of demonstrating that the task of harmonizing dissipated ruins with illuminations was naturally necessary and therefore imperative to art. If toning down harshness and brightening up darkness were so deeply founded in the nature of eyesight as to be reduced to the formula of a natural law (Fechner's, so called)[34]—then how could painting escape! On the contrary, its job was exactly to crown such a noble faculty and provide its beholders with the emotions and confirmations that Helmholtz superlatively depicted as follows: "Sensory pleasantness, the purely beneficial but never exhausting excitement of our nerves, the feeling of well-being in them corresponds here, as elsewhere, to the conditions that are most favorable to perceiving the outer world, that permit the finest discrimination and ob-

* Ibid., p. 89.

servation."* In this way, illumination serves to produce a comfortable medium pleasure, which light could only disturb. Transfiguration had become cheap, for people had learned how to get it on their own.

THE GAS WORKS

The less outside light was admitted, the more inside illumination there had to be. It was only when the drapes were fully drawn that the polychrome coating over the enclosure was perfect on all sides, and now the inner Enlightenment could begin, signifying something different from, and more than, the lighting. Its home was likewise the Orient: Geibel's *Oriental Myth* sketched the magical matrix:

> *Now the moon went down and in its final*
> *Silvery gaze, the swarthy danhash, coming*
> *Here from India with the gracious burden,*
> *Saw the lofty Saleh mountains and the*
> *Faery's castle built by hands of spirits*
> *Boldly on the jagged peak. The danhash*
> *Hovered like a cloud of smoke above it*
> *Soon, and flying slowly then descended,*
> *Landed on the roof and strode down fifty*
> *Wide steps till he reached the halls below him.*
> *Sleeping gently like a child, however,*
> *Rosy Badur in his arms lay nestled,*
> *Innocent.—A silken curtain, richly*
> *Pleated, swished across the lofty gateway.*
> *And the genie stood bedazzled. Sudden*
> *Brilliance poured into his purblind vision.*
> *For, enclosed upon the ceiling, blazing,*
> *Burnt a giant diamond, shooting blissful*
> *Light in gentle radiance, like sunbeams.*
> *All around on walls so richly sculpted,*
> *Green entwinements; Countless shrubs lunged snow-white*
> *Blossoms and deep calyxes of purple*

---

*   Ibid., p. 89.

In the flashing brightness; and a myriad
Scents were wafting through the warming ether.

[Juniuslieder*]

What the dark, smoky spirit, called a danhash and a genie, sights here is the fascinating illumination of the ghostly castle by the unborrowed inherent power of the earthly stone, the "diamond," which so resembles the sun that even the white and purple blossoms reach for its light. And similarly, the bourgeois rooms and chambers of that century, with their richly pleated curtains and their shrubs, were lit by their own light, a light hauled up from caverns bored into the bowels of the earth, even if mineral coal did not shine with a crystal shimmer like that fairy diamond but had to be combusted to release the luminous gas. The flames of coal gas are light from darkness, wrested from the night by a different magic, namely chemistry. To be sure, the potence of hard coal, according to the law of energy preservation, is nothing but stored-up solar heat once given to prehistoric plants over vast periods of time; but this means, of course that lighting gas comes from the dark energy storehouse of the whole of nature and, more precisely, from the heavenly right that once plunged down into the bowels of the earth.

"What a splendid invention gas lighting is!" exclaims Gottfried Semper. "With what devices it enriches our festivities (aside from its infinite importance for the needs of life)!"† This strange priority of the festive over the daily or rather nightly purposes (urban night itself, thanks to general illumination, became a kind of permanent, exciting festivity) plainly divulges the eastern character of this illumination. Its history commenced with the radiance of two gas-fueled "Bengal" lights, kindled at Amiens to celebrate the peace treaty in 1802; and there was something quite analogous about the first outdoor gaslights, the ones on the Pall Mall in London, which the stockholders, brought together by the adventurous German privy councilor Winzler, from Znaim, expressly intended as a public exhibition. The reason for this, of course,

---

*   Stuttgart and Tübingen, 1848. Quoted from the seventh edition, 1851.
†   Gottfried Semper: *Wissenschaft, Industrie und Kunst. Vorschläge zur Anregung nationalen Kunstgefühles. Bei dem Schlusse der Londoner Industrie-Ausstellung*, p. 12. Brunswick, 1852.

was that the practical use "for lighting whole districts of the city" had not yet been sanctioned by the London authorities.

That took place in the year 1808. In Germany, pursued partly by German, partly by competing, sometimes superior English enterprises, gaslight on a large scale began with the 1820s, taking its greatest upswing from 1850 to 1870, two decades that were crucial in every respect. "Thus we see," goes an historical sketch (in Schilling's *Handbook for Gaslight Illumination*),

> that the fifties, and even more the sixties, were the years in which gas illumination actually broke through in Germany despite the simultaneous emergence of petroleum and despite the great political occurrences which had such a disturbing effect on other circumstances during those decades. The need for light had become also literally irresistible, and a prolonged and heightened activity had gained ground everywhere.*

Also literally—the allusion to the figurative sense, as if this were the primary one, evidently implied the light of scientific "enlightment," which illuminates nature inwardly just as gaslight does towns and homes.

However, the most essential historical fact chiming with the spread of such inner enlightenment, promoting it and in turn promoted by it, is that "prolonged and heightened activity" about which Knapp speaks: Simply the opening up of the city night or the introduction of night life. In the Berlin of 1846, after a gasworks had been operating for twenty years, only a scant ten thousand private flames were burning, and the same historian explains this in a highly penetrating way: "The major responsibility . . . resided with the general social and sociological circumstances; there was still no real need for increased activity during the evening and nighttime hours." But then, when social conditions enabled or necessitated nocturnal labor in factories, plus night school for assiduous workers, the light shone here, albeit dimly; and indeed, these flames were not provided with bell-shaped reflectors as in the homes of the owners, or mounted in sun-burners," or united in "bouquets" of sconces on the walls; they lacked all such Oriental sparkling and enhancing

*   *Handbuch für Steinkohlengasbeleuchtung*, ed, by N.H. Schilling, p. 21. Third edition, Munich, 1879.

paraphernelia. Issuing from the iron pipes, they not infrequently emitted that uncanny soughing that seemed so closely to recall their subterranean origin.

Nevertheless, it was the same "steady firework," although in its most wretched form, and no doubt that was why the want of illumination became an outstanding literary token of industrial misery, for illumination was one of the most intrinsic motifs, one of the noblest purposes of the century. Even the poorest area (as we read earlier) can be transfigured by the rays of a sunset. Nothing, on the other hand, can make an area, a locale poorer and the sight of it more dreadful or disgraceful than the absence of the transfiguring element; and nothing provoked the bitterness of the poor so sharply as the nimbuses of bouquets and sun-burners, the glitter of "diamonds" at a nocturnal festivity in the halls of the rich. The magic of illumination, endlessly spellbinding, thus became perhaps the strongest expression of the arrogance of exploiting natural energy; or so it must have seemed to those left out in the cold and therefore unable to perceive this light as a mere gift of nature. The same gas having fairylike—that is, demonic—light effects turned, when streaming flameless out of the iron pipe, into a new, universally accessible, easy-to-handle means of suicide, an element of death in the kitchens of the desperate. The brilliant face and the venomous face of this natural energy scintillated into one another, bewitching and baleful, but the simple, beneficial serviceability was lacking.

The fear or anxiety unwilling to trust the thing was an inevitable companion of the marvelous invention, and it is quite characteristic that, when planning factories and containers, the gas engineers were forced, very much against their will, to pay homage to that feeling.

> One will always be well advised to heed as much as possible the anxiety of the public if one would rather not be exposed to all kinds of rules and measures that can ultimately become bothersome and expensive. One will therefore seek to choose a somewhat isolated place, one will favor that side of the town where the prevailing winds remove the air from the town, and one will, finally, if there is a flowing water, try to use the same below rather than above the town.*

*   Ibid., p. 459.

What was here articulated (with a somewhat irritated sign of the in-
sensitive expert as a piece of good advice that goodness knew ought to
be followed) has remained the rule. Gas factories are located on the outskirts of cities, with those monstrous black spheres from the gas containers, whose shapeless and indelicate presence exceeded and offended
any normal standards. At first, for a long time, attempts were made—
and for good reason, I think— to have architecture tame and render
more bearable and more familiar those tanks of the underground element, which were erected so colossally and importunately, and yet,
given the situation, so irrevocably. Schilling observes in his handbook as
early as 1879 that there is a special English custom of building containers "out in the open," but then he promptly recommends not emulating
that habit in Germany, because of the harsher climate. Now one can
hardly presume that the German climate could be more harmful to iron
spheres hanging freely and perhaps shielded by paint, when the corro-
sive dampness of the English climate was something much more to be
feared. We can only assume that this expert had fished up a cogent and
intelligible argument when in truth he merely felt an urge to deal in
some human way with the terrifying monstrosity. Of course, this attempt was ineffectual. The gigantic black sphere (a euphemism in both
English and German—*Glocke*, or bell), floating in its stone or iron basin
and kept mobile on the outside by iron pillars and tracks, was misshapen
and horrifying enough. Yet how much more abstruse a brick temple
must have seemed, filled out on the inside with its odd sanctum, which
could not be reached except, at best, by a high, encircling gallery! The
more recent champions of engineering art have ferociously campaigned
against the "falsehood" of architectural disguises for utility constructions, and yet not one of them has ever cared to behold the naked monument of the gas container as testimony to such technological beauty.
(In this case, however, something quite utilitarian would have to be
called ugly—if this were not such an inadequate term.) The gas container is no less unfortunate after being stripped of its masonry than before. At most, this dull, dark boil no longer has the character of a "reverse side" today, now that its contents are used predominantly for
cooking and heating and almost never for lighting.
    Inside the cities, anything above ground was instantly put in an ar-

tistic form. Lanterns and candelabra in particular only had to be perf-orated lengthwise and mass-produced in cast iron to take in the natural element of gas. They were columns, as fluted as in the days of imperial Rome, or else provided with animal feet, winding leaves, or masks, but simply—hollow. Such a candlestick of cast iron was not a decorated pipe, but a hollowed light-bearer forfeiting its massivity—not the mere-ly concealed prolongation of the iron tube hidden under the street, but an autonomous object (with an Achilles heel, that hollow interior, to be sure).

Only towards the end of his manual does Schilling speak about these "higher problems" and interests, but he does treat them with an earnest-ness that clearly shows taste to be no fata morgana for him.

> Whereas in all the apparatuses and appliances heretofore dealt with, the gas engineer focused essentially on their utility and soli-darity, the illumination facilities challenge him with a third de-mand, that is, their decorative appointments. Even for sidewalk candelabra and consoles, it is crucial that their form and disposition be pleasant, so that these objects may not be an eyesore for the town during the daytime either; but considerations of taste are of a much higher significance in regard to the lamps and lusters meant to deck out the rooms and salons of private homes and pub-lic buildings; those objects must be executed in the same style as the place for which they are intended, and they must be given the degree of elegance harmonizing in richness with the rest of the furnishings.*

The mere chemical substance of gas, the naked pipe, sticking out of the wall or pulling down from the ceiling, was underworldly, virtually pro-letarian. It had to be captured and concealed by art, an art that received (and could not deny) its specific character from the reverse process of concealing, adorning, of overcrusting nature. The elegance of the chandelier in the parlor was what first made the fairy world come true; it was a witchly beauty, disintegrating and dissolving by day. A mirage.

The black freak of the container and the decoration of candelabra and lusters on the front of the opera and inside the parlor—those were

---

*   Ibid., p. 534.

the two aspects essential to coal-gas lighting. Essential because gas, unlike modern electricity, is a transportable mass, both "energy" and "matter" at once. Gas lighting, according to Knapp's admittedly somewhat vague definition, is "that manner of illumination in which the development of combustible gas for the purpose of light development lie [sic] far apart in space and time. This very separation in space and time is extraordinarily meaningful."* And that two-fold aspect, the industrial and the decorative, is intimately bound, in terms of its potential, to the fundamental circumstance that production and consumption are widely separated in place and time, and that the fuel itself is pumped in as an alien natural element from the outside.

ILLUMINATION OF HISTORY

The bourgeois interior, pallid during the day and with a thick and colorful coat during the evening, was thus illuminated by a gaslight that glittered Orientally and whose flamelets emerged from bat's-wing gas burners or twin nozzles (Auer's queer "mantle" or "hood," frail but more peaceful, was not invented till later[35]) and multiplied by the enameled iron plates into seeming suns. In the same way, history, which had otherwise darkened, was artificially illuminated by flashes of genius when the final little stars of hope, freedom, enlightenment, humanity, and world peace had turned blind and cold.

Listen to Richard Wagner in his jubilee essay on Beethoven (a pretended lecture to a huge auditorium), written in 1870, the year of the glorious victories in France: "Since it is fully impossible to discuss the true essence of Beethoven's music without instantly lapsing into a tone of sheer ecstasy . . . we shall first, if we wish to avoid the impossible, have to fix our fascination on Beethoven's person, the focus of the light rays of the wondrous world emanating from him."† A metaphor, one might say. Certainly, a metaphor (self-contradictory, by the way)—but with what repercussions! If the works of the genius are like emitted rays or even emit rays, we can then, astonished by their effect, set about investigating the source or else the "focus ("Where did Beethoven ob-

---

*   Ibid., p. 4.
†   Richard Wagner: *Gesammelte Schriften und Dichtungen*, Vol. IX, p. 107. Leipzig, 1883.

tain this energy?"), and then, after familiarizing ourselves with the personal circumstances, go back to the rays and, more content, bask in their light. Thus all this may be fascinating, nay, enrapturing radiance, yet remains an enclosing and enclosed circle. It merely leads deeper and deeper into new caverns of the subject, and these caverns keep on illuminating themselves magically. Later in the same essay, when talking about Beethoven's deafness and total alienation from the world, Wagner says: "And now the musician's eye illuminated itself from the inside. Now he also cast his gaze on the manisfestation that, illuminated by his inner light, reimparted itself to his interior in a wondrous reflection." So much light, so much reflection, so much inwardness. Things are so entangled by now that one can barely distinguish the source from the mirroring. The rays of eyesight and the sight of rays are confused, the fantastic spectacle is complete. And the enclosure of the newly illuminated inner world, the wall surrounding on all sides and keeping off the "disturbances of the outer world," is reliably massive: "Thus a few years ago, when viewing the remains of the dead man, we saw, in concordance with an extraordinary strength of the entire bone structure, that the skull was quite unusually thick and solid." That too can be found in Richard Wagner's essay on Beethoven.

This was a single genius. But the nocturnal space of history was not dependent on a single light source. If no one else clearly articulated it earlier, Houston Stewart Chamberlain did so at the close of the century not failing to utilize several peculiarities of radiation and back radiation, and also, finally, an ingenious zoological metaphor from the wealth of Darwin's or Haeckel's experience. Here is the highly significant passus, from the "General Introduction" to *The Foundations of the Nineteenth Century*:

> Not only the *Iliad* and *Prometheus Bound*, not only the *Worship of the Cross* and *Hamlet*, but likewise Plato's ideology and Democritus' world of atoms, Chandogya's Tat-twam-asi and the celestial system of Copernicus are works of immortal genius; for as indestructible as matter and energy are the lightning bolts that flash from the brains of men endued with creative power; generations and nations ever keep mirroring one another, and, though sometimes temporarily paling, they light up again as soon as they fall

upon a creative eye. Our century has discovered that in those depths of the sea whither the sunlight never penetrates, there are fish that light up this nocturnal world electrically; by the same token, the dark night of our human knowledge is lit up by the torch of genius.*

The dark night of our knowledge? Were not people once tempted to leave it by the shine of Truth?

THE BLIND GIRL

"The sun shone mightily; but the girl did not blink her lashes. Her eyelids were wide open, the way a flower turns its wide-open cups to the sun, and the expression of the sweet features with their childlike purity was as lovely as a flower." That is, so far as I recollect, the only scene in Spielhagen's *Storm Tide* to have a sun that shines mightily.† And it shines mightily only for the blind girl, indeed, as a kind of attribute of this blind girl. For she—the daughter of a bookkeeper with the humdrum name of Kreisel, who passes through the courtyard every morning to bring her father two sandwiches in his office—she does not see the sunshine, and that makes up the essence of this mighty sunshine, the fact that it is not seen. It appears precisely and exclusively where it is not seen and because it is not seen.

The indubitable idyll to which it belongs as much as ever is not what the idyll used to be, namely a place of earthly happiness, but rather one of sorrow, the only place in which innocence is completely secluded and at home, deeply submerged in the medium of poignancy. "What are our purest, our holiest feelings," calls out the hero of the novel after witnessing that scene, "compared with the heaven of purity and goodness in the soul of this poor, blind girl who knows as little of her charm and beauty as the lilies in the field." The evangelical parable alluded to here is, of course, used somewhat differently from when it was first uttered: It implies no demand, but merely strengthens the unattainability of such innocence, such purity and goodness. The mere contemplation

---

*   H.S. Chamberlain: *Die Grundlagen des neunzehnten Jahrhunderts*, p. 27. Munich, 1889.
†   Friedrich Spielhagen: *Sturmflut*, p. 139 ff. Berlin 1876.

of these qualities tugs at the heartstrings, arousing the beneficially doleful memory of the paradise lost that shall remain lost forever. In paradise, however, the sun shines mightily—unseen, for the blindness is here the earnest of both innocence and poignancy. "This poor blind girl!" Were she not so pitiful, so immutably "poor," she would have no heaven in her soul, and were she not blind, the sun would not shine over her mightily. It is unfortunate, one might say, but the fact that it is so unfortunate is necessary here and makes up the essence.

Poignancy is a sentiment that has nowadays fallen into disrepute under the name of "sentimentality." There is no question that on certain occasions, especially in the darkness of motion-picture theatres, rivers, nay, oceans of tears are shed even today, and tears of poignancy at that, but people are mostly ashamed of them. They feel caught off guard and are gladly prepared to take vengeance for this defeat by simply writing off the causes of such tears as kitsch, thereby regarding the matter as settled and the defeat as made up for. That defeat seems forgivable, but really quite unworthy. People are convinced (and rightly so) that there is really no such thing as a heaven of purity and goodness, not even in the souls of blind girls. People know what people are like. And thus sentiment or sentimentality, for tending to be evoked by such and similar untrue things, is considered unauthentic, even mendacious. Especially considering that this feeling overcomes people, both women and men, who, in the reality outside the movie darkness, i.e. in practical life, are not moved by anything, but pursue their goals and advantages ruthlessly. This observation has a critical tone: Should these people, if properly constituted, be moved to tears? What should they be moved by if there is nothing to move them in that selfsame reality? The fact that there are sorrows and sufferings galore, but no suffering innocence? That in this bad world, the suffering man or woman will prove to be thankless, nasty, guilty by the very latest when someone has only just been moved to tears? Hence, one must conclude, sentiment or sentimentality may be quite praiseworthy under certain circumstances, not just at the movies but also in practical life, yet they will always be displaced and therefore basically unworthy, even despicable. Might then the magnate who, importuned by a wretched beggar, tells his servants: "Throw him out, he's breaking my heart!"—might he be on the right track? That is, after all, the behavior of the film viewers when they wipe away their embarrassing tears, stand up triumphantly, and indulge in the security of having watched kitsch. They throw it out, that kitsch, for it has broken their hearts. The behavior in and vis-à-vis tears is highly contradictory—but it is time to terminate this insertion.

The cruel fate that stole the poor girl's eyesight but left the heaven of her soul occasioned a poignant lament, scarcely any indignation, and certainly no heroic struggle. All the less so since, under the sway of fate, a lovely innocence does thrive, after all, though suffering. It is destiny in the age of stock corporations (*Storm Tide* is the classical novel of the *Gründerzeit*, the period of promoterism) that manifests itself in the implacable guise of the market curves, in the mask of a new and very deceptive Fortuna, in the roaring of the uncertain sea and the Storm Tide. It is the destiny of a crisis-rocked socially jeapordized, politically not yet anchored financial power. This destiny let innocence flourish in the hidden nook of the bookkeeper's cottage, in the milieu of the unsuspecting "little people"; it preserved the idyll (which was always the expression of innocence) and made the sun shine mightily where it could not be seen. This destiny surrounded charming innocence with the safe protection of suffering, of blindness, and exposed it only to sentiment (never to laughter), unleashing tears of commiseration and granting humaneness this last, moist haven. Tears are as hopeless as they are powerless; indeed, they enjoy their powerlessness but are full of brooding reminiscence. They demand no consequences (which is why they are today called "mendacious") and they do not kindle rebellion, they are virtually a cul-de-sac for humaneness. They salvage the memory of a better condition—and promptly drown it.

The "poor blind girl" was, in any event (for the time being and for a long time), the only creature on whom the sun shone mightily in that wan world. But nevertheless, it did shine.

NOTES

1.   Oddly, the first appearance of panorama painting occurred almost exactly in 1800, its decline being sealed around 1900. These round numbers are not so much an amazing coincidence as a sign that "the nineteenth century" is more than a chronological indication. The history of the panorama has been forgotten for so long that the various lexicons and compilations mentioning it do not even spell the inventor's name consistently. He was an Irishman named Robert Barker (if we follow what seems to be the most reliable orthography), and he lived from 1739 to 1806. His first panorama showed a view of the city of Edinburgh; it was exhibited there in 1788 and a year later in Glasgow and London as well. Supposedly, the picture and thus the "invention" itself drew little attention. Evidently, the view of Edinburgh was still highly imperfect in its technique, more of an assemblage of several landscapes than a real panorama, i.e. one constructed in terms of a rigorous perspective from a single central point of observation. Barker's later works which applied this principle more purely and more regularly and which seemed to have been more perfect in the illusionistic portrayal of nature, quickly became popular and were emulated. A major example was a survey of London from the Albion Mills, and there were views of Elba, Athens, Lisbon, and especially a depiction of the naval parade at Spithead. The latter, painted around 1793-94, was, according to news reports of the day, the first to be shown in an especially constructed rotunda, and thus only now was that the panorama complete in its essential elements.

    Barker's priority (allegedly, after his first few works, he took out a patent for his invention, characteristically calling it "*La nature à coup d'oeil*") was later challenged and attributed to a German professor of fine arts named Breysig (by S. Hausmann, in an article entitled *Die Erfindung der Panoramen*—"The Invention of the Panoramas"—in the

fourth volume of *Kunst für Alle*, 1889, pp. 198 ff.). Breysig had trained
with a stage designer in Coblenz, studying perspective and perspective
illusionism then and later, and he had also published a piece on bas-relief
perspective in 1798. Hausmann quotes a passage from Breysig's *Skizzen*
(*Sketches*) of 1799, and it is given here—not because of the priority
issue, but because it very nicely characterizes the social and theatrical
sphere in or for which this early and purely conceptual panorama was
intended: "Some ten or more years ago, I hit upon the idea of a hall for
concerts, balls, etc. to be used in the evening or at night, and to be dis-
posed in a very particular way, so that people would be in it as if out of
doors. The edifice would have a circular interior and a vaulted form,
like a hollow sphere. No windows for illumination, but merely concealed apertures for circulating the air. The cupola and the round walls
would depict a free, open scene, whose visual point would be the center
of the vault. The best possibility would be a garden scene, since it would
offer the chance of a lovely illumination. The entrances could be real
doors on painted constructions (pavilions), which would make it seem
as if the people entering were actually coming out of these buildings
into the outdoors."

The fact that Breysig independently framed such notions and prepared to realize them was already alleged and described in a "Letter
from Magdeburg" published in the *Journal des Luxus und der Moden*,
Vol. XV, 1800, edited by F.J. Bertuch and G.M. Kraus, pp. 642 ff.
There the Baroque origins of his idea are pinpointed: "He owed his
thought to certain landscape prospects that he occasionally chanced
upon in princely gardens. He noted that the illusion was in a higher
degree than in ordinary garden paintings often to be found in private
gardens. . . . Those prospects had been set up in such a way as to be
seen from dark buildings, i.e. from a standpoint at which no light from
the real (only from the painted air) could fall immediately into the beholder's eye. . . . Never did it strike him that such paintings would
someday become showpieces of great cities and objects of financial
speculation. At the time, he intended this idea for beautifying a park in
English style."

The author of that article in *Kunst für Alle* emphasizes among other
things that the "real doors on painted houses" at least theoretically made
a start toward "that grand connection of real objects with the contents
of the panorama, a connection that is not the least basis for the overwhelming impression"—in other words, a fusion of nature and artifice.
This essential factor in the panorama, incidentally, was not lacking in
Barker's cyclorama of the fleet at Spithead: Here the viewing platform
was arranged as the deck of a frigate, the space from there to the wall

being filled with some kind of painted cover. Breysig, for his part, executed his idea exactly in the year 1800; together with two Berlin painters, Tielker and Kaaz, he did huge-scale versions of his Italian sketches, which had been intended for that very purpose; and in the same year, the *View of Rome from the Ruins of the Imperial Villa* was put on exhibit inside a wooden rotunda in Berlin.

Aside from the painters Barker and Breysig, two other men were of characteristic importance for this early period of the panorama, an engineer and an officer. The former was the renowned American Robert Fulton (1765-1815), who actually started out as a portraitist and historical painter—during his stay in England, around 1790, his works formed the basis of copper engravings that depicted *Louis XVI and His Family in Prison, Mary Stuart Praying*, and also *Jane Grey Praying*. A short time later, however, he was working in Watt's machine factory in Birmingham, England. This remarkable man, whose life embraces such essential and such contradictory elements of the century, also spent several years in Paris, around 1800. It was during this sojourn, in any event, that he mounted the rotunda on the Rue des Panoramas, even though the paintings shown here were not by him. This was the self-same Fulton who presently, in the harbor of Brest, tried out his submarine, an invention that fired torpedoes, and who then piloted the first steamboat, on the Hudson River. (The earliest panoramas in France were painted by Pierre Prévost, with whom Daguerre also studied.) However, the officer who supplied this configuration of technology and decorative illusionism with the exact military interest that became so crucial to later panorama painting, and for such men as Anton von Werner, was Charles Langlois (1789-1870). He is described as the inventor of the battle panorama, even though Barker, in 1795, had already done a highly illusionistic portrayal of the Anglo-French naval battle of 1794, benefiting from the advice of two captains who had been present at the scene. Langlois himself fought at Wagram and Waterloo, then studied painting with Horace Vernet and others during the Restoration, joined the army again in 1819, took part in the Spanish campaign and the Algerian expedition, and went to St. Petersburg as an attaché in 1832. During this Russian phase, he undertook studies for panorama pictures near Borodino and Moscow. In 1850, he traveled along the Nile; by 1855 he was fighting once more, this time in the Crimean. His most famous panoramas, for which he wrote explanatory texts, were: *The Battle on the Moskva, The Battle of Borodino, The Battle of Eylau, The Burning of Moscow.* A large sketch for *The Battle of Borodino* has been preserved at the Musée des Invalides in Paris, and the city of Caën actually has a Musée Langlois.

In order to complete the essential first dates and figures in the history of panoramas, we must still recall an invention by Louis Jacques Mandé Daguerre—not the daguerrotype, but the diorama, whose technique he regarded as important and interesting enough to make public its explanation along with that of the daguerrotype in 1839, after concluding his well-known contract with the French government. The construction and impact of the Paris diorama (an international tourist attraction) have been more thoroughly researched than the previously mentioned data, since the historians of photography have focused on this topic; Eder's *Geschichte der Photographie* offers the most about it. Here, instead of individual items, let me quote the description by one of the first German translators of Daguerre's piece. This evidently first-hand account of the dioramas is a footnote in the edition published during 1839 by the Metzler'sche Buchhandlung in Stuttgart: *Das Daguerrotyp und das Diorama oder genaue und authentische Beschreibung meines Verfahrens und meiner Apparate zu Fixierung der Bilder der Camera obscura und der von mir bei dem Diorama angewendeten Art und Weise der Malerei und der Beleuchtung von Louis Jacq. Mandé Daguerre*: "The depictions of the diorama, as Daguerre called this invention of his, used a painting applied to both sides of a vertically stretched canvas and various directions and modifications of the reflected and translucent light, either joined together or in proper sequence, in order to attain the various effects of daylight, moonlight, or firelight; they were among the most interesting productions of artistically applied optics, or, if you prefer, of painting that, by applying the laws of optics, achieves visual illusions. The spectator sits in a small amphitheater; the scene appears covered with a curtain enshrouded in darkness. Little by little, however, this darkness gives way to a twilight and the scene commences on the curtain itself: A landscape or prospect emerges more and more distinctly thereupon, the dawn lightens, the scene grows lively, trees loom out of the shadows, the outlines of mountains, of houses become visible, human and animal figures appear in the foreground which turns brighter and brighter as if from the rising sun; day has broken. The sun mounts higher and higher; through the open window of a house, one sees a kitchen fire gradually blazing up; in a corner of the countryside, a group of bivouacking soldiers sit around a mess-kettle under which the fire is increasing bit by bit; a smithy heaves into view, and its smoldering fire seems to be fanned more and more by an unseen bellows. After a while, and the spectator's interest has no yardstick for the brevity of the time, the daylight wanes, while the red glow of the artificial fire gains in strength; the twilight returns and then at last comes night. Soon, however, the moonlight re-enters into its rights, the landscape is once again visible in the soft tints of the illuminated night, a ship's lantern kindles in the boat anchored in the foreground of a harbor; the candles on the altar in the background of an excellent church prospect light up, the heretofore invisible congregation is shone upon by rays from the altar; or lamenting people stand on the edge of the avalanche whose devastations are moonlit in the same place where hitherto Mount Ruffi formed the backdrop of the charming Swiss countryside of Goldau.—These are the magical effects of the both ingenious and tasteful changeable painting of Daguerre's diorama in Paris."

2.   This poem, "Here Comes the Band" ("Die Musik kommt"), first appeared in the volume of verse entitled *Struggle and Games* (*Kampf und Spiele*), the seventh volume of the complete works (*Sämtliche Werke*) in Berlin. The flying associations of almost random metaphors (the Persian shah and the day of doom, i.e., the Bengal and the eschatological, or the operatic and the ecclesiastic) function as a cluster of opening signs in the initial stanza. After that, for five stanzas, the actual procession of the guard detachment passes, together with the "little girls" at their heels. In the seventh and last stanza, however, the whole thing, simply by being over and merely sounding feebly from the distance, is resolved with enigmatic lightness in a completely different image, which does not so much evoke what is past as belong quite typically to Liliencron's modern *"plein-air* soul":

> *So softly, boom-boom-boom-ching—why,*
> *Was that a gaudy butterfly,*
> *Ching-ching boom, round the corner?*

3.   It comes as no surprise that Anton von Werner himself conspicuously evades, or does not seem equal to, the aesthetic discussion as to whether the panorama really is or can be art. At one point in his memoirs he brings up the topic, quotes the opposing arguments with a considerable admixture of bitterness in his tone, counters them with all the many approving judgments from his high and highest contemporaries and patrons, and ultimately winds up without any theoretical justification of his own. "At times," he says, "the question has been raised as to whether panorama painting can be looked upon as an artistic task and accomplishment like easel and monumental painting, even though panorama art makes the very highest possible demands on the intellectual and technical abilities of the executing artists and their staffs." Citing the technical and artistic achievement, i.e. "Should so much work have been for naught?", may at first glance appear as a retreat; but that means

something extremely essential for a man like Werner. He goes on to say that the highest demands are made here, "especially on veracity and honesty, because the semblance of reality is meant to be feigned, and even a fly crawling on the brightly painted air or a visible fleck can destroy the feigned semblance of reality." Now, since that fly cannot be prevented by the painter from settling on the painted air, one could therefore write off the entire undertaking as hopeless. But for Werner, on the contrary, it follows that the artist must adhere all the more strongly to the principle of paramount accuracy in constructing or copying all those leaves and roof tiles, for only if the spectator fails to discern any lacunae or imprecisions can the painter hope to fend off any disabusement occasioned by the fly. If he could not feel with a clear conscience that he has done everything possible in this respect, the fly would have to be highly dangerous to him, and without that resource to fall back upon, he would soon go astray in the labyrinth of the concepts of art and reality. However, he, the panorama painter, knows no way out of this maze—and after all, his highest goal is actually to construct it and lead the spectators into it.

The skepticism about whether the panorama is or is not art accompanied its history from the very outset. That very same volume, 1800, of the *Journal des Luxus und der Moden*, containing the first news about panoramas, also voices doubts. Thus, on page 283: "The judgments of many more rigorous cognoscenti have, from the very outset, not been very positive about this optical phantasmagoria. Painters have seen in it nothing but a costly botchery for entertaining older and younger children and in whose favor nothing can be reckoned but the observation of perspective and the fidelity of depiction. Nonetheless, the thing has won unlimited applause in London itself, and both noble and common people pour in at every renewal of the spectacle in order to let themselves be so pleasantly deceived for an hour." Even this reporter is somewhat helpless toward the criticism and can only resort to the general plaudits in London. The supporters and defenders of panorama art, on the other hand, were already citing "naturalist" arguments by relating that self-same fidelity of depiction—which those "painters" had grudgingly allowed—to the venerable aesthetic law of "imitation of nature." Thus a Paris report on the panorama of the harbor of Toulon (p. 408 in the same volume) goes: "The eye dips into the womb of the billows, it follows their rocking. We see the foaming swell strike against the coasts or vanish on the horizon at an immense distance. It is nature itself, from which art must never deviate."

Other objections, expressing greater scorn, speak of "mere stage sets" or a "big peep show"—which reveals that, at the very same time, the peep show had dropped to the lower realm of the county fair and that theater design was a lesser-ranking artistic practice. Still, there are favorable opinions, especially from educated people who are glad to be back at the sublime places of, say, classical Italy: "In this way," runs an account dealing with Breysig's panorama in Berlin and published in the *Jahrbücher der preussischen Monarchie*, July 1800 (p. 638), the new panorama of Rome offers not only a pleasant view, but also a great spiritual enjoyment, which has the additional advantage that the enjoyer owes it to himself."

In many ways, these pros and cons were similar to the controversy sparked a century later by the film and before that by photography and are as unsettled today as the panorama controversy was then. There is, of course, no dearth of theoreticians who firmly assign the panorama within the boundaries of its own inherent and unique laws, just as theoreticians do today in regard to the characteristically "cinematic." Thus an ingenious anonymous in the 1801 volume of the *Journal des Luxus und der Moden* (pp. 143 ff), in a piece entitled "What Subjects are Suitable for the Panorama?", undertakes to grant it only "dead" nature, i.e. a nature not filled with any irritating movement. The sublime landscape, especially when grand memories cleave to it (the graveyard of Vevey, Rousseau's setting, Chamonix with Mont Blanc and all the glaciers and mountain torrents, Waldstätt Lake with the deathly terror of its rocky shore); this and this alone ought to be the field of panorama painting, and here it is art. "Replicas with which memory will celebrate as never before its 'I too was in Elysium' and to which the tyro entering this highest Temple of Nature bows as to the Primal Image itself." The tumult of war and the hubbub of the street, however, anything too transitory, ought to be banished, and this will decide whether the panorama will remain a new genre of art or a fleeting fad—appearing and vanishing on the horizon of the day like a flaming meteor, and as quickly forgotten as it was admired."

The historical course of things proved this anonymous commentator right. Today, the abstract aesthetic question is as boundless as it was then. The art of perspective, once the signal of a new era, nay, the birth of a special domain of art, subsequently perfected as illusionism and achieving autonomy as such (a sublime illusionism in counter-Reformation churches and in opera, a playful though not unmysterious illusionism in the princely gardens of the late Baroque), this strange and dangerous, magical, indeed black art, bringing along all elements of its earlier stages, finally brought forth the panorama. It was its ultimate miracle, that eventually became insipid and seemed quite ordinary. The question of whether it is "art" is, in the last analysis, idle if we recall what Citizen Dufourny described as the utmost effect of this invention to the Paris National Institute in the year VIII of the Republic: "It deluded the viewer to such an extent that he could scarcely distinguish between nature and art" (*Journal*, 1801, p. 143).

4.   In Eduard von Hartmann's philosophy, fashionable in the salons around 1870, "the Unconscious" was nothing less than the shaping power that the Romantic Carus had thus dubbed decades earlier. The physiological mechanisms have their full rights here and total autonomy. Only, according to Hartmann's reasoning, as explanations of vital processes they all have a certain tiny gap. Their causal connections (by dint of that psychophysical telegraphy from the brain to the muscles) are completely closed; there always remains, according to Hartmann, that one cause-and-effect question that cannot be answered by mechanics: How does this telegraphy operate correctly? Or how do the "transmissions" always function exactly in the necessary fashion? Here is one of his answers: "Every arbitrary motion presupposes the unconscious idea of the position of corresponding motor nerve endings in the brain" (*Philosophie des Unbewussten*, p. 68). Plainly, such an "unconscious idea" is in no way distinguished, by its character, from a rational, a factual knowledge—it is merely an unconscious knowledge. The unconscious, constructed in this manner, steps like a *deux ex machina* (or rather *in machinam*,) into the different gaps of the physiological apparatus and, in itself, it basically fulfills only the mechanical function of a "regulator." "Let us now," says Hartmann when discussing the motor nervous system, "contemplate electric current, which is so closely akin to the nervous currents" (p. 152). The nervous current, he explains, is produced when the molecules turn in such a way that their electric polarities are parallel. How can this occur? This is once again the question about the tiny gap, i.e. the unconscious. In this context, it is called the "will": "The turning of the molecules is thus the least mechanical performance left up to the will, and the polarity of the nervous molecules is the stored-up mechanical energy."

This unconscious neither forms nor produces anything, it is virtually the technician who is indispensable for running the organic mechanism, who stands at the lever and always "knows" what to do. This is almost occultism, and indeed it was precisely the affirmation and justification of many occult "facts" as "facts" that made Hartmann's work so sensational and modern. Although thereby contrasting sharply with prevailing "materialism," this attitude and theory of his does not so much overcome as merely form an exact pendant to materialism. Just as the unconscious enters the gaps of mechanics, so too the phenomena of second sight or those of mesmerism, blithely hailed by many people, enter the gaps in the world of power and matter. Here, hideouts of the supernatural are assiduously tracked down, and the supernatural itself, in some guise or other, is reified as a scientific fact to make the world of solid objects complete.

5.   The first railroad tunnel in Germany was bored in 1857 for the Aachen-Cologne line, near Königsdorf. The construction of the St. Gotthard Tunnel, which kept the world in suspense, lasted from 1872 to 1878. (The Thames Tunnel, the work of the "iron-headed" Sir Marc Isambart Brunel, was begun quite early, in 1825, after older abortive attempts, and completed in 1843.) The iron bridge between Strasbourg and Kehl was built in 1858-61, the one between Mannheim and Ludwigshafen in 1865-68.

6.   This song is cited in volume five of Treitschke's *Deutsche Geschichte im Neunzehnten Jahrhundert* (Leipzig, 1894), when the author discusses the various roots of the German workers' movement (p. 516). He calls the song the "Worker's Marseillaise" of the Chartists. Their alliance was already concluded in 1835. The Silesian weavers rebelled nine years later; the house of the Zwanziger firm in Peterswaldau was destroyed on a June day in 1844. In the weavers' "Scaffold" song, likewise in Treitschke, steam does not become king, but instead the entrepreneur becomes a demon:

> *You scoundrels all, you satanic breed,*
> *You hellish, demonic horde,*
> *You devour what belongs to the poor,*
> *And a curse is your reward!*

7.   Actually, it was Robert Mayer (1814-78) who first came upon the law that was later known simply as the energy principle. His investigations were prompted by an observation quite remote from all later systematic proof—namely, that in the Dutch Indies, human blood contains many fewer red corpuscles than in our climes, the cause for which Mayer ascribed to the difference in the average temperatures. This circumstance led him to the relationship between heat and work in the organism, which he defined as a relationship of equivalency. In the area of mechanics, scientists had already recognized the principle of the preservation of "living energy" (this term derives from Leibniz). Mayer discovered the validity of that principle for all conversions of energy in animate and inanimate nature. His first work on this topic appeared in

1842 (in Liebig's *Annalen*, Vol. 42). He summed up his research from the angle of the theory of heat in *Mechanik der Wärme (Mechanics of Heat)*, published in 1867.

The Englishman Joule (1818-89) mainly investigated the heat effect of an electric current that performs no mechanical work, and he found that the effect had the thermal equivalent of the chemical processes occurring in the elements. However, he did not attain more universal grasp of the principle reaching beyond that phenomenon. Joule brought out the results of his experiments in the years 1841, 1842, and 1843. There were still only a few individuals who could free themselves from conventional ideas and follow the newly opened paths of knowledge. (This is noted by E. Hoppe in *Die Geschichte der Physik; Handbuch der Physik*, Vol. I, Berlin 1826.) On the other hand, independently of Robert Mayer, the Danish engineer Colding, essentially on the basis of theoretical considerations, declared the universality of the law in a paper that also came out in 1843. He too experimented to compute the mechanical heat equivalency. Helmholtz's renowned lecture at Berlin's Physikalische Gesellschaft was not delivered until 1847. Later on, after the thing was fairly widespread, Joule, Colding, and the Frenchman Séguin laid claims to having their discoveries acknowledged as independent. However, these claims were publicly rejected at the forum of the Natural Science Convention, which met in Innsbruck in 1869.

We may add in passing that Hoppe's *Geschichte der Physik* marks 1842 as the start of a new characteristic era in the science of physics because of the discovery of that principle.

8.   The very same historical instant in which physics, by dint of the notion of energy and by computing the equivalency relation, made an arithmetical and finally technical connection between the most disparate phenomena and areas in nature—the very same historical instant brought the first, if not objection, then decisive attack against the notion of "vital energy," which prevailed in medicine, as an independent, solidly substantial, and directly influenceable entity. In 1842, Hermann Lotzte, teaching medicine and philosophy at Leipzig, published *Allgemeine Pathologie und Therapie (General Pathology and Therapy)* with the characteristic, quite aggressively meant subtitle: "As Mechanical Sciences." The foreword leaves no doubt as to the author's intention; it closes with the abrupt sentence that the writer is dissatisfied with much in his work, but satisfied with "what will be most criticized, namely the thorough consistency of a rigorous mechanical view." Lotze tests and rejects the notion of a peculiar "vital energy" precisely on the basis of the concept of physical energy: "We speak not of a peculiar leverage

in the physical sense, as though it were one of the fundamental energies in nature, to which the possibility of certain phenomena would have to be traced back; we do mean this in a mechanical sense, namely, the various motion capacities of larger or smaller loads, capacities derived from the varying use of the laws of motion . . . as the final resulting size of the performance." Lotze admits vital energy only in the very same sense and degree; it can only be the size of the performance from "the fusion of infinitely many partial forces under certain circumstances" (pp. 19-20). For medicine, this critique inevitably leads to the consequence that neither the disturbances causing disease, nor even the medical healing measures can bear upon such vital energy, either influencing or altering the strength or weakness thereof.

It is quite fascinating and informative for today's reader of Lotze's work to witness, as it were, the fresh performance of the drama taking place here: As soon as the previous entity of "vital energy" is reduced, by that physical analogy, to a purely functional connection, then, beneath or behind it, a barely surveyable field of special mechanical and chemical "forces" or processes opens as the real field of medicine and physiology. This diversity is of course not yet a decay. The same polemical framework that yielded those previous lines of Lotze's contains an ingenious phrase offering a proof of that by sharply distinguishing between the idea (of the living body) and the virtually mythical notion of vital energy: "It is not difficult to note the strange inconsistency of this view, which, on the one hand, regards the physical forces as too ignoble to produce the movements of life, and yet, on the other hand, demotes that idea shining forth in the guise of a fusion, demotes it to a new operative energy and regards it in terms of the laws of such a force."

9.   "The heyday of capitalism is also the era of the railroad. Only this means of transportation was 'epoch-making.'" (Werner Sombart: *Hochkapitalismus*, p. 292.)

The development during the sections of this "epoch" (this word is now meant purely in its chronological sense) can be seen in the well-known figures, of which a few follow here for the sake of orientation.

The total length of the world's railroad network:
   1840:   7,679 km.
   1860:   107,961
   1880:   372,429
   1900:   790,125

Even more eloquent is the average annual increase, which according to

Sombart was as follows in these years:

        1841-50:   3,000 km.
        1851-60:   7,000
        1861-70:   10,000
        1871-80:   16,000
        1881-90:   24,000
     1891-1900:   17,000

Even the average annual number of workers building the railroad has been computed. It we take just the three middle decades of the century, we see that the total number per year during 1861-70 was about two million; during the following decade, about three million; and in the decade after that, about five million.

10.   Aside from Stanley's Congo travels, the events behind the scenes of the Kaiser Diorama were still quite recent by the time of the opening. Dr. Gustav Nachtigal had begun his journey in April 1884, as an imperial commissioner; on July 5 and 6 of the same year, he had run up the German flag after negotiating with two native chieftains at two points on the Togo coast, in Cameroun, and four other places during late July; in October, still on the *Möwe*, he had landed in Lüderitz Bay in Angra Pequena and concluded a defense treaty with the captain of Bethania, which laid the foundation for the colony of South West Africa; and on April 19, 1885, a year after setting sail, he died on the way home.

Captain Kurt von François's expedition for exploring a few Congo districts was undertaken in 1885.

The scene of the Blood Brotherhood between Dr. Peters and the sultan of Nguru refers to the first voyage of this enterprising man, which commenced with so many unedifying hindrances: Upon arriving in Zanzibar in early November 1884, he and his companions were told by the German consul there, on behalf of Bismarck, that the Reich would not give them any protection. Nevertheless, he ferried over to the East African mainland and, on the basis of Stanley's accounts, he followed the Wami River into the interior, where he concluded treaties with several chieftains, who agreed to make over their territories to his company. One of these chieftains was the sultan of Nguru.

Then, after Peters's company obtained the Imperial Letter of Safe Conduct, the conflict began with the sultan of Zanzibar, who claimed the questionable part of the East African coast as his legal property. In order to make him yield, Berlin sent out five man-of-wars, which reached Zanzibar on August 7, 1885. This is the Naval Demonstration of Zanzibar. It was successful.

11.   Twenty years before Stangen's tour of Egypt, Richard Lepsius, on behalf of King Friedrich Wilhelm IV, had made excavations on the field of Gizeh (among other places), uncovering necropoles, finding previously unknown pyramids, and having numerous sketches made of buildings, sculptures, and inscriptions. The Sphinx (usually feminine in German, but masculine here) is described in a letter dated January 2, 1843, "at the foot of the largest pyramid": "I even had them dig in front of the great Sphinx in order to bring to light the little temple lying between his paws and to reveal the colossal stele made up of a block of granite . . . forming the back wall of the temple and covered with sand to a depth as great as its own height." Richard Lepsius: *Briefe aus Ägypten, Äthiopien, und der Halbinsel des Sinai,* 1862, p. 25).

However, Lepsius's pupil Georg Mority Ebers, an Egyptologist and author of those strange footnoted novels, gave an account of climbing the pyramid of Cheops in his Egyptian *Cicerone* (1886). His description finally offers the complete picture of the touristry that lets the travelers find some rest only up on the platform. Reaching the Sphinx, the imaginative man meditates on its former appearance: "Even today this figure measures twenty meters from the crown to the ground on which the paws rest, and what a sight it must have been when the servants of the necropolis saw it free of sand and one could survey the figure fully together with the stairway leading up to it!" (Georg Ebers: *Cicerone durch das Alte und Neue Ägypten,* Stuttgart and Leipzig, 1886, Vol. I, p. 144).

12.   As points of orientation, here are the dates of the two most important nineteenth-century travelers in Italy, whose writings are still or once again generally known. In February 1852 Ferdinand Gregorovius reached the soil which he then so thoroughly traveled; during the fifties and sixties, his main Italian books of wanderings came out. Jakob Burckhardt's *Cicerone,* meant as a guide and companion for many voyagers, namely as a *Manual for the Enjoyment of the Art Works of Italy,* was first published in the year 1855. The earliest German tours, those organized by Stangen, followed somewhat on the heels of these famous "Lone Travelers."

13.   *Bohême* or *Bohémien (Bohémienne)* has always been a French term for the vagabonding gypsies in a literal, ethnographic sense. Yet Littré's *Dictionnaire de la langue française* records a figurative usage of the word in a few eighteenth-century writers, especially in such expressions as *mener une vie de bohême* and *maison de bohême* (i.e. a disorderly, also fantastic house). Béranger has a song entitled "Les Bohé-

miens," dated 1827 or 1828, and this work, almost intentionally dissolving the ethnographic specificity, seems to be the first to tie the glorification of unbound roving to this word, a glorification that later became universal:

> Sans pays, sans prince et sans lois,
>   Notre vie
>   Doit faire envie,
> Sans pays, sans prince and sans lois,
> L'homme est heureux un jour sur trois.

> No land, no ruler, no laws,
>   Our life
>   Wakes jealousy,
> No land, no ruler, no laws,
> A man is happy one day in three.

In the next few stanzas, this ideal anarchy is elaborated in every desirable direction, including the erotic. "*Voir c'est avoir*" it goes, and this more than anything perhaps announces the figurative transfer to artistic life, especially that of painters, whose eyes grasp the world. The final stanza says:

> Oui, croyez en notre gaîté,
>   Noble ou prêtre,
>   Valet ou maître,
> Oui, croyez en notre gaîté:
> Le bonheur, c'est la liberté:

> Yes, just believe in our gaity,
>   Priest or earl,
>   Master or churl,
> Yes, just believe in our gaity:
> Happiness is liberty.
> [Béranger: Oeuvres complètes. Paris, 1847. Chansons, p. 418]

The definitive fixation of the word to the world of the miserably beautiful studio took place with Henri Murger's *Scènes de la vie de bohème*, published in 1851.

14.   The Venus was discovered on the island of Melos or Milo by a farmer named Georgios, while he was plowing. According to the report

of consular agent Brest, who, next to the discoverer, was the earliest eye witness, the statue, broken in two, lay in a niche painted brownish-red on the inside; both arms, separated, reputedly were next to the figure, with the left hand perhaps holding a similarly painted apple. The right arm vanished totally by the time the statue reached Paris; and as for the left arm, all that arrived was a set of fragments whose connection to the statue was soon challenged.

15.   The interpretation of the Venus de Milo as mirroring herself in Ares's shield was first presented by Otto Jahn (in *Berichte der sächsischen Gesellschaft der Wissenschaften*, 1861) and then concretely realized by the sculptor Wittich (published in *Zeitschrift für bildende Kunst*, 1870, with notes by the publisher Carl von Lützow, who was not totally convinced). Several other scholars, on the basis of the excavation reports, tended to think that the Venus was holding her garment with her right hand and an apple, perhaps the apple of Paris, in her left hand high over her head. (Fröhner: *Notice de la sculpture antique du musée impérial du Louvre*, Paris, 1869; Jean Aicard *La Vénus de Milo*, Paris, 1874; C. Doussault, *La Vénus de Milo*, Paris 1877; Friedrich Baron Goeler von Ravensburg: *Die Venus von Milo*, Heidelberg, 1879.) The theory of the Venus as the survivor of a group of statues was forwarded by Geskel Saloman, a Swede (*La Statue de Milo dite Venus Victrix*, Stockholm, 1878 and 1880). Finally the Breslau anatomist C. Hasse, on the basis of anatomical reflections, concluded: "The Venus de Milo is a sublime, charming, chaste woman about to descend into the waves. Her right hand is reaching for the garment falling over her left hip, already dropped past the right hip, and essentially supported only by the hidden left leg that rests on a pedestal, while, with her raised left arm, she tries to loosen the hair band and the diadem and thus fully release the hair. Her eyes are dreamy and self-oblivious as they stare with infinite grace into the distance" (*Die Venus von Milo, Jena*, 1882). This completer, too, made sketches and then had a sculptor use them to reconstruct the figure in half life-size and in multiple replicas. A closer colleague, W. Henke, scornfully polemicized against him in the *Zeitschrift für bildende Kunst* (1886, pp. 194 ff.). He declares quite sharply that the Venus is climbing not into, but out of, the waves, and that the garment is no garment, but a bathing towel "which, after she is dried off, is slung around the hips as a provisional semi-garb until the completion of her toilette." In support of this reversed "bathing situation," Henke add the curious "aesthetic" argument that the "unclad woman" does not represent such a low (i.e. lascivious or at best teasing) genre of art as the woman before the bath. The countless owners of copies,

whether armless or finished off in all conceivable materials, must have
had similar reflections or emotions.

16.   The concept of *genre* was applied to very vast areas of ancient
sculpture by renowned archeologists during the nineteenth century.
Adolf Furtwängler, for instance, offers the following definition: "By
genre in the wider . . . sense, we mean all those subjects that, in contrast
to the mythical and historical, make a random, daily, ordinary, anonymous action representative of its entire genre" (*Der Dornauszieher und
der Knabe mit der Gans, Entwurf einer Geschichte der Genrebildnerei
bei den Griechen*; Berlin, 1876, pp. 12-13). Here, however, genre forms
not just a contrast but also, peculiarly, a preliminary stage to the mythical in that the Greeks, allegedly, progressed from everyday life to the
sublime in their continuous "ideal" direction. In the very oldest pieces,
the vase pictures and Homer's shield of Achilles, Furtwängler finds an
almost exclusive dominion of genre. Nor is there any want (however
abstract the concept may be) of the relation to the viewer, something
that can always be easily created. The era's taste for the thorn-puller,
writes Furtwängler, is easy to explain: "A trait that touches us so humanly, closely wafts from those works," and their truth "holds us more
permanently, more universally than those few completely graspable
ideal figures of deities can do; whereas the latter may always remain
alien to the noninitiate, the former have long been like dear relatives."

17.   The worldwide success of *Uncle Tom's Cabin* brought a kind
of sentimental Christianity of a specifically American origin to Europe
and thus to Germany as well. Here it found a well-prepared soil, but its
extreme development was something quite new.
      Harriet Beecher, the seventh child of Lyman and Roxana Beecher,
was born in 1811, in Litchfield, Connecticut. When she was four she
lost her mother, and was then brought up mainly by her older sister
Catherine. This factor was characteristic in designating the phenomenon
of a joint and independent life of women or girls in a way that was still
unknown in Europe. Catherine founded a school (in Hartford), where
her sister studied and then later taught. In 1832, her father became president of Cincinnati's Lane Theological Seminary, where he was accompanied by both daughters. There, Harriet married Professor Calvin
Ellis Stowe, who likewise taught at the seminary. She spent eighteen
years in Cincinnati, "separated only by the Ohio from a slaveholding
commonwealth." There she gathered experience that provided the
actual material for her most famous work. *Uncle Tom's Cabin* was written during the years 1850 to 1852, in the very northern town of Bruns-

wick, Maine, to which her husband had meanwhile transferred. The novel (this too is characteristic) was first serialized in the (generally abolitionist) newspaper *National Era* and then put out as a book on March 20, 1852. It spread at an enormous clip, being translated, according to reliable sources, into at least twenty-three languages. In Germany alone, that same year and the following, no fewer than thirteen publishers printed translations and adaptations. Hard on the heels of the novel, Harriet Beecher Stowe came out with a volume of documents and testimony on slavery, entitled *Key to Uncle Tom's Cabin*. From then on she wrote regularly for various newspapers, including the New York *Independent* and the *Christian Union*, which her brother Henry Ward Beecher copublished. This brother is an essential part of the picture: He was one of the most famous orators in the United States, but characteristically, he was unable for a long time to frame a definite opinion in the practical moral question that his sister had so decisively answered. Supposedly, Henry Ward Beecher chose his vocation not out of a definite, i.e. dogmatic belief, but because he loved oratory. Harriet died in Hartford, in 1896.

18.   The slave trade was first legally prohibited and abolished in England, through the Abolition Act of Slavery, in 1807. After long-drawn-out international negotiations, France, Spain, and Portugal followed her example. England likewise made a start in the express manumission or emancipation of slaves when the government freed all crown slaves in 1830; the planters in English colonies did the same in 1833, with a large compensation for their losses. In Jamaica alone, 322,000 slaves were thus freed at one time. The French colonies followed suit when the Revolution of 1848 effected this act. During those years, the contrast between the northern and southern states in the U.S.A. became visible, especially since in the South, the number of slaves was actually still growing. The election of the Republican abolitionist Abraham Lincoln as president in 1860 brought the moment of truth nearer. The Civil War broke out. The Emancipation Proclamation of January 1, 1863 was made a law one year later by Congress, and, after another year, it became effective in practice when the southern states were defeated. Harriet Beecher Stowe's novel contributed a great deal to preparing the mood for the Civil War, although that was surely not her aim.

     In the later years of the nineteenth century, European interest concentrated on the flourishing abduction and slave trade within Africa. The fight against them was always an essential argument for the colonial policies of the major powers.

19.   England was at the fore again when she passed the law of 1876
limiting vivisection after a widespread reaction against it. A similar edict,
which likewise permitted vivisection only in physiological institutes,
was issued by Prussia in 1885 thanks to the efforts of Ernst von Weber.
Overall German laws, however, have been in existence only since the
Law for the Protection of Animals of February 1, 1934, according to
which vivisection is permissible only under certain conditions, mainly
in connection with scientific aims and expected usefulness. It can be
practiced pedagogically only when other pedagogical means are wanting; horses, dogs, cats, and monkeys are to be replaced to as great an
extent as possible by lower creatures.

20.   Harriet Beecher Stowe also undertook activating female hearts
in this way. A year after *Uncle Tom*, she went to Europe to establish
an *entente cordiale* between English and American women.
        This province also includes a phenomenon like Florence Nightin-
gale, incidentally a granddaughter of Will-Smith, who pressed for
abolishing slavery in England during the time of Pitts. Of a delicate
constitution herself, she worked all her life for founding new hospitals
and reorganizing old ones. The feelings of all women and many men
were with her when she tended the wounded and comforted the dying
on the battlefields of the Crimean War and, with the example of her
self-sacrificing life, kept getting the sometimes clumsy apparatus of
field hospital provisions to function again. A true saint of genre humanity!

21.   The classic "Essay on the Principles of Population" by Thomas
Robert Malthus had already appeared in 1798; after considerable expansion on the basis of new thorough studies, it came out again in 1803.

22.   "Linnaeus' immortal merit resides in his introducing the concept
of species into biology" (E. Radl: *Geschichte der biologischen Theorien
in der Neuzeit*, Berlin-Leipzig, second edition, 1813, p. 267). Linnaeus's
(1707-78) understanding of species and genera can be gleaned from his
sentence: "We count as many species as there were various forms
created *in principio* (in the beginning)." Likewise: "We distinguish as
many genera as similarly constructed generative apparatuses are produced by the various natural species. . . . Every genus is naturally created as such *in principio* and must not therefore arbitrarily or by any
theory be frivolously split off from or lumped together with others"
(*Systema naturae*, Lugd. bat. 1735.)
        Georges Cuvier (1769-1832) based his classification not on the dif-

ferences of an organ, the "generative apparatus," but on a uniformly understood structural plan of the animal organization. That is why this author brought all of Linnaeus's mammals, birds, reptiles, and fishes together as a single class, that of the vertebrates, despite their different means of propagation.

23.   From 1855 to 1902, there were altogether twenty editions (not counting the popular edition) of *Kraft und Stoff*; the first fifteen were put out by Meidinger in Frankfurt, the later ones by Thomas in Leipzig. Unfortunately, there is no way of determining how large the printings were. Since they were always truly new editions, containing changes, additions, new forewords or introductions, and quite different paginations, one is justified in concluding that more than one such edition was not a schematic "thousand," but a perhaps significantly higher number of copies, corresponding to the demand.

24.   In regard to this self-evident use of the conception of the atom, let us cite a passage from Hoppe's *Geschichte der Physik (Handbuch der Physik*, Vol. I, Berlin, 1926) that characterizes the entire epoch: Next to, or in league with, the struggle for the energy principle, "another struggle is waged, the struggle of atomistics against the view of the continuum. Both aspirations have a particularly intimate contact in the area of ether research, i.e. in optics, electricity, and magnetism, so that the end of this period may be described as the victory of atomistics" (p. 125).

25.   The role played by Hans Makart in his time is so thoroughly forgotten, and all memory of him so entirely vanished, that it is worth listing some data and judgments. Makart was born in 1840, the son of a minor court servant at the summer residence of Mirabell in Salzburg. His father disappeared when Makart was still a child. At school, all that interested him, supposedly, was drawing, which is why, when he was sixteen, his teacher advised sending him to the Academy of Vienna. There, he was sent away again after six months. Fortunate circumstances, however, brought him to Munich in 1859, and he worked there at home for two years since Piloty could not take him into his studio for lack of space. He studied with Piloty from 1861 to 1867, painting his first large canvases. Next, he set up his own studio, and the frieze he painted for it, the so-called Modern Putti, soon became the object of keenest sensation, enthusiasm, and also indignation. Pecht writes about it: "The whole thing, in its mixture of half-naked and modernly cos-

tumed figures, looming against the gold background with its trees and bushes, seems so intoxicating in its wild chaos full of enchanting beauty, that its exhibition prompted an out-and-out uproar in an otherwise so phlegmatic Munich, such as could have had its equivalent only at the appearance of Delacroix's *Dante and Virgil* in the Paris Salon" (*Geschichte der Münchener Kunst im neunzehten Jahrhundert*, Munich, 1888, p. 316). In Vienna, where the frieze was then shown, the violent protests seemed to dominate. "Just like the provocative Richard Wagner," writes Pecht, "the innocent Makart now became an object of wrath for all aestheticians and art scholars." Even more sensational was *The Plague in Florence* (formerly titled *The Seven Deadly Sins*), which, "lavishly provided with radiant female beauty," was displayed a year later, in 1868. The three parts of the painting (stock exchange or house of joy, men and women in the bath, wild bacchanale) together constitute the classical "tableau of passion." According to Pecht, Makart did not paint a more ingenious work. It apparently conquered the resistance against this "neo-Romantic art," as shown when the Austrian Kaiser invited Makart to Vienna, offering him a house and garden on Gusshausgasse. It cannot be doubted that this artist, a man of few words, and of a rather slender physique, became distinctly popular during the next few years in Vienna. His famous *Entrance of Charles the Fifth in Antwerp* (once again, as Pecht puts it, teeming wth marvelous Viennese women) was viewed by some forty thousand visitors in five days when it displayed at the Künstlerhaus. Makart died in fall 1884—"for the restless activity and the wastage of his energy in every direction, ultimately climaxing in a far from brilliant marriage, prematurely exhausted his nature."

If one wishes to comprehend the historic role and popularity of this man, one must not forget the impact of his ever active arranging taste on the art industry and the effect of the world-famous interior design of his studio on bourgeois decorating. "Makart hats," "Makart roses," "Makart bouquets" were available everywhere. One can now scarcely realize the enthusiasm aroused by his artistic genius, and, as contemporary opinion demonstrated, he fulfills precisely and even lavishly the desired concept of the "ardent" and intoxicating, the joy-pouring, sensual, and splendid artistry, the Bohême, which, attaining riches and fame, no longer hinders social recognition, the Bohemia of prosperity. Pecht calls him the immediate successor to Paolo Veronese and especially Rubens. The most informative comment on Makart's renown was by Carl von Lützow, the (for his time) highly prominent editor of the *Zeitschrift für bildende Kunst*. The latter praises him (1886, p. 22) as the total artist, who, far from embracing art for art's sake, as his sumptuous parties demonstrated, understood and realized art as a way of shaping life.

26.   It was only a short time ago that Franz Schnabel (in an essay for the *Frankfurter Zeitung*, August 15, 1937) first called attention to the significance of monuments, the money collections for erecting them, and the great unveiling ceremonies for shaping a pan-German consciousness. The earliest event of this sort, according to him, was the dedication of the Gutenberg monument in Mainz, in 1837. No less characteristic was the dedication of the Bonifatius monument in Fulda, which, by contrasting with the heraldic Baroque figures opposite on the quondam sovereign abbot's palace, still leaves every visitor in the town with a sharp impression of the epoch-making significance of these street monuments. A contemporary author, Heinrich Koenig, who was close to the German Catholics, clearly enough articulates the decisively worldly, secularizing tendency of this sculpture: "The clergy, initially opposed to the entire enterprise, ultimately, when it could not succeed without clerical help, managed to take the ceremony into its own hands. The worldly dedication was turned into an out-of-doors devotion; the festive procession became a pilgrimage, the aspersorium encircled the bronze effigy." And all that, despite the fact that the sculpture itself, cast by Werner Henschel (the forebear of the well-known machine factory), had a thoroughly different intention, namely a nonecclesiastic one: "The cross is made of little fir staffs; one can still see the stumps of the broken-off twigs. . . . The Gospel has conquered the woods and now, from there, it brings the simple weapon for conquering hearts. The beard and hair of the saint are so full as to reveal the strength of his nature. . . . Something shaggy and tousled in these curls suits the apostle's inattentiveness to tending his body; indeed, it mirrors the wilderness through which the wandering preacher followed his pious impetuousness. . . . Of course, the people do not find the well-known crook, the old familiar miter, and the book split by the Frisian sword. Viewers forget that the aim was to represent not the croziered priest, not the martyr, but the traveling apostle of Germany, who did not dash through the woods in a miter. . . . Bonifatius is not to be regarded here as a saint, as which he could already be seen, according to the clergy, in the cathedral, but as the founder of a secular culture, as the man who established a state" (H. Koenig: *Stationen*, Frankfurt, 1846, pp. 104 ff). Thus taken in a secular fashion and put up as a monument out in the open, this Bonifatius, amid that culture, represents the element of the wilderness, whose attributes (wooden branches, shaggy hair, and a disheveled beard) he so visibly bears on his own person.

The confusion soon inflicted by the equivalent adjacency of so many disparate cultural and national saints was expressed incomparably in a conversation in Niebergall's *Datterich* about the recent unveiling of a monument in Gernsheim: In the alcohol-dulled minds, the monumental figures of Gutenberg, Armin, and "Marshal Forwards" are indifferently entangled, and we can understand all too well why the conversation ends with the comments:

"If yav seen one monnerment, yav seen'm awwl!"

"Dat's eggzackerly de way ah feel!"

27.   The idea of constructing the Walhalla came to Ludwig of Bavaria, still a crown prince, during 1807, a time when all national hope seemed totally wrecked. Later, he took counsel with educated men, especially Johannes von Müller, about the choice of the great figures to be united in this temple, and in 1821 he commissioned Leo von Klenze to construct it. But with procuring and preparing the marble and other preliminary work, nine more years passed until the cornerstone was laid—the cornerstone (as State Minister Von Schenk said) "of a monument to German greatness, which the king fulfills, and to German troth, which his upright nation has maintained for centuries and will keep maintaining." In 1842, the construction was done. Schwanthaler's external gable groups showed Germania with the personified federal states and Armin as victor of the Teutoburg Forest. Inside the building, there is a huge relief by Martin Wagner, depicting ancient German history in eight scenes: The migration of wanderers, the Druids and Bards, the Ducal Election, the Alpine migration of the Cimbri and Teutons, etc., and finally Bonifatius felling the oak tree of Thor. A "Valhalla Song" and a "Bardic Chant" were specially composed for the opening-day celebration. The long series of 160 Valhalla Comrades (as they were designated), glorified partly by plaques and partly by busts, began chronologically with Hermann, Marobod, and the legendary Seer of Velleda, and ended with Stein, Gneisenau, and "Göthe"(*sic*). Included were not merely German and Austrian, but also a few Dutch, Scandinavian, and even Baltio-Russian names.

28.   The sculptor of the Hermann Monument in the Teutoberg Forest, Ernst von Bandel (1800-1876), born in Ansbach as the son of a high judiciary official and educated at the Munich Academy, was connected, though in very changing relationships, to the men of Walhalla, Thorwaldsen, Schwanthaler, and Martin Wagner. He also contributed a bust. In 1836, during an outing from Göttingen to Detmold, he climbed Mount Teut: "I recognized this mountain, which rises as a cone amid the

chief valleys of the mountain chain (the poor Romans who were entrenched in these ravines could not have been saved by even Jupiter
himself) as a proper location for my monument. From here, one could
view all the valleys, and a monument placed upon it could be seen from
the utmost distance" (Dr. Hermann Schmidt: *Ernst von Bandel, Ein
deutscher Mann und Künstler*, Hanover, 1892, p. 113). It is perhaps of
interest to learn that he also had the idea at that time of using one of the
external rocks, which he also visited, as a pedestal for the Armin. In early
1838, a seven-foot-high plaster model of the Armin figure was displayed
at the royal castle in Hanover. That same year, Bandel appealed to
Prince von Lippe: "In the event that Your Highness grant me permission to execute my project, I intend to erect the Armin monument for
the entire German nation, as supported by the German people through
voluntary contributions. All my work will be donated as my gift and
present." That very same year, a few prominent men of Detmold
formed the Association for Erecting the Hermann Monument. In July,
preparations of the site commenced. Initial difficulties, including Bandel's rejection of a competitive monument design by Schinkel and
Rauch, brought the association's participation to a halt. To spur it on,
Bandel, supported by King Friedrich Wilhelm the Fourth, prompted a
cornerstone celebration in 1841. By 1846, the substructure was complete. Bandel says of it: "What kind of architectural style ought the substructure to have? What kind of architectural style did Germany have
in Armin's times? . . . No architectural style ought to predominate in
this substructure; therefore, I have included the transition from round
arches to pointed arches as the only unavoidable ornament on this structure. The oakleaf garlands at the points of juncture are cheerful tokens
of glory." From 1846 to 1862, the work on the monument lay dormant
—at first because of the events of 1848, then because of lasting alterca-
tions between Bandel and the Detmold Association, which managed the
affair. It was only now that Bandel brought about the founding of a
new association in Hanover, where he had been living all that time; the
new initiative raised new funds. Armin's figure, supported on the inside
by a peculiar system of pipes, was cast in copper; the steel sword was
donated by Krupp in Essen. Since the monument treasury was again
empty, particularly during the war years 1864-66, the head of the association hit upon the idea of activating school children; he wrote to the
head of the class in every high school, and his efforts paid off. A considerable sum was donated by King Wilhelm I after his visit to Detmold in
1869. Finally, the only thing lacking was the money to put together the
finished parts of the giant figure and to erect the whole thing. After the
Franco-Prussian War and the founding of the Empire, the monument

association petitioned the German Parliament for a one-time subsidy of
10,000 talers; but even this amount, though granted, did not suffice, and
the Kaiser contributed another 9000 talers from his reserve funds. On
August 16, 1875, in the presence of the Kaiser, many princes, and a huge
crowd of people, the monument was unveiled, and Bandel was highly
honored. A year later, he died. The long-drawn-out history of this construction thus stretches from the dream world of the mountain wilderness and national sanctuary to the monumental achievement of political
unity, from the eve of the March Revolution of 1848 to the Empire.

29.   Eugenie Marlitt (1825-87; real name Eugenie John) was a mer-
chant's daughter in Arnstadt, Thuringia. At seventeen, she became the
ward of the reigning princess of Schwarzburg-Sondershausen, who had
first noticed her because of her musicality and lovely voice. An exclusive finishing-school, a musical education in Vienna, the stage—those
were her further stations. Forced by a hearing impairment to abandon
the theatre, she came to court and into the close proximity of the princess, as her reader and travel companion. Anyone who knows a few or
even one of her novels can easily see that these social circumstances are
a crucial motif in them. In 1863, she returned to Arnstadt, where she began her long series of novels, usually published in the magazine *Garten-
laube*. Her first were *The Twelve Apostles* and *Golden Else*. Common
to all is the attitude against "class arrogance" and speculative capitalism,
and for true nobility and merit. The prevalent judgment of the times is
represented in a line from *Meyers Konversationslexikon* of 1876: "All
these works . . . excel in the narrative talent, which, with extraordinary
liveliness, puts the reader into the very midst of events and manages to
lucidly depict as well as express inner sentiments." The thorough demolition of her renown, which nowadays has provided wide circles with
laughter, was basically caused by "modern realism." Its chief critical
organ, M.G. Conrad's *Gesellschaft* (Society), began in the very first issue (January 1, 1885), in the very first article, with the sentence: "Our
'*Society*' primarily intends the emancipation of periodical belletristic literature and criticism from the tyranny of the 'upper-class daughters'
and 'old ladies of both sexes.' "

30.   *The Trumpeter of Säckingen*, first published in 1854, went
through 140 editions by the time of Scheffel's death in 1886 and exactly
250 by 1900, each edition probably running to about 1000 copies. The
spread of Scheffel's works was estimated as having reached some 500,000
copies by the time he died: "There is one volume of Scheffel for every
hundred Germans."

31.   Even the European carpet industry seen on a large scale, is a specific hallmark of the nineteenth century. Carpets as meant for the floor, according to modern usage, had of course already appeared in the eighteenth century, but, in Germany at least, initially only in the highest strata of society, and even there merely as a luxury article, serving appearance more than usefulness. Toward the end of the century, the demand increased among the well-to-do, who sought not so much the costly Flemish as the cheaper English products. Around 1790, to fill this demand, German production was launched, first in Berlin, and then slowly in other places during the following decades. The Germans at first manufactured mainly the cheapest kinds, according to the British model, so-called checkered "wool blankets," on the hand loom; they turned to more complicated sorts during the late 1820s, especially Jacquard carpets. Soon, however, attempts were made, by such people as Schinkel and Semper, to give the new industry an artistic impulse, and in 1831, the first "Sunday school for designing industrial fabrics" was established in Berlin. From 1846 to 1861, German carpet production increased by 151 percent; the number of workers, however (because of mechanized weaving) by only 23 percent. As of 1865 or so, the well-to-do bourgeoisie started carpeting entire floors, whereas earlier they had generally used only small rugs in bedrooms. At the same time, the German output reached a level truly competitive with foreign production. Now Germany could not fully satisfy the domestic market, but during the last four decades of the century, the carpet exports did increasingly outstrip the imports. (Cf. Alfred Häberle: *Die deutsche Teppichfabrikation*, "Münchener volkswirtschaftliche Studien," 143rd piece. Stuttgart-Berlin, 1919.)

32.   "Sunshine, you highest human joy" is the last line of a poem, "Resignation," in Otto Ernst's collection *Stimmen des Mittags*, published in 1901. Cäsar Flaischlen's volume of poems *Von Alltag und Sonne* came out in 1898. The sun is the midpoint of his poetry, a possession, postulate, and homeland in one. One of his poems begins as follows:

> *The man who does not love the sun*
> *Is not my friend....*
> *He must love the sun, if he*
> *Wishes to be my friend....*

And with an expression of the same cheerful self-confidence, another poem terminates:

My mother is the sun,
And I know she loves me!

As in Otto Ernst's poetic house and garden, "Appelschnut" and "Heidede," the children frolic likewise through the Jugendstil-Biedermeier rooms, whose illustrations the Swede Carl Larsson, enamored of his own new form of life, joined together in the book *Das Haus in der Sonne* (*The House in the Sun*). It appeared in 1895.

33.   Semper was not the first to bring up and defend the archeological thesis of the polychromy on ancient buildings and sculptures. He had been preceded by the French art scholar Quatremère de Quincy, who had expressed and supported this allegation in *Jupiter olympien, ou l'art de la sculpture antique* Paris, 1814), then especially the architect Hittorf, who had tried to reconstruct a temple of Selinunt in such terms *Restitution du temple d'Empédocle à Sélinunte*, Paris, 1930). However, these were merely the first scattered voices in an era of otherwise consistently "white" classicism, to which such a thesis had to be quite repugnant. During the early 1830s, Semper himself returned from travels in Italy, Sicily, and Greece with colored drawings, including a colored restoration of the Acropolis of Athens, and he presented his conviction to the public in 1834, in a small piece entitled *"Vorläufige Bermerkungen über die Anwendung der Farben an den Werken der Architectur und Sculptur bei den Alten* (Preliminary Remarks on the Use of Colo· in the Works of Architecture and Sculpture of the Ancients). The article aroused vehement, nay, violent protest from scholars, as best evinced by Frank Kugler's book *Über die Polychromie der griechischen Architectur und Sculptur und ihre Grenzen* (1835). Semper then held his tongue about this topic for seventeen years, offering the following explanation in his introduction to *Die Vier Elemente der Baukunst* Brunswick, 1851): More . . . than the criticism of scholars and connoisseurs, I feared the misunderstanding of the enthusiasts. In truth, the first polychrome experiments in Germany were no encouragement to pursuing an enterprise whose modernity I began doubting." And in a footnote, he says: "The various systems of ancient polychromy found their practical employment. Whereas a delicately faded marchpane style prevailed as Greek here, a blood-red butcher's style blossomed there, claiming likewise to be Greek." Meanwhile Germany had discovered Romanic "polychromy" and France Gothic "polychromy," employing them practically, especially in restorations. Furthermore, scholars had begun studying paleo-Christian art, especially mosaics. Now, finally, Semper once again joined the fray, replying to his critic Kugler. Oddly,

but crucially, the archeological theory was promptly accompanied by an immediately applicable aesthetics. "I must" so it says in *Die Vier Elemente*) "—and even if the aestheticians were to anathematize me doubly as a heretic—repeat what I once owned to: namely that I cannot regard huge white edifice masses, whether in the North or in the South, as beautiful."

34.   Gustav Theodor Fechner's chief intention was generally to measure "the psychical." He construed this basically as "sensation," and made sensations consequent on external stimuli. Physical stimuli, he said, were virtually the ell for measuring psychical sensations. The difficulty lay, however, in finding a constant, numerically graspable relation between stimulus and sensation. He took this relation to be as follows (*Elemente der Psychophysik*, first edition 1860; second 1889): "The psychical measure will always remain less easy and simple in both construction and application than the physical; especially, because in the physical the even divisions of the yardstick generally match the even divisions of the object to be measured, whereas we know the circumstance) quite universal in experience) that with an increase of stimulus and sensation greater additions of stimuli are needed to cover the same increase in sensation; and that circumstance is, to an extent, like the case of having uneven divisions in a measurement correspond to even divisions in the object to be measured." After countless experiments, particularly with increasing and decreasing intensities of light, Fechner ultimately felt he had discovered a very precise mathematical formula expressing the relationship between stimulus and sensation: Sensation was equal to the logarithm of the number indicated by the amount of stimulus (E-log R). Quite essential is the assumption required for the validity of Fechner's law; he names that assumption himself: it is a "constant sensitivity under normal or average conditions." Such constant sensitivity, never really occurring in human beings, is like the reaction of a perception apparatus that is bound fast and not moved by anything but the arriving isolated "stimuli"—or like the panorama viewer, who is nailed to his prescribed standpoint and for whom his harmonious, perspective painted world would be astonishingly distorted, were he to leave that standpoint. The scale of sensations thus has a much smaller scope (smaller in the logarithmic proportion) than the scale of stimuli. Furthermore, the scale is limited above and below by the "stimulus thresholds." Between these thresholds, nothing violent can happen to the feeling or perceiving, to that abstract being, especially since we always observe merely the relative "increase" of sensation, and not the sharpness of the absolute brightness or darkness.

Today's physiology and psychology of perception generally reject Fechner's law. Armin Tschermak, for instance, writes: "A true measuring of the doubtless intensely graduated quality of sensation known as "brightness," like any psychical measuring system at all, is beyond us." ("Licht-und Farbsinn," in *Handbuch der normalen und pathologischen Physiologie*, Vol. XII, 1, p. 393.)

35.   Gas burners were first made of metal, later of porcelain, and finally of soapstone. There were a huge number of different forms, which Schilling's manual divided into four groups: 1) One-hole burners: their lighting was unfavorable; 2) split burners (also called bat-wing burners, butterfly burners—*bec papillon*); here, the gas streamed out of a narrow cut instead of a hole; 3) two-hole, fishtail, or Lancashire fishtail burners: the gas streamed out of two piercings that leaned toward one another, so that both streams met immediately, forming a lovely flat flame together; 4) Argand or round burners: these were made up of a large number of adjacent one-hole flames, together forming a flat, cylindrical wall. They were all rapidly superceded by Auer's incandescent gaslight.

. . . we must meantime occupy ourselves with a less resplendent, but still meritorious, task, namely, to level the ground and to render it sufficiently secure for moral edifices of these majestic dimensions. For this ground has been honeycombed by subterranean workings which reason, in its confident but fruitless search for hidden treasures, has carried out in all directions, and which threaten the security of the superstructures.

—Kant

MOLE EDITIONS
AN EDITORIAL STATEMENT

Our series MOLE EDITIONS would like to show a possible way out of a quandary. Though social science and social history cannot exist without theoretical foundations, there exists today no adequate philosophy and no comprehensive social theory capable of informing research without imposing dogmatic distortions. Realizing the intimate interdependence of theory and practice in the social, intellectual and political processes, the editors of MOLE EDITIONS think that the present dilemma is rooted in the inadequacy of the answers provided by theory and in the inability of narrow empirical research to ask questions which could solicit meaningful explanations—as though there were only quick answers or no answers at all, with the enjoyment of detail destroyed in either case.

A possible manner of confronting this impasse—and the general malaise that extends from everyday life to intellectual discourse—would not seem to lie in yet another program, yet another grand scheme. Rather, it seems more useful to examine the history of theory itself, rediscovering the roots of the problems which have produced the impasse, concentrating simultaneously on the details of social, political and cultural history so as to let these details speak for themselves. Through this retrieval, we hope to be able to arrive at new, more adequate, theoretical frameworks. We are therefore prepared to entertain a more contemplative scholarly sensibility and to rework material which has either been ignored or has escaped the grasp of inherited theories. We hope that this will help to restore some of the pleasure that social science lost when its mode of discourse was divorced from literature.

MOLE EDITIONS
Available in 1977

Pierre Clastres	Society against the State	$12.95 cloth
Norbert Elias	The Civilizing Process: Vol. 1	$15.00 cloth
Dolf Sternberger	Panorama of the 19th Century	$15.00 cloth

In active preparation for 1978

Reinhart Koselleck	Enlightenment and Hypocrisy	$12.95 cloth
Wolf Lepenies	The End of Natural History	$12.95 cloth
Norbert Elias	The Civilizing Process: Vol. II	
Robert Jaulin	The White Peace	
Wolfgang Schivelbusch	The Industrialized Traveller	

In active preparation for 1979

| Pierre Clastres | Chronicles of the Guayaki Indians | |